The Uses of Fiction

Essays on the Modern Novel
in Honour of Arnold Kettle

Edited by
Douglas Jefferson
and
Graham Martin

The Open University Press
Milton Keynes

The Open University Press
A division of
Open University Educational Enterprises Limited
12 Cofferidge Close
Stony Stratford
Milton Keynes MK11 1BY, England.

First published 1982

British Library Cataloguing in Publication Data

The Uses of fiction.
1. Kettle, Arnold 2. English fiction – 19th century – History and criticism 3. English fiction – 20th century – History and criticism
I. Jefferson, Douglas II. Martin, Graham
III. Kettle, Arnold
823'.7'09 PR861

ISBN 0-335-10181-X ✓

Text design by W.A.P.

Phototypeset by
Rowland Phototypesetting Limited, Bury St Edmunds, Suffolk
Printed in Great Britain by
St Edmundsbury Press, Bury St Edmunds, Suffolk

Contents

Acknowledgements

The editors would like to thank Barbara Hardy, Mark Kinkead-Weekes, and Dipak Nandy for invaluable help and advice in the planning of this volume; and to express their appreciation to Mrs Pat Wallace, Faculty of Arts, The Open University, for secretarial assistance in preparing it for publication.

List of contributors

Douglas Jefferson
Emeritus Professor, School of English, University of Leeds.

Graham Martin
Professor of Literature, The Open University.

Miriam Allott
Professor of English Literature, Birkbeck College, University of London.

Angus Calder
Staff Tutor in Arts, The Open University.

David Craig
Senior Lecturer in English Literature, University of Lancaster.

P. N. Furbank
Reader in Literature, The Open University.

Andrew Gurr
Professor of English Literature, University of Reading.

Barbara Hardy
Professor of English Literature, Birkbeck College, University of London.

Cicely Palser Havely
Lecturer in Literature, The Open University.

Jeremy Hawthorn
Professor of English, University of Trondheim, Norway.

Margot Heinemann
Sometime Fellow in English Literature, New Hall, University of Cambridge.

Mark Kinkead-Weekes
Professor of English Literature, Rutherford College, University of Kent.

Sylvère Monod
Professor of English Literature, the Sorbonne, Paris.

Kenneth Muir
Emeritus Professor of English Literature, University of Liverpool.

Dipak Nandy
Deputy Chief Executive, Equal Opportunities Commission.

W. R. Owens
Research Assistant in Literature, The Open University.

Arthur Ravenscroft
Senior Lecturer in English Literature, University of Leeds.

Kiernan Ryan
Fellow in English Literature, New Hall, University of Cambridge.

Alistair Stead
Lecturer in English Literature, University of Leeds.

Robert Weimann
Professor of English Literature, Akademie der Künste, Berlin, German Democratic Republic.

Raymond Williams
Professor of Drama, University of Cambridge.

Introduction

I

The retirement in 1981 of Arnold Kettle from the Chair of Literature in the Open University marked an epoch in the history of the University itself and will be associated in the minds of many colleagues and former students with the course on the *Nineteenth Century Novel*, then in the process of revision and about to enter upon a new phase. But it also marked the thirtieth anniversary of the publication of the first volume of his *Introduction to the English Novel*, which appeared when he was a lecturer in the University of Leeds and had taken over the Novel course from Bonamy Dobrée. This volume appeared at an appropriate moment. F. R. Leavis's *Scrutiny* essays leading to *The Great Tradition* in 1948 had given direction to the more serious approach to the novel that was to characterize the post-war period. His sequence of authors and texts had a moral and historical coherence and an authority which has continued to influence our thinking. That Arnold Kettle was influenced is apparent from the fact that he incorporated central elements of that sequence, such as *The Portrait of a Lady* (which had been virtually nobody's book and now became everybody's book); and in a number of places he acknowledges the value of Leavis's critical observations. But Arnold's emphasis is different and so is the design of his book, in that it encompasses a much larger area of English fiction. Leavis's policy of identifying and concentrating on the few novelists whom he regarded as truly great was invigorating, but it involved the exclusion from discussion of some authors for whom much could be said, as Leavis himself acknowledged. Whereas Leavis described *Vanity Fair* as 'in a minor way a classic', Arnold Kettle wrote an essay on that novel, an admirable combination of appreciation and limiting judgements. Leavis saw that *Clarissa* was 'a really impressive work', but with certain disabling defects, and his comments on it are very brief. Arnold Kettle gave it six excellent pages. No one would wish to challenge Leavis's unique place among the critics of that time, but his austere terms of reference created opportunities for other critics, and one of the remarkable qualities of *The English Novel* is the range of works on which it makes a critical contribution of lasting value. In the first volume, the chapter on *Oliver Twist* is a key document in the gradual and most heartening movement of thought which has now placed Dickens higher than ever before. Criticism of Dickens had been in a rather disgraceful state, what with Forster's absurd ideas about his 'flat' characters and the infelicity of Lubbock's reference to the 'odd and amusing' figures in novels like *Bleak House* (Skimpole? Krook? of whom was he thinking?). Edmund Wilson's 'The Two Scrooges' is a landmark, but stresses mainly the thematic elements. Leavis recognized Dickens as a 'great genius' but primarily as a 'great entertainer', singling out the untypical *Hard Times* as the book worthy of serious discussion (although later he and Q. D. Leavis made a fine contribution to Dickens criticism). Good criticism often states what one feels should always have been apparent. The power of the first eleven chapters of *Oliver Twist*, which Arnold so well demonstrated had not previously been emphasized. His gift for effective illustration was never more finely exercised than in his quotation in full of the trial of the Artful Dodger. How *had* people managed to miss this extraordinary, wantonly brilliant episode? But it has a social and moral point ('this ain't the shop for justice'), which, characteristically, Arnold also recognizes.

So too, in his account of *Wuthering Heights*, where his concern is with the hard facts of economic and social relationships even to the neglect of the visionary elements (some readers have repined at this). He finally arrives, most movingly, at Heathcliff the man, and we become aware of Emily Bronte's wonderful sense of the recognizable realities (a gift not hitherto much stressed) as well as of the mysteries of human nature.

II

Until the publication of *An Introduction to the English Novel*, Marxism had hovered uneasily on the margins of the orthodox literary-critical enterprise, and something must be said, however brief, of Arnold Kettle's distinctive achievement in bringing to bear on criticism as then practised the insights of Marxism in a manner which did violence to neither. This can be done without preliminary discussion of such figures as Lukács and the early English Marxists, which would be essential in any adequate historical account of the place of his work within the Marxist tradition. Much of this earlier work is limited by rigidity and insensitiveness, and Arnold Kettle's own practice is distinctive as much for the absence of any irritable reaching after theoretical system, as for its unusual sensitiveness towards specific literary works. And this sensitiveness embraces at once a scrupulous conception of a novel as a creation of its own time and place, and a recognition of its continuing power as a present force for life.

There are perhaps three features of literature to which all critics, particularly Marxists, must attend. The first is that a literary work is relatively closed. It creates a world which insists on being taken on its own terms, and when those terms are violated by inappropriate questions the result is a palpable sense of absurdity. But, secondly, the closure is only relative. A work of art is a product of time and place, and our first apprehension of it is in terms of its period. There are a few points at which the relatively closed world of the novel opens out, to admit evidence from outside its own covers. The art of the critic requires the tact and sense of relevance to be able to judge where this evidence lies and how much of it is admissible; and the art of the Marxist literary critic is largely an ability to find those points where the specific insights of Marxism can be brought to bear on the novel without doing violence to it. But, thirdly, great novels are not only products of their time. Their essential feature, which needs remarking on afresh for each generation, is their capacity to communicate across gulfs of time, space and culture. The task of the Marxist literary critic then is to be able to respect the relative closure of a novel, to be able to detect those points of openness where the character of the epoch and its illusions have a direct and unavoidable bearing on our understanding of it, and to be able to account for its persistence as a living force beyond its age.

Alone among the critics who might have been cited as Arnold Kettle's predecessors, Walter Benjamin grappled consciously with this threefold requirement, and Charles Rosen has lucidly summarised Benjamin's perception of the task:

> 'For Benjamin, the significance of the work is not exhausted by the meaning given to it by the author and his contemporaries, and is often not even adequately realized by them. The work is 'timeless' in that it is not limited to the moment of its appearance. It transcends history, but its transcendence is only revealed by its projection through history . . . The work detaches itself both from the life that produced it and from the specific cultural milieu within which it was conceived; nevertheless it keeps a sense of that past life as an effect of distance from us . . . [Benjamin's] formulation of [his] task was to relate the work to history while respecting its essential function of stepping out of the historical time and space in which it was produced. The achievement of Benjamin was . . . to have developed a way of interpreting the historical significance of a work that does not question its supra-historical integrity.

Even more germane is Rosen's account of Benjamin's doctrine of the autonomy of the work of art, and of the essentially provisional nature of literary criticism:

> 'It does not imply that a text does not refer outside itself, or, even more absurdly, that it is intelligible without a knowledge of the universe that surrounds it. It merely guarantees that no elucidation of the text – not even the author's own exegesis – can ever attach itself permanently to it or pretend to be an integral or necessary condition of experiencing it . . . No critical theory whatever has a valid and lasting claim upon the work. This autonomy requires that one return to the work itself, and that the interpretation is never in any way a substitute for it, or even, more modestly, its necessary accompaniment.'[1]

Arnold Kettle's best criticism does in practice just what Benjamin thought the Marxist critic ought to do.

Of all the chapters in the *Introduction to the English Novel* none is quite so remarkable as that on Richardson. So much that is acute and just about a novel of over two thousand pages is compressed into a mere six pages of criticism. Having placed Richardson securely in his age, Arnold turns directly to the question of what gives *Clarissa* a trans-historical vitality:

> 'Here we reach a point at which [Richardson] ceases to be merely of historical interest. For in his delving into the private feelings and secret motives of his characters he achieved something quite different from the

> mere evocation of the sentimental moment which he seems to have intended. He got deeper into the subtle, wayward and contradictory feelings of human beings than any previous novelist had managed, and he did so because, in his search for the easily pathetic, he stumbled on a situation fully tragic . . .
>
> Tragedy occurs when a situation arises which men, in the particular point of development that they have reached, are unable to solve. Such a situation in the eighteenth and nineteenth centuries – and the problem is not yet answered – was the growing consciousness of women of the necessity of their emancipation . . . Clarissa *has* to fight her family and Lovelace; they for their part *cannot* let her win without undermining all that is to them necessary and even sacred. It is from the examination of such situations that the artist makes contact with the stuff and movement of life. The actual material of tragedy changes. Clarissa today could solve her problem, at any rate after a fashion. But we still respond to Richardson's novel because in the world of the novel the problem is not soluble and yet the direction of the solution is indicated in the quality of sympathy which Clarissa herself (silly as she often is) evokes . . . It is in this sense that works of art are timeless; they capture the tensions and movement of life which, though for ever altering in form, are nevertheless perpetually going on.
>
> . . . We shall not enjoy *Clarissa* unless we approach it sympathetically, through history. But if we approach it *only* through history we shall not enjoy it either. The past and the present are at once different and inseparable. It is precisely because he stumbled on one of the real, contemporary dilemmas of his own time that Richardson achieved an art which has relevance to ours.'[2]

Another fine example is the chapter on *Middlemarch*, which begins with a tightly focussed concentration on some ten lines of text and then, after two more extended passages, fastens on the passage in which Lydgate is first introduced, with its disastrous sentence: 'Destiny stands by sarcastic with our *dramatis personae* folded in her hand.' This is 'A pretentious and unhelpful sentence,' in Kettle's view, 'calling up a significance it does not satisfy. Who, one feels tempted to ask, is this Destiny, a character previously unmentioned by the author?' And from there he can move to the three central judgments in which he puts his finger on the weaknesses as well as the enduring vitality of the novel:

> 'Because the Middlemarch world is the given, static reality, the characters of the novel must be seen as at its mercy. They are free to make certain moral decisions within the bounds of the Middlemarch world, yet they are held captive by that world. Hence the temptation of George

> Eliot, once she accepts the social implications of her story, to introduce an unconvincing, unrealised 'Destiny'. The artist in her does not believe in this Destiny . . . But it is always lurking in the background and it eats into the overall vitality of the novel.
>
> For though George Eliot hates Middlemarch she believes in its inevitability . . . She, whose noble humanity informs the whole novel, even its weaknesses, cannot submit emotionally to a philosophy that binds her people for ever to the Middlemarch world. Hence the significance of the Saint Theresa theme, both as to its place in the novel and as to the rather breathless, uncontrolled, even embarrassing emotional quality it exudes.
>
> In spite of all our reservations it is Dorothea who, of all the characters in the novel, most deeply captures our imagination. It is her aspiration to a life nobler than the Middlemarch way of life that is the great positive force within the novel and the force which, above all, counteracts the tendency to present society as a static, invincible force outside the characters themselves.'[3]

And there we witness the scrupulous discharge of the three tasks of this kind of criticism: a respect for the relative closure of the fictional world of the novel; a capacity to perceive the crucial detail, in the text, signalling the fact that the closed world has opened out to permit a legitimate comment on the author's philosophy and its effect on the work; and a readiness to venture an account of what it is about this work which gives it its power to address us, not as an historical document, but as a living, contemporary comment. There is a sentence in the chapter on George Eliot in which Arnold asks: 'Can we perhaps . . . put our finger on a note in *Middlemarch* which may justly be described as a shade flat?' It is a recurring phrase in his work: 'put our finger on' – tact. And this sense of touch goes together with that other kind of tact, moral rather than technical, which respects each thing for being what it is and not another thing. It is the necessary tact of the good critic.

III

In the second volume of *The English Novel*, Arnold's selection of novelists from the 1920s to 1950s, when the best work was being written by people of very different outlook from his own, illustrates other marks of his critical distinctiveness: his forbearance, honesty, and sheer delight in anything good of its kind. Like his critical tact, these were also human virtues which became the delight of those who knew him in professional life. He was all that a colleague could be. His affection for people, the affection he inspired, his high and generous conception of friendship gave a special quality to relationships in the School of English at Leeds University, as in the Arts Faculty of the Open University. His salutary wit and humour enlivened many a situation in the academic round. To work with him, as a colleague, was to learn what intellectual and academic fellowship might be. Many who were taught by him remember this as a great life-giving experience. And with the passion to share knowledge and enjoyment, he combines a rarer gift. He can convey the value and quality of his own response to literature in a lithe and subtle prose style, a matter for the special admiration of his colleagues in the Open University, where so much of the tutorial task must be carried by means of written language. It is a quality which Open University students have directly praised: his ability to write straightforwardly on complex issues; yet also densely, with an imaginative flair that never interposes itself between the reader and the object of tutorial attention; and with a variety of tone – asking, prompting, qualifying, joking – which as far as writing can, gives the reader immediate access to Arnold's thinking and feeling for the work.

Speaking of Arnold's commitment to the ideals of the Open University, one student remarked upon his sure understanding of 'that pursuit of an enhanced self-respect, and not just of a university degree', that moved so many men and women, of many ages, to embark upon their demanding courses. Arnold's sense of literature's ability to open up such opportunities for self-realization, and at the same time to open up the world of objective historical conditions within which such self-realization must happen, if it is to happen at all, are brilliantly expressed in the range of his writing for Open University students.

In this collection of Essays in his honour, we wished to include a discussion of authors from this century, and particularly of the last thirty years. Whether the choice is precisely what Arnold would himself have made is a matter on which we can trust his diplomacy and forbearance. But it is fitting that a volume presented to a critic with such generous and sustained concern for the needs of his fellow human-beings should contain some studies of the fiction that has played, and will continue to play, so interesting a part in the expansion of consciousness and the struggle for identity and human fulfilment in countries of the Third World. We hope that the volume as a whole, conceived and written in celebration of Arnold's achievements, as teacher, as critic, and as writer, will make its own indirect contribution to the continuing influence of his work.

Douglas Jefferson
Graham Martin
Dipak Nandy

Notes

1 Charles Rosen, 'The Ruins of Walter Benjamin' and 'The Origins of Walter Benjamin', *The New York Review of Books*, 27 October, 1977, pp. 33 and 35, and 10 November, 1977, p. 37.
2 Arnold Kettle, *An Introduction to the English Novel* (London: Hutchinson, 1951), Vol. I, pp. 70–71.
3 Ibid, pp. 184–5, 187–8, 188.

The Uses of Fiction
Edited by
Douglas Jefferson
and Graham Martin

I

"Fictionality" and Realism: Rabelais to Barth

Robert Weimann

When we consider recent critical interest in realism as a part of the extraordinary growth in the contemporary criticism of fiction it seems surprising that the tools we use to understand and evaluate realism in the novel are still rather rudimentary. Looking at some of the most widely used anthologies of criticism on the novel we find, among the 'Materials for a Poetics', the customary sections on plot, character, and point of view, with related ones on narrative technique, style, symbol, etc.[1] But as soon as we begin to examine the relation to reality of certain works of contemporary fiction, especially those of an experimental and post-modernist cast, these categories and concepts seem as unsatisfactory as when they are applied to the works of early modern fiction, such as Rabelais' *Gargantua*, Nashe's *Jack Wilton*, or even Cervantes' *Don Quijote*. In both cases, it may be claimed, these categories furnish no very helpful instruments with which to discuss some of the most basic problems arising out of the relationship between the novel and society: by which I mean between authors and their works, the institutions and conditions involved in the circulation and reception of those works and, finally, their readers. Criticism of the traditional novel has its own appropriate language and style, and this is only partially applicable to the problems and meanings of certain other forms and traditions of prose narrative. In these areas the concepts of mimesis, or the representation of reality in terms of plot and character (let alone 'order' and 'symmetry', as the disposing of parts towards a single end) may provide an incomplete and irrelevant frame of reference – especially when they are brought to bear on the central tension in realist fiction: the tension between socially accepted truths and fictionally created images.

If 'realism' points beyond the representation of empirical reality, the whole question of the meaning and value of fiction must be reconsidered. Once the concept of 'meaning' is related to the contradiction between image and society, between the fictional structure of the text and its actual function in reality, some of the most influential modern theoretical approaches to fiction may be seen in a critical perspective. Take, for instance, the recent approaches by the hermeneutic and new formalist critics who, even when they have gone a considerable way towards a more subtle reconsideration of the problem of achieving and perceiving meaning in fiction, must appear biased in one central respect. For despite some recent signs of convergence between formalism and hermeneutics their criticism has usually been either text-oriented (so that the problem of meaning was defined as a textual or formal one) or it was reader-oriented (so that the problem of meaning was defined as functional, with the reader sometimes conceived as an abstraction out of time and place). Whereas the latter tendency is, in Michael Riffaterre's words, 'towards an autonomous semiotics of the narrative'[2], the former is still (in the tradition of the New Criticism) haunted by memories of the 'affective fallacy'.

Obviously, the question of realism in the novel cannot be reconsidered without rejecting both the modern formalist view that art conflicts with reality *and* the nineteenth-century assumption that only 'formal' realism can exist, and therefore must preclude stylization or fabulation. But the definition of 'meaning' must be functional as well as structural: *structural* in the sense that the structure of the text itself (and not the sociology of its author and its readers) provides the central object of analysis and evaluation; *functional* in the sense that in the last resort 'meaning' itself is a function of the relationship between the fictional world of the novel and the social world inhabited by both authors and readers. This relationship, to be sure, is a subject of debate.[3] But the glory, as well as the difficulty of the problem of 'meaning' in realism is that the relationship of fiction and society is itself fraught with values both moral and aesthetic. This relationship involves an intense interaction between social function and novelistic structure and, ultimately, the conflicting views of the meanings of realism cannot be separated from conflicting senses of the meaning of reality itself.

I

A discussion of *Fiktion* and the rise of realism is a case in point. I use the German term to emphasize my concern not with 'fiction' (as a category distinct from, e.g., documentary writing) but with the rising practice and consciousness of 'fictionality', as a process and a product of particular significance in the pre-history and the early history (as well as in some contemporary developments) of the modern novel.[4] My proposition, then, is that in sixteenth and seventeenth-century fiction there is, for authors as well as readers, a new sense of *Fiktion*, or fictionality, a heightened awareness of both the links and the distinctions between the playful illusion of art and a realistic sense of life.

Paradoxically, this new consciousness of the fictional nature of the novelistic world interacts with a new awareness of the realities of experience. Such interaction involves problems as well as achievements; and an exploration of these might prove helpful in considering the forms and functions of realism in the novel as a social and aesthetic mode of imaginatively apprehending and comprehending whichever truths are ascertainable about the world as it actually exists.

To elaborate this point properly calls for a foundation in the social and literary history of the sixteenth century. Since this would be inappropriate here,[5] let me briefly glance at the new type of social consciousness involved in the writer's and reader's sense of fictionality. In sixteenth-century Western Europe there is a newly individualized and more highly communicative type of consciousness, asserting itself in the form of increased social mobility, sharing in, and profiting from, that wider exchange of goods and ideas following on from the dissolution of the feudal structure of society. Writers of narrative prose, like Rabelais in Lyon, Fischart in Strassburg, or Nashe in London, now living beyond the self-sufficient mediaeval communities and in touch with a wider audience, were able to break with some of the traditional social norms and corresponding conventions of rhetoric. In searching for and addressing such an audience the author is conscious of both the new freedom and the new burden of this recently achieved independence – a precarious independence between the decline of aristocratic patronage and the nascent market for books. But at this stage an enhanced sense of personal autonomy on the part of the author does not conflict either with the use of popular traditions or, for that matter, with a heightened capacity for communicating a personal vision to the particularized expectations of his audience. The paradox of the writer's independence and the new reader's isolation is expressed in a felt need to explore and communicate motives, perspectives and causes. But by questioning the traditional subjects and treatments and inventing new ones, the author expects the reader, as it were, more creatively, to perceive the contradiction between matter and meaning, between traditional symbols and their new significance.

Once the matter is no longer traditional, no longer the well-known *matière*, the modes of establishing its meaning drastically change. The meaning of each new version of traditional material (including allegorical treatments) had been achieved by way of variations on and contrasts with, previous versions of this material. But the meaning of the untraditional matter was conceived like that of the Italian *novella* not exclusively, or even primarily, in reference to established literary codes. If the *novella* can be defined (as in Arthur Heiserman's study of *The Novel before the Novel*), as a 'story whose material is fresh, untraditional'[6] then the genre's very name suggests that the material was no longer to be understood in reference to a traditional *literary* canon, but in reference to the writer's or reader's own experience in society, to the contradiction between imagination and reality: a contradiction which involves a permanently active correlation between the world of the story and the world of history.

In the traditional forms of mediaeval literature, such as the courtly epic, some such correlation was of course already implied, at least to some degree. But the centrality and the complexity of the new *Fiktion* involved particularized inventions in the interest of a generalized truth about society. In its feigning images of true meaning, this novel type of fiction goes beyond not only, say, the Arthurian *matière* or the Amadis cycle, but also beyond the theoretical premises of the neoclassical poetics of Castelvetro, Pontanus and Sidney. There, the customary distinction was between *fabula* and *historia*, in the sense that (as Sidney has it) 'Poesie dealeth with . . . the universall consideration, and the Historie with . . . the particular'.[7] The neoclassical concept of 'Historie' (as being 'captivated to the trueth of a foolish world') was worlds apart from what Sidney called 'the fained Image of Poetrie'. But in the new fiction the feigned images of story did not contradict 'the trueth of a foolish world'. On the contrary, the maker of narrative images – rather like Sidney's historian – felt 'bound to tell things as things were'.[8] Thus, the feigning element of *fictio* and the truth of history engaged in a mutually rewarding relationship; but they did so only in the process of a more exacting kind of literary communication where social norms and private responses had to accommodate one another.

It is in this context that *Fiktion*, the age-old convention, serves a new kind of function. Once the matter, or material, is no longer traditional, allegorical or poetically removed from 'the trueth of a foolish world', the modes of establishing and perceiving its meaning begin to change. In the language (though not quite in the sense) of Wolfgang Iser,[9] the first code, or 'schema' (that is, the 'repertoire' of social norms and literary conventions), becomes less invariable, less secure, more contradictory, whereas the second code, the so-called 'equivalence system' or 'correction', greatly enhances its variability and heterogeneity. The result is that the new communicative transaction becomes both more intense and less predictable: the newly abundant rhetoric of the novel is a necessary mode of achieving and perceiving meaning. At the same time, the new meaning becomes more historical and less literary. In the words of Sidney's poetics, *fabula*, 'the fained Image of Poetrie', took up the task that was relegated to *historia*. But in doing so, it went beyond both the historian's and the epic poet's demands on the reader's cooperation in grasping the contradiction between generalization and experience, between the symbolic representations and the true meanings of narrative.

If the resulting contradiction is at the centre of the new sense of fictionality, it also has structural consequences, especially for the emerging narrative point of view. For this contradiction simultaneously involves the congruity as well as the discongruity between author's and readers' actual perception of the world of history and that of the characters in the world of their story. In accordance with that, the world of history in the process of narration, and the processing of the world of the story interact: the product and the process of the literary transaction engage in a more active relationship. The *product* (or result) of the narrative (in form of whatever 'character', plot, description we have) and the *process* of achieving and, from the reader's point of view, comprehending it, become more highly interactive. The tale and the telling, the story and its understanding are intensely related through both rhetoric and structure. Again, in the words of Sidney's poetics, though in defiance of its doctrine, the 'fained Image of Poetrie' provided a 'universal consideration' of the particular 'trueth of a foolish world' by making the fiction historical and history fictional.

II

At this point, an illustration may serve to reveal the three-fold problem of language, meaning and social function. The passages which I have chosen from Thomas Nashe's *Unfortunate Traveller* and Rabelais' *Gargantua* are quoted at length because they suggest some of the problems and achievements of fictionality as part of a new attitude to the meaning of fiction.

> 'On the hard boords he threw her, and used his knee as an yron ramme to beat ope the two leavd gate of her chastitie. Her husbands dead bodie he made a pillow to his abhomination. Conjecture the rest, my words stick fast in the myre and are cleane tyred, would I had never undertooke this tragicall tale. Whatsoever is borne, is borne to have an end. Thus ends my tale: his whorish lust was glutted, his beastly desire satisfied; what in the house of anie worth was carriageable, he put up, and went his way.
>
> Let not your sorrow die, you that have read the proeme and narration of this eligiacall historie. Shew you have quick wits in sharp conceipt of compassion.'[10]

> 'Les couleurs de Gargantua feurent blanc et bleu, comme cy dessus avez peu lire, et par icelles vouloit son pere qu'on entendist que ce luy estoit une joye celeste; car le blanc luy signifioit joye, plaisir, delices et resjouissance, et le bleu choses celestes.
>
> J'entends bien que, lisans ces motz, vous mocquez du vieil beuveur et reputez l'exposition des couleurs par trop indague et abhorrente, et dictes que blanc signifie foy et bleu fermeté. Mais, sans vous mouvoir, courroucer, eschaufer ny alterer (car le temps est dangereux), respondez moy, si bon vous semble. D'aultre contraincte ne useray envers vous, ny aultres, quelz qu'ilz soient; seulement vous diray un mot de la bouteille.
>
> Qui vous meut? Qui vous poinct? Qui vous dict que blanc signifie foy et bleu fermeté? Un (dictes vous) livre trepelu, qui se vend par les bisouars et porteballes, au titre: *le Blason des couleurs*. Qui l'a fac it? Quiconques il soit, en ce a esté prudent qu'il n'y a poinct mis son nom. Mais, au reste, je ne sçay quoy premier en luy je doibvc admircr, ou son oultrecuidance ou sa besterie: son oultrecuidance, qui, sans raison, sans cause et sans apparence, a ausé prescripre de son autorité privée quelles choses seroient denotées par les couleurs, ce que est l'usance des tyrans qui voulent leur arbitre tenir lieu de raison, non des saiges et sçavans qui par raisons manifestes contentent les lecteurs; . . .
>
> En pareilles tenebres sont comprins ces glorieux de court et transporteurs de noms, lesquelz, voulens en leurs divises signifier *espoir*, font

protraire une *sphere*, des *pennes* d'oiseaulx pour *poines*, de l'*ancholie* pour *melancholie*, *la lune bicorne* pour *vivre en croissant*, un *banc rompu* pour *bancque roupte*, *non* et un *alcret* pour *non durhabit*, un *lict sans ciel* pour un *licentié*, que sont homonymies tant ineptes, tant fades, tant rusticques et barbares, que l'on doibvroit atacher une queue de renard au collet et faire un masque d'une bouze de vache à un chascun d'iceulx qui en vouldroit dorenavant user én France, après la restitution des bonnes lettres.

Par mesmes raisons (si raisons les doibz nommer et non resveries) ferois je paindre un *penier*, denotant q'on me faict *pener*; et un *pot à moustarde*, que c'est mon cueur à qui *moult tarde*; et un *pot à pisser*, c'est un official; et le *fond de mes chausses*, c'est un *vaisseau de petz*; et ma *braguette*, c'est le *greffe des arrestz*; et un *estront de chien*, c'est un *tronc de ceans*, où gist l'amour de m'amye.

Bien aultrement faisoient en temps jadis les saiges de Egypte, quand ilz escripvoient par lettres qu'ilz appelloient hieroglyphiques, lesquelles nul n'entendoit qui n'entendist et un chascun entendoit qui entendist la vertu, proprieté et nature des choses par icelles figurées; . . .'[11]

While Nash's highly rhetorical climax seems to present little initial difficulty, the passage from the 9th chapter of the First Book of *La Vie très Horrifique du grand Gargantua* is complex on more than one level. Here, the new post-allegorical type of relationship between matter and meaning, between symbols and their signification, is discussed on the basis of a strikingly original interpretation of the various colours and their varying significances. But whatever their significance, there are two modes of establishing meaning which, according to the narrator, seem unacceptable. One is the mode of those who, on no authority but their private interpretation, seek to establish which things shall be signified by which colours. The other mode, equally unacceptable, is that of two punning courtiers who illustrate their heraldic devices by a ludicrous play on words.

So rather than following such private interpretations or such fantastic analogies the narrator proposes a new method of achieving and perceiving significance in fiction. Both Rabelais and, on a different level, Nashe set out to discuss the most effectual relationships between stories and their meaning, between the various images and representations on the one hand and the mode by which their proper significance can be achieved and comprehended, on the other. To begin with, there is an exploratory concern with rhetoric – rhetoric as a means of probing into, and guaranteeing the efficacy of the communicative process. Since the act of communication cannot be achieved outside the narrative terms of textual structure, note how the process of communication and the product of narration tend to be balanced. In Nashe's case the desperate *outcome* of his story and the organized despair in the *telling* of it ('would I had never undertooke this tragicall tale') coalesce in a proverbial *sententia*: 'Whatsoever is borne, is borne to have an end.' The jingling identity in the suffering consummations of both the narrator and his heroine is, of course, outrageously witty. But since the telling process of despair is as superficial as its told product is sensational, the wittiness (together with the *sententia*) is not profoundly correlated to either the story or the rendering of it. The product does not achieve the depth in the dialectic of illusion and reality that we have in *La Vie très Horrifique du grand Gargantua*.

What Rabelais is concerned with is no more and no less than the premises on which, and the process by which, symbolic statements and their meanings engage, in modern fiction, in a more deeply functional, but still highly precarious relationship. The true mode of symbolization must reject both the preordained 'autorité privée' and the courtly affectation and the rustic barbarism of those traditional 'transporteurs des noms'. Instead of either the preordained mode of abstract meaning (white for 'faith') or the arbitrary form of allegorical and homonymous meaning (such as 'lict sans ciel' for 'un licentié') an alternative mode of symbolization is suggested. The truly functioning relationship between illusion and reality, imagination and truth, must not be conceived 'sans raison, sans cause et sans apparance', but from the point of view of those 'sages et sçavants, qui, par raisons manifestes, contentent les lecteurs'. It is by basing the literary communication on 'raisons manifestes', that is, on more universally acclaimed and applicable standards, that the feigning and the meaning can best be correlated in the new fiction.

The language of fiction may have its own laws, much like those 'hiéroglyphiques' used by those Egyptian sages who 'nul n'entendoit qui n'entendist et un chascun entendoit qui entendist la vertue, proprieté, et nature des choses par icelles figurées'. Ultimately, the fictive images and their symbolic meanings are indivisible. The direct reference of the sign to the nature of things may, from the point of view of modern semiotics, be considered fallacious; but, at this stage, the emphasis on *things* does not as yet reduce the signs and *figures*: their close connection is emphasized by a phrase like 'des choses par icelles figurées'. What finally counts is the symbolic relationship between the things of history and the figures of the story, and it is this relationship which informs both the outcome (the 'product') of the narration, and its mode, the 'process', for authors and readers, of arriving at a coherent meaning.

The reader is made to share in the interplay between the two. But such interplay, with Nashe even more than Rabelais, involves the achievement of balance between empathy and distance. Thus, the reader is summoned: 'Let not your sorrow die . . . Show you have quick wits in sharp conceipt of compassion.' Here, the complexity of the appeal to the reader's faculties seems characteristic. On the one hand, it places an emphasis on his 'personal opinion, judgement or estimation' (to quote the OED's definition of 'conceit') which is expected to be 'sharp', that is, 'acute or penetrating in intellect or perception'. The reader is urged to have a critical intellect of his own or, as Cervantes puts it in the Preface to *Don Quijote*, he is taken to have his 'own mind and free inclination'[12], just as the orator (and the poet) are expected, again in *Jack Wilton*, to have 'invention or matter . . . of theyr owne'[13]. But to expect the reader to use his 'quick wits' is only part of the author's appeal; on the other hand, the reader's 'compassion' is alluded to. Obviously, his 'wits' and his 'compassion' are taken to be perfectly reconcilable, a reconciliation between rationality and empathy which enhances the momentary balance between distance and illusion promoted by the very structure of this prose. The reader, at any rate, is actively involved, and once his 'equivalence system' is simultaneously set to work on several levels he may be the better able to respond to that point in the artistic transaction where process turns into product, product into process.[14]

In a different manner, Rabelais' readers, solidly reassured of the world they live in ('car le temps est dangereux'), are confronted with the world (and the process) of the author's narration. The reader, in fact, is challenged to consider an issue which, despite its playful tone, is of fundamental importance to the way fiction, through the symbolic dimension of language, is related to reality. If, as we have noted, the knowledge of the reality of material things is stressed, it is also because the reader, in the opening paragraph of the following chapter, is summoned to verify his own experience, relinquishing traditional notions of the preconceived correspondence between the shades of colour and the states of reality ('Ce que pourrez vérifier, si arrière mise vos affections, voulez entendre . . .').

However, for Rabelais to reject the merely verbal and the traditional correspondence ('que blanc signifie foi, et bleue fermeté') is not to make room for some 'primitive purity and shortness'[15] (Bishop Sprat's terms) in a pragmatic one-for-one correspondence between terms and things. Instead, something richer than seventeenth-century empiricism is envisaged: a mode of writing which provides room, still, both to raid and to enjoy the quibbling feasts of language, and to ask the reader, not simply to unsettle the feudal tenor of metaphorical language but to build up again a new system of equivalence, a new set of imaginary correlations, more in line with the spirit of the times ('après la restitution des bonnes lettres'). The remarkable thing is that the reader is made to join, not only in the enjoyment of the imaginary products of the new Renaissance mode of symbolization but in the imaginative process of bringing them about.

III

This is not the place to read the passages in their full context. That would require an awareness of the social energies and contradictions involved in the authors' own positions (for instance, the political imagery of Rabelais' attack upon 'l'usance des tyrans qui voulent leur arbitre tenir lieu de raison'). Nor could an appreciation of the social implications in the proposed mode of symbolization disregard the paradox of Rabelais' rejection of an 'autorité privée'. (The emancipatory force and pathos of the rising conscience of modern fiction ultimately derive from the very same grounds of individuality which, as a criterion of symbolic meaning, are here exposed in their limitations). But even though the unformulated poetics of sixteenth-century fiction must be viewed as a part of a wider constellation of forces – social, ideological, rhetorical – this cursory glance at a selected text in a limited context may, perhaps, suffice to draw attention to the need for a reconsideration of the problem of realism and meaning in the context of an author–text–reader relationship which is not exclusively that of the nineteenth-century novel.

For the problem is not a purely historical one. There is an obvious connection between the rise of a new sense of fictionality in the sixteenth century and its crisis in the twentieth. New forms of opposition between imagination and reality have come to the fore, the relationship of feigning and meaning, illusion and reality, has again become a subject of practical experiment and theoretical debate. Today we know, much better than in the eighteenth and the nineteenth centuries, that art and life are not the same. The work of Bertolt Brecht and the avant-garde of our own day has made us less likely to accept the facile identification of art and reality. 'The world and the world as we are made conscious of it'[16] are not identical, yet the achievement of modern fiction cannot – despite Gabriel Josipovici and other critics – be measured alone by the degree to which the gap between perception and reality, ideology and *Praxis* is conveyed to us. If the tradition of the novel of realism, from the seventeenth to the nineteenth centuries, means anything, fiction is also vitally concerned with challenging this gap. If there is 'a dogmatic factor in realism', as Geoffrey Hartman thinks, this should not be identified with the 'assumption that a direct contact with life – with things themselves – is always available'.[17] As the multiple consciousness of fiction in the sixteenth and in the twentieth centuries shows, the gap is there all right; the question is whether it can be turned into a source of strength: whether it provides us, novelists and readers alike, with a profound challenge or an insoluble dilemma. Hence, to conceive the gap as purely ontological is not good enough for an understanding of the problem either in its modern or in its sixteenth-century context. If, instead, the varying modes of fictionality are seen as part of a changing world of history, they can be viewed as functional within a varying social context: as an imaginative vehicle of meaning within a larger process of social and literary communication which, then as now, is never outside the changing relationships and ideologies of society.

The element of historical change within the modes of fictionality can be said to reflect, more than anything else, the changing forms and functions of the communicative process between author, text and reader. In the sixteenth century, as suggested above, the need for the author to communicate his particular story and vision to the particularized expectations of his readers involved experimental forms of rhetoric and multiple modes of fictionality. The newly achieved flexibility and variability of the authorial presence (and distance) corresponded with a more variable 'system of equivalences', norms and 'corrections' on the side of the readers. At that stage the newly abundant rhetoric, the variable blending of authorial statement and mimetic illusion became a necessary mode of exploring and assuring the communicative effect of the 'true' (intended) and universal meanings of particularized images 'of a foolish world'. The product-as-process structure of the narrative reflected the unexplored needs, the nascent tensions as well as the unique possibilities and the new intensities in the interaction between what was prefigured in the writing and what was to be achieved in the reading.

When in the eighteenth and nineteenth centuries, the novel had become a widely accepted cultural institution, many initial tensions between authorial prefiguring and receptive equivalence had given way to some more common ground – social, cultural, conventional – between writers and readers. As the middle classes became pre-eminent, the ideological premises of both writing and reading were developing towards an unstable kind of consensus. On that basis many of the early functions of authorial rhetoric and several of the modes of multiple fictionality were discontinued, or replaced by self-confident sentiment and more consistent forms of mimetic reference, illusion and empathy. While Defoe and Richardson still saw fit to claim a background of fact for their fictional prefigurations (the 'true history' or authentic 'letters' of hero or heroine) as part of the significance, and while Fielding deliberately devised laws in 'the science of authoring' with 'the sanction of great antiquity' (*Joseph Andrews*, II, i), for Balzac, Scott, Jane Austen, Dickens, Turgeniev and Tolstoi, the mode of fictionality already served as a securely established convention – a convention unquestionably appropriate to a balanced relationship between prefiguration and achievement, authorial repertoires and readers' responses. The balance in that relationship was such that the fictionality of the text emerged as a confident convention which meant that communication between 'sender' and 'receiver' was both disciplined and remarkably relaxed and flexible. Continuing and consummating some of the novelistic conceptions of Rabelais, Cervantes and the early moderns, these novelists avoided the extremes of either a literal interpretation (as, say, a one-for-one correspondence between images and things) or the seven-door castle of allegory or ambiguity. Instead, their modes of fictionality allowed 'particular characters' but not in equation with 'individuals', 'general descriptions' but not as a signature of 'universals' (*Jospeh Andrews*, III, i). On premises such as these the relationship between the representation of reality and the meaning of fiction was as complex as it seemed simple: fictionality served as a metaphorical vessel of reality; form and truth seemed satisfyingly compatible. The imaginative autonomy of the fictional world helped to sustain a balanced traffic between the author's intentions or suggestions, and the reader's discovery and interpretation of meaning. Because the 'particular characters' in the text were at more than one remove from actual 'individuals' (and yet so life-like, so like them), the true meaning of the text seemed perceptible within the mode of fictionality itself. If meaning was by itself the natural test of a successful communication, the fictional realism in the process of writing and a true sense of reality in the process of reading became, as a matter of course, consonant with each other. The representation of the world in the novel and the presentation of the novel to the world of its readers constituted, or so it seemed, a self-generating circuit of considerable vitality.

This, of course, is not to deny that the author's norms and choices and the individual reader's norms and 'corrections' were quite distinct and not at all identical; for the understanding of a fictional text required readers to operate a system of equivalences as derived from differing areas of social and individual experience, and to expose, seriously or playfully, their own more pragmatic frames of reference to that operative in the text.[18] But whatever divergence there was, it was still possible for the majority of the middle-class reading public to be approached in terms of that honorable abstraction, the 'general reader' who – as the novelist's partner in dialogue – was both willing and competent to measure his own sense of value and reality in relation to that of the fictional text. The text might challenge and, occasionally, broaden his norms of perception and interpretation without actually forcing him to surrender the substance of his own social and individual identity. On that basis fictionality served as a perfectly unselfconscious vehicle of communication: imagination and truth were seen as interrelated on the levels of both writing and reading as well as through the emotional effects of the communicative transaction between them. But at that stage the product and the process were kept rather more distinct; there was little need for the kind of rhetoric which, in early modern fiction, had set out to organize that process by which the new narrative syntheses of representation and fabulation might best be communicated to what was then an inexperienced reading public.[19]

However, from the end of the nineteenth century the traditional modes of fictionality underwent considerable changes. They began to be involved in those contradictions, economic, social, ideological, which reflected the decline of bourgeois society as based on the principles of liberalism, *laissez faire*, and entrepreneurial capitalism. Against a background of economic crises, social revolution and international conflict, the position of the writer and of his middle-class audience changed radically. Since the keenly experienced contradictions between the liberal-humanist ideology and a not-so-liberal and in no way humanist praxis began to affect the writer's sensibility, his sense of value and reality began to contradict, at times to reject, the traditionally oriented norms and values of his middle-class audience. The communicative process between author, text and audience was, again, deeply affected. The traditional modes of fictionality, with their semi-autonomous assumptions of symbolic truth, could no longer provide unquestioned areas of imaginative concurrence between authorial prefigurations and readers' expectations and achievements. Novelistic truth and the social form of its reception no longer corresponded and fictionality as a mode of literary communication once more became problematic. Once the standards of realism (and the criticism of the middle-class world) in the process of writing began to reject, rather than challenge and broaden, basic premises of the general reader's ideology and sense of identity, the traditional narrative transaction was increasingly jeopardized.

But whereas Proust, Joyce, Musil, and the early *avant-garde* novelists, in rejecting traditional forms of mimesis, plot and character, cared little for the effectiveness of the novelistic transaction, many contemporary writers of fiction respond differently to the needs and problems of a more heterogeneous (and much larger) audience. This is not the place (impossible task!) to generalize about the contemporary novelist's response to his readers, yet the point should be made that today the novelistic transaction is still, perhaps more than ever before, confronted with the need for coming to terms with the gap between imagination and reality, feigning and meaning. In confronting this gap contemporary writers are all, positively or negatively (whether they recognize it as such or not) confronting the basic practical problem of a realist aesthetic: how to put across the true meaning of their statements about art or society via the fictional forms, conventions, conditions of publishing and circulation which are the tools to hand. If today the 'gap' between 'the world and the world as we are made conscious of it' presents an ever greater challenge for fiction, the ways and means of liberating and communicating this consciousness are at the centre of any realistic solution to the contradictions between ideology and praxis, art and reality, communication and publicity.

IV

As an illustration, let me cite the voice of an author sharply aware of the dichotomy between communication and publicity in contemporary American society. This is how J. D. Salinger opens *Seymour: An Introduction*:

> 'At times, frankly, I find it pretty slim pickings, but at the age of forty I look on my old fair-weather friend the general reader as my last deeply

contemporary confidant, and I was rather strenuously requested, long before I was out of my teens, by at once the most exciting and the least fundamentally bumptious public craftsman I've ever personally known, to try to keep a steady and sober regard for the amenities of such a relationship, be it ever so peculiar or terrible; in my case, he saw it coming on from the first. The question is, how can a writer observe the amenities if he has no idea what his general reader is like? The reverse is common enough, most certainly, but just when is the author of a story ever asked what he thinks the reader is like? . . . It would be too much of a good thing to hope, of course, that my very own general reader should turn out to be one of the three people who have actually seen the curlew sand-piper's nest, but I feel, at least, that I know him – you – quite well enough to guess what kind of well-meant gesture might be welcomed from me right now. In this *entre-nous* spirit, then, old confidant, before we join the others, the grounded every-where, including, I'm sure, the middle-aged hot-rodders who insist on zooming us to the moon, the Dharma Bums, the makers of cigarette filters for thinking men, the Beat and the Sloppy and the Petulant, the chosen cultists, all the lofty experts who know so well what we should or shouldn't do with our poor little sex organs, all the bearded, proud, unlettered young men and unskilled guitarists and Zenkillers and incorporated aesthetic Teddy boys who look down their thoroughly unenlightened noses at this splendid planet where (please don't shut me up) Kilroy, Christ, and Shakespeare all stopped – before we join these others, I privately say to you, old friend (unto you, really, I'm afraid), please accept from me this unpretentious bouquet of very early-blooming parentheses: (((()))).'[20]

It is almost because the narrator Buddy Class (the author's curiously undisguised *alter ego*) 'has no idea what his general reader is like', that he attempts to recreate and redefine him. There is no doubt about authorial intention here. The dedication of the book records Salinger's 'untellable affection and gratitude' to the 'amateur reader', but on a note of scepticism: 'If there is an amateur reader still left in the world . . .' The passage, despite the relaxed, genial tone of 'this *entre-nous* spirit', has something artificial and embarrassing about it. The gist of it is rhetorical artifice with studied (or scarcely suppressed) ambiguities, such as the 'amenities of such a relationship, be it ever so peculiar or terrible'. The 'terrible' quality of the welcome links between writing and reading may of course be ironically or at least deliberately stylized, as when, a few sentences later, the 'prose writer' is blamed for being 'no longer in a position to look after the reader's most immediate want; namely, to see the author get the hell on with his story'. Against that, witness in the same context the narrator's declared intention 'to jump up personally on the reader's back when I see something off the beaten plot line that looks exciting . . .' And finally, towards the end, there is the good-humoured but desperate charge: 'good night! Good night, all you infuriatingly uncommunicative people!'

It is, of course, not the irony of the narrator's protests which is disturbing. On the contrary, the ironic quality of the statement is scarcely consistent enough; rather the ambiguity of his appeal to his 'old fair-weather friend the general reader' is such that it can easily be stretched to include 'the Dharma Bums, . . . the Beat . . . , the chosen cultists, . . . Zenkillers' and such like symbols of *chic* contemporaneity (1959). If this, too, is a studied case of that 'indiscrimination' which, in *Raise High the Roof Beam, Carpenters*, is said to point 'the way of the Tao'[21] it reflects the same kind of dilemma that the narrator, as 'a discriminating man' is up against in the story. For the meaning of the story and the mode of conveying it to the reader seem to be opposed and yet linked at the same time. While the story is not actually a story about Seymour, rather a story about the writing of such a story, so the direct address to the reader is not so much a genuinely functioning mode of communication but, rather, a communication about how to communicate. The general reader, since he does not exist, is literally projected into the novel. Direct address, which used to be a convention of rhetoric, is treated as a novelistic subject matter or theme itself. The stylized process of fictional communication is not so much correlated with, but turned into, a narrative product.

The thematic function of such rhetoric points to a similarly ironic use of fictionality which is so marked among contemporary American writers like John Barth, Donald Barthelme, John Batki, Ronald Sukenick, and others. If 'the most important impetus for this sort of fiction' is said to have been 'the expression of anxiety over the epistemological validity of the fiction-making process'[22] then this anxiety is the opposite of the awareness of fictionality in early modern fiction. To put it very simply: the anxiety does not reflect a concern to bridge the gap between the world and the narrator's consciousness of it but, rather, a despairing inability to confront it realistically.

Now it should readily be admitted that out of such anxiety there has resulted an intense concern with narrative form, process and language. This may indeed stimulate the business of writing and reading by making us more fully aware of the fact that the act of perception itself – like any act of consciousness – is never a neutral one and that fiction is at more than one remove from reality: through fictionality a direct contact with life – with things themselves – is not available. But to recognize this does not by itself justify the doubt about the validity of the fiction-making process, nor does it refute the realist argument. It is only when a writer surrenders, in despair or out of frivolity, to the gap between the world and his consciousness of it that the supreme dissociation of imagination and reality ensues. At that stage the whole mode of fictionality must once again become problematic – not, as in early modern fiction, through the initial process of exploring the gap but in a final refusal to connect.

As a result, the creation and reception of meaning are radically affected. Again, if 'meaning' is defined as a function of the relationship between the poetic perception of the world in the novel and the readers' perception (and reception) of the novel in the world, then, indeed, for the 'irrealist' the question is: 'can nothing be made meaningful'? Witness, for instance, the terrifying consistency in the opening paragraphs of 'Title', from *Lost in the Funhouse*:

> Beginning: in the middle, past the middle, nearer three-quarters done, waiting for the end. Consider how dreadful so far: passionlessness, abstraction, pro, dis. And it will get worse. Can we possibly continue?
>
> Plot and theme: notions vitiated by this hour of the world but as yet not successfully succeeded. Conflict, complication, no climax. The worst is to come. Everything leads to nothing: future tense; past tense; present tense. Perfect. The final question is, Can nothing be made meaningful? Isn't that the final question? If not, the end is at hand. Literally, as it were. Can't stand any more of this.[23]

This is the story of a story which does not proceed beyond reflections on its impossibility. It is a fictional process without, properly speaking, a fictional 'product'. The narrator's activity leads to no other 'result' than the self-recording of that activity under a heading whose very namelessness pointedly suggests that 'exhausted parody of itself' which the narrator considers as one of the possibilities 'to fill in the blank'. Like Donald Barthelme's 'Sentence' or Joyce Carol Oates' 'Plot' this story sets out to 'make something out of nothing'. But Barth's rejection of the referential dimension is so extreme that the wilful acknowledgement of the chasm between fiction and reality is inverted, as it were, in the process of their absolute dissociation.

There is a paradox involved in this. If the traditional story is believed to be 'penned in red ink, to make a figure out of a fact' the practiced method of 'irrealism' attempts 'to make a fact out of a figure'.[24] The alternative is, of course, as facile as it is potentially misleading but it does emphasize the process of a *making* which, somehow, points beyond the mere filling in the blank. For one thing, the correlating function of fictionality reasserts itself and in doing so transfers, if not reality to literature, then literature back to the reality of making it. This amounts almost to a *volte-face*; for the solipsistic premises of the rejection of reality as well as its narcissistic consequences ('it's myself I address') tend to be suspended in the making and the using of the artefact itself. Over and above the fragments of whatever image and story we have, the recorded reality of the fiction-making process asserts itself out of 'nothing': nothing *is* made meaningful. The shock of recognition is derived from that: turning the negative into a quibbling positive ('there's nothing to say. Say nothing.') The chasm between the statement and its potential meaning and function is as considerable as 'the difference' – noted by Barth himself – 'between the *fact* of aesthetic ultimacies and their artistic *use*'[25]. The formulated paradox and the unformulated contradictions within such writing and reading are brilliantly explored.

The depth of the crisis in which this fiction finds itself can hardly be more cogently rendered. As prisoner of his nihilistic consciousness the narrator cannot but welcome the discontinuation of a fiction-writing activity ('the end is at hand') when everything else is finished: 'Everything's finished . . . story, novel, literature, art, humanism, humanity, the self itself.' The one exception ('Wait: the story's not finished.') seems to find itself in a complete isolation which becomes unbearably painful as soon as it is referred to the human activity of rendering it. But at this point the image of an existential situation is locked up with the technical process of composition: hence the ambiguous force of the threatening 'end' which adumbrates both the story and the life behind it. The fictional and the non-fictional meanings of 'end' become interchangeable. (The qualification – 'Literally, as it were' – only points to what is beyond the 'literal' meaning.) If this is meta-fiction at the moment of its self-styled literary exhaustion and self-destruction, it does suspend its dehumanized poetics: the process of technique and the images of a biography are reassociated. As Robert Scholes has noted, 'for Barth, it is clear in the *Funhouse* that being an artist is only a poor substitute for being a lover'[26]. In the teeth of its extinction a traditional function of fictionality asserts itself in the achievement of a momentary correlation of art and life.

This, indeed, may be a poor triumph for realism but even so it provides food for thought about the paradoxical consequences of the attempt to disparage the mimetic dimension and (more resolutely consistent even than the *nouveau roman*) 'humanism, humanity, the self itself'. For the re-emerging image of the suffering self in 'Title' sets a pattern which is more thoroughly developed in 'Autobiography', another piece of 'Self-Recorded Fiction', or in Joyce Carol Oates' 'Plot' where, again, the fictional difficulties of the author are reflected in the inseparable ties between the narrator's plot and the narrator's experience – that experience conceived as 'The record of someone going crazy'. The re-emergence of an authorial self may – as we have seen with Salinger – take the curiously undisguised form of an image of the author-narrator, but it may also point back to sophisticated patterns of fictionality, as in Barth's *Giles Goat-Boy* and *The Sot-Weed Factor* as 'novels which "imitate the form of the Novel by an author who imitates the role of Author" '[27].

In these works the mode of fictionality – so different from that of early modern narrative – has become a precarious convention, a style, but even as a style it embodies (as any style does) 'an epistemological decision, an interpretation of how and what we perceive'[28]. In that sense, the chosen mode of fictionality is still a 'statement about perception and about the relationship between fiction and life.'[29] In John Barth's case the statement may be almost totally negative but even so his turning away from some of the early functions of fictionality is revealing. This is so not only because of his acknowledged admiration for Rabelais and his own reference to Shakespeare ('*The Tempest* is the example *par excellence* – the master of illusion uncloaking his illusions on one level while maintaining them on another'). Even more significant is the way in which he has deliberately formalized the earlier dialectic of product and process: 'The process is the content, more or less'[30]. This, at any rate, seems characteristic of a good deal of experiment in contemporary fiction. For these contemporary versions of rhetoric and fictionality do not reflect the attempt to explore afresh the social function of fiction so much as they artfully respond to the absence of any such idea. In contrast, the writer of early modern fiction had to cope with a communicative situation in which the new genre had to introduce (and justify) itself by opening up both new channels of literary communication and unorthodox areas of experience. Early fiction endeavoured to help create its readers in reality; the artifice in these endeavours was taken for granted, for they were functionally related to the needs and possibilities of the literary transaction in society. Hence, the process and the content of fictionality were not identical; they were related, no matter how haphazardly, so as to involve the reader in a perception of the need for (and the pleasure of) a fictional treatment of ordinary experience. Whereas the earlier fiction reflected the readiness to face and to appropriate the tension between feigning and meaning through the contradictions of fictional form and novelistic truth, the post-modernist writers tend to redefine the gap between the real world and the poetic consciousness by moving, not beyond the contradictions of fictional form and novelistic truth but beyond the hope of ever being able to challenge and face them realistically.

Notes

1 See, for instance, *Approaches to the Novel, Materials for Poetics*, ed. Robert Scholes, rev. edition (Scranton, Penn., 1966); *The Theory of the Novel*, ed. Philip Stevick (New York, London, 1967); *The Theory of the Novel: New Essays*, ed. John Halperin (New York, 1974). There is, of course, a 'veritable log-jam of conflicting theories' on the novel which is not adequately reflected in these categories. See David Lodge, *The Novelist at the Crossroads* (London, 1971), pp. 37–68, 247–86; the citation, from the first editorial of *Novel* (Fall, 1967), p. 37.

2 Michael Riffaterre, 'The Reader's Perception of Narrative: Balzac's *Paix du ménage*', in *Interpretation of Narrative*, ed. Mario J. Valdés and Owen J. Miller (Toronto, 1978), p. 28. Mario Valdés' 'Preface' (pp. vii ff.) contains a penetrating discussion of areas of conflict and convergence between formalism and reception theory.

3 See, for example, David Lodge, 'Onions and Apricots; or, Was the Rise of the Novel a Fall from Grace? Serious Reflections on Gabriel Josipovici's *The World and the Book*', in *Critical Quarterly*, XIV (1972), p. 171.

4 As discussed, for instance, by Käte Hamburger; see Roy Pascal, 'Tense and Novel', in *Modern Language Review*, LVII (1962), 1–11.

5 I have discussed this background at some length in a German study of *Realismus in der Renaissance*, ed. Robert Weimann (Berlin, 1977), pp. 47–182.

6 Arthur Heiserman, *The Novel before the Novel* (Chicago, London, 1977), p. 221.

7 Sir Philip Sidney, *The Prose Works*, ed. Albert Feuillerat (Cambridge, 1912), III, p. 12.

8 *Ibid.*

9 Wolfgang Iser, *The Act of Reading. A Theory of Aesthetic Response* (Baltimore, London, 1978), pp. 92 ff. This is a pioneer study of great profundity but will have to be read in the light of the fact – so well brought out by J. M. Hawthorn (*Identity and Relationship*, 1973, p. 99) – that a literary response is both an individual and social phenomenon . . . is both unique and shared. It is from a position like this that the reader's response can be shown to be very much an activity in history.

10 *The Works of Thomas Nashe*, ed. R. B. McKerrow (London, 1904–10), II, p. 292.

11 François Rabelais, *Œuvres complètes*, ed. Pierre Jourda (Paris, 1962), I, pp. 40–42. The English translation follows: Gargantua's colours were white and blue, as you may have read above, by which his father meant it to be understood that he felt a heavenly joy. For white signified to him gladness, pleasure, delights, and rejoicing, and blue anything to do with Heaven.

I quite realize that on reading these words you will laugh at the old boozer, and consider his interpretation of colours most ungentlemanly and infelicitous. You will say that white stands for faith and blue for steadfastness. But without getting excited, annoyed, heated, or chafed – for this is dangerous weather – be so kind as to answer my question. I will put no other constraint upon you, or on anyone else whatever; but merely tell you a saying of the bottle.

Who is exciting you now? Who is pricking you? Who is telling you that white stands for faith and blue for steadfastness? A mouldy book, you say, that is sold by pedlars and ballad-mongers, entitled *The Blason of Colours*. Who made it? Whoever he is he has been prudent in one respect, that he has not put his name to it. For the rest, I do not know which surprises me more, his presumption or his stupidity: his presumption in daring, without reason, cause, or probability, to prescribe by his private authority what things shall be denoted by what colours; which is the custom of tyrants who would have their will take the place of reason, not of the wise and learned, who satisfy their readers with display of evidence . . .

. . . In a like darkness are involved those vainglorious courtiers and jugglers-with-names who, when they wish in their devices to signify *hope* (espoir), portray a *sphere*, put birds' *plumes* (pennes) for *pains*, *aquilegia* (l'ancholie) for *melancholy*, the *horned moon* for a *waxing fortune*, *a broken bench* for *bankrupt*, *non* and a *corselet* (un dur habit) for *non durabit*, *a bed without a tester* (lit sans ciel) for a *licentiate*: such an absurd, stale, clownish, and barbarous collection of puns, that anyone henceforth attempting to use them in France – since the Revival of Letters – ought to have a fox's tail tied to his collar and his nose rubbed in a cowpat.

With as good reason (if I should call it reason and not raving) I could have a *panier* painted to show that I am much *pained*, and a *mustard-pot* to stand for the *tardiness* of my heart. A *piss-pot* will denote an *officer*; the *bottom of my breeches*, *a jar full of wind*; my *codpiece*, *a lance in rest*; and a *dog's turd* (estront de chien), *the firm lance within* tronc de ceans), wherein lies the love of my lady.

The sages of ancient Egypt followed a very different course, when they wrote in letters that they called hieroglyphs – which none understood who did not understand, and which everyone understood who did understand, the virtue, property, and nature of the things thereby described. (Translated by J. M. Cohen, Penguin edition, 1979, pp. 57–8.)

12 Miguel de Cervantes Saavedra, *El ingenioso hidalgo Don Quijote de la Mancha*, edited by Clemente Cortejôn (Madrid, 1905), I, 16. This image of the reader is highly charged with middle-class values: 'tienes tu alma en tu cuerpo y tu libre albedrío como el más pintado, y estás en tu casa, donde eres señor della, como el rey de sus alcabalas . . .'
13 Nashe, *op. cit.*, II, p. 251.
14 On the role of the reader as collaborator cf. Jeremy Hawthorn: 'By thus seeing a literary response as something to which both reader and work contribute, we can escape both from an unreal "objectivity" resting on an assumed sameness of the work of literature which all must recognize, and a hopelessly subjective interiority which makes of a literary response something asocial and inaccessible.' (*Identity and Relationship* p. 109.)
15 *Critical Essays of the Seventeenth Century*, ed. J. E. Spingarn (London, 1908), II, p. 118.
16 Gabriel Josipovici, *The World and the Book* (Stanford, Cal., 1971), p. 139.
17 Geoffrey Hartman, 'The Heroics of Realism', in *Beyond Formalism* (New Haven, 1970), p. 62. Hartman is here concerned with a 'realism' which is '*a priori* or formal' (p. 64).
18 Cf. Johannes Anderegg, *Fiktion und Kommunikation. Ein Beitrag zur Theorie der Prosa* (Göttingen, 1973), p. 107: for the reader to perceive fictional meaning is both to supply, and tentatively to abstract from, his own frame of reference ('*dass er sein Bezugsfeld als Basis der Deutung ins Spiel bringt, daß er es aber deutend aufs Spiel setzt*').
19 Cf. William Nelson, *Fact or Fiction. The Dilemma of the Renaissance Storyteller* (Cambridge, Mass., 1973), p. 67, for the wider context of 'representation' in Renaissance narrative.
20 J. D. Salinger, *Raise High the Roof Beam, Carpenters – Seymour: An Introduction* (Penguin Books, 1964), pp. 75–7.
21 *Ibid.*, p. 58.
22 *Superfiction, or The American Story Transformed*. An anthology ed. J. D, Bellamy (New York, 1975), p.15.
23 John Barth, *Lost in the Funhouse* (New York, 1969), p. 102.
24 *Ibid.*, p. 104.
25 John Barth, 'The Literature of Exhaustion', in *Atlantic Monthly*, 220 (August, 1967), p. 31.
26 Robert Scholes, 'The Allegory of Exhaustion', in *Fiction International* (Fall, 1973), p. 107; cited by Jerome Klinkowitz, *Literary Disruptions. The Making of a Post Contemporary American Fiction* (Urbana, Chicago, London, 1975), p. 10.
27 J. D. Bellamy, *The New Fiction*. Interviews with Innovative American Writers (Urbana, Chicago, London, 1974), p. 18.
28 Susan Sontag, *ibid.*, p. 120.
29 The interviewer's question, *ibid.*
30 John Barth, *ibid.*, p. 10.

The Uses of Fiction
Edited by
Douglas Jefferson
and Graham Martin

2

The Novel and Its 'Resemblance to Life'

P. N. Furbank

Let us examine a hackneyed and familiar turn of speech about the Novel, *viz.* that certain novels exhibit 'photographic realism'. Or, reprovingly, that they are 'merely photographic' – a vice, for art demands more than just 'putting everything in'. Or again, that their photographic quality is 'deceptive': closer inspection reveals that it is the result of skilful 'selection'. This way of speaking, once extremely popular, is now distinctly old-fashioned. Nevertheless, critics and reviewers still sometimes fall into it, in an absent-minded sort of way. And, though this is not my main concern in this essay, that fact should surprise us, so I feel, even more than it does.

For, why did anyone ever think of novels as being 'photographic', with the implication that there is some straightforward, quasi-mechanical, manner in which a novelist could 'record' life – could convey to the reader an untransmuted copy of it? Or, to re-define the question more broadly: why did anyone ever speak of literature, and novels in particular, as being 'like' life? Clearly, literature is about life; and equally clearly it often describes life, in the intervals of doing other things like exhorting, or lamenting or persuading. But a description is not 'like' what it describes. It is a device for inducing the reader to conjure up what is described, in the mind's eye; resemblance does not seem to be involved. Indeed, I think the only reason why anyone would think it was involved, is because of the age-old habit of talking of literature in terms of painting. A painter's portrait, of the old-fashioned kind, or a photograph, is said to be 'a good likeness'; and this relates to the fact that someone might not *quite* impossibly mistake the portrait for the reality. Whereas, evidently, no-one ever mistook a chapter of *Middlemarch* for Dorothea Brooke.

But anyway, we don't commonly praise any particular description in a novel for its 'likeness to life'. We could hardly call George Eliot's Mr Casaubon 'a good likeness', since there never was such a person. And to speak of the description of the meeting of the Middlemarch Board of Hygiene as 'lifelike' would be vapid praise indeed. Phrases like 'photographic realism' or 'likeness to life', if used at all, have normally been applied to a novel considered as a whole. And in this essay we have not so far found any literal circumstance – like the possibility of mistaking a picture for the reality – from which, in the case of fiction, such metaphors might have developed. (You could, it is hardly necessary to add, be encouraged by a novelist to believe that his novel is actually an authentic historical document – a device exploited powerfully by Defoe, and later by many others. But what such a device prompts is not the remark that the novel is 'like life' but that it is like another sort of document or 'copy' of life. Roland Barthes, whom I shall quote later, believed indeed that 'realism' in fiction always means copying a copy.)

Meanwhile I am strongly solicited by reasons why you might want to say fiction was *not* like life. After all, our relationship to the events and people in novels could hardly be more different from what we experience in life. First, and most important of all, we can stop the events happening – the hangings, the revolutions, the marriages – by the mere decision not to turn the page: it is a gratifying and more-than-imperial situation, but could anything be less like life? And then, if one believed the stories in novels to be true, how different would be our attitude to their author. What would one feel about the author of *Madame Bovary*, that monster who spends his days perfecting sentences, and seeking the *mot juste*, to depict the agonies of arsenical poisoning? The point was excellently expressed in that brilliant essay of Fitzjames Stephens, 'The Relation of Novels to Life'[1] written in 1855; '. . . a person who went to see a man die because he liked it,' says Stephens, 'would receive very different impressions from one who saw such a sight because he could not help it.' And again, speaking of a man who attended a murder-trial:

> A man really present on such an occasion, and personally interested, would probably bring away impressions which a life-time would not destroy. In a novel, such a scene is at once more and less interesting than it is in fact. There are more points of interest, more dramatic situations; the circumstances are more clearly defined, and more sharply brought out, than they ever would be in real life; but at the same time, that from which such circumstances derive their interest is wanting: the necessity of thought and attention, the consciousness that what is passing is most real and serious business, which it is not open to the spectators to hurry over, or to lay down and take up again at pleasure. In one word, the reality.[1]

One could ask again – and the reader must forgive a question so painfully trite – where, in ordinary life, do we look for many of the features standard in novels? What, shall we say, corresponds in ordinary life to the sentence-construction, with its parenthesis, "'The will I hold in my hand,' said Mr Standish, who, seated at the table in the middle of the room, took his time about everything, including the coughs with which he showed a disposition to clear his voice, 'was drawn up by myself and executed by our deceased friend . . .'?"[2] I mean, what in ordinary life does it *resemble*? The sentence, with its rules of syntax, is the novelist's medium, as paint and canvas are those of a portrait-painter; and if, in the relationship of the sentence to 'life' there is likeness involved, it is certainly not plain for all to see, as it is with paintings, and we are going to have to dig for it.

Equally tritely, let us think of plot for a moment. If a Victorian novelist mentions that his hero, while going down the street, catches sight of a face that seems half familiar, we know, if nothing else, that we shall hear more about the owner of that face. What does this correspond to in our own life? Certainly nothing to do with walking down the street and noticing half-remembered faces – for this, in our own life, leads to no such sure prophesy and indeed tells us nothing about the future. Now this is a crude example for me to use; not all novels, I need hardly say, have 'plots' in this unashamed Victorian sense. Nevertheless it happens to lead us in a useful direction. For there is a likeness involved. There is something in life as we know it which corresponds to at least this Victorian type of plotted novel: I refer to nothing more nor less than *someone telling us a story* – in a car or a railway-carriage or by the fireside. This is a real similarity between fiction and life, and we must cling on to it, for all that it may seem very boring. And it is perhaps not as boring as it appears. Why it would be boring would be because the resemblance was too close, and in fact it is really not so close as all that. For one thing, it makes no difference to our comparison whether the story told by a real-life story-teller be true or made up. Moreover the real-life story-teller takes the initiative – unlike the case of the novel, where it is the reader who turns the page. In fact the differences are extensive and would be more obviously so, were it not that professional story-tellers, in so far as they were not supplanted by novelists, learned to model their technique and their language on those of the novelist.

So here we have what we are seeking, a likeness between fiction and life. It is a likeness-across-a-difference, and this is the only interesting kind. David Lodge, in *The Modes of Modern Writing*, remarks: '"Like" is an ambiguous word because it can denote either a relationship of similarity between things otherwise dissimilar ("My love is like a red, red rose") or a quality or representativeness deriving from an original contiguity between part and whole or unit and set ("All the roses in the garden are like this one")'[3] I once made a roughly similar remark myself in *Reflections on the Word 'Image'*: "One should remember that there are two senses of the world "like". The giant and the bearded lady at the fair are more "like" each other, in the sense of having more in common, than the roses on wallpaper are like roses in the garden.' And I went on to say, assuming what I am now questioning: 'But when we say that books are like life, or reading is like living, we mean it in the sense in which the roses on wallpaper are like the real ones.'[4]

Now as we know novelists used to love to exploit the likeness-across-a-difference between novel-writing and oral story-telling. They would playfully pose as a buttonholing *raconteur*. And some, like Emily Brontë and Conrad, would find much of their material in the likeness-across-a-difference between *raconteur* and novelistic narrator, as an area in which to suggest motive. They might choose, as Emily Brontë did, to dramatize such a likeness-across-a-difference, so that much of what we learn about Nelly Dean is inferred from her unreliability as *raconteur*. Or they might, by means of it, tacitly indicate characteristics and personal motives in an ostensibly neutral or 'invisible' narrator. And, as Roland Barthes has shown in *S/Z*, '*raconteurs*' and 'narrators' can be considered as anthropomorphizations of narratives, which themselves can reveal motives, or at any rate compulsions – i.e. economic ones, to do with their own survival and self-protection.[5]

It will be noticed that the resemblance between fiction and life that we have been talking about is between just one aspect of novels (plot), though a very important one at least for the nineteenth-century novel, and just one aspect of real life (anecdotage and story-telling), not a very important one in literate Western society. Thus we shall find no warrant here for talking of novels as 'like life' in general (or 'photographic', or whatever), these being terms (as I have said) which always imply speaking of life as a whole and novels as a whole. And as for 'photographic realism', the phrase has nothing much to do with the grand and heroic achievements of nineteenth-century French Realism and Naturalism and mainly relates to the British 'slice-of-life' school of fiction of the 1930s, which was rather a muddle anyway; so that all that a critic needs to do is simply to throw the phrase away, if he has not done so already, and with it the one about art residing in 'selection'.

On the other hand, when considering that great nineteenth-century French school of fiction, I am attracted by Roland Barthes' way of explaining it in terms of 'likeness-making'. The basic equipment of a French Realist or Naturalist novelist, according to Barthes, is not an easel but an empty frame. Faced with a collection or continuum of objects, his only way of turning it into words (and it becomes almost a Laurel-and-Hardy eccentricity) is to put his frame round it.

> 'In order to speak about it, the writer, through this initial rite, first transforms the "real" into a depicted (framed) object; having done this, he can take down this object, *remove* it from his picture: in short: de-depict it (to depict is to unroll the carpet of the codes, to refer not from a language to a referent but from one code to another). Thus, realism (badly named, at any rate often badly interpreted) consists not in copying the real but in copying a (depicted) copy of the real.'[6]

According to this, 'likeness to life' in Balzac (and Flaubert) comes in as the result of a very arbitrary, and as you might say unnatural, decision on the part of writing to take painting as its model. And it raises the all-important question of why the novelist should thus want to frame reality and put it at a remove; or in what spirit, to quote Barthes:

> this famous reality, as if from a fear forbidding it to be touched directly, is *set farther away*, deferred, or at any rate taken hold of by means of the pictorial matrix or "setting" in which it has been embedded as a preliminary to turning into words.[7]

It does, moreover, bring in the notion, if not of photography, at least of mechanical copying. For, as Barthes points out, there is in Balzac's descriptions a sort of 'infinite regress' or circularity involved, so that, in order to describe a real body, he will habitually refer it to works of art.

But are there other ways in which novels are 'like life'? (We can forget the complementary question of life being like novels, since it can never rise above the trivial – a matter of remarking to a friend 'What a Balzacian situation' or 'What a very Ivy Compton-Burnett conversation'. Though the reasons why this should be so, .if we troubled to pursue them, would also tell us much to our purpose.) I will quite another telling *mot* of Fitzjames Stephens: 'Marriage in novels occupies almost always the position which death occupies in real life: it is the art of transition into a new state, with which novelists (with some very rare exceptions) have little or nothing to do'[8]. This seems to me a very true remark. Marriage was, for the nineteenth-century novelist, the regular and most dependable embodiment of the fiction that repercussions are not infinite and that certain events do really have an end and a quietus. It was the most familiar of answers to Henry James's 'exquisite problem':

> 'Really, universally, relations stop nowhere, and the exquisite problem of the artist is eternally but to draw, by a geometry of his own, the circle within which they shall happily *appear* to do so.'[9]

It is also a true likeness between life and fiction, and all the more rewarding by being so very much a likeness-across-a-difference. And on the other hand the marriage-novel (from Fielding to Forster) is a particularly strong discouragement, should we still need one, to any lingering tendency to think of novels as replicas of life – in that their form, a set of events all tending towards a marriage, so little suggests a 'slice of life' and so loudly announces a purpose. The purpose, of course, may take various forms: it may be ethical, marriage being seen as the reward for right moral behaviour; or it may be eugenic, showing how and by what mating the best kind of soul or citizen is to be engendered; or it may be, as in *Howards End*, to exemplify the reconciliation of warring qualities, for the health of the individual or society or the nation. And, as Fitzjames Stephens implies, the form has a weakness, one which infects even *Middlemarch* to some degree – I mean, the haloing of marriage, the end-term of the novel, with a nimbus of hopes and possibilities, undefined and (because of the THE END sign) undefinable.

I would like to digress on the subject of the 'marriage-novel'. What I want to say concerns Proust. His account of how Swann came to marry Odette could, with a little straining, be said to be a 'marriage-novel'; and if this were allowed, it would have to count as one of the greatest examples of the *genre*, though a most sophisticated and astringent one, quite free from that weakness I have just referred to. Swann, cured of his passion, reflects with surprise: 'And she wasn't even my type.' And that is that. A most convincing novel ends here; and soon there begins an entirely different one, that of Swann's married life. But what also calls for comment is the use to which the Swann 'novel' is put in the larger work. Proust must, one feels (it is characteristic of his 'concrete' methods) have placed this story where it is, near the outset of the book, to serve as a specimen of nineteenth-century fiction in this twentieth-century novel. Metaphors about 'development' must be involved, since the fictive date of the Swann episode corresponds to that of the Naturalist school of fiction-writing. However, it was necessary for Proust to justify the presence of such a specimen, and the justification he found was a most satisfying one and is instructive for our present theme. When the narrator first got to know Swann, the Swann-Odette affair was already over; but his gradual coming to hear the story, and effort to reconstruct it, was his first introduction to adult experience, and for that reason a permanent model and point of reference for him (a fact we are continually reminded of later). Thus he came to know the story *backwards*, from the familiar figure of the older Swann, the family friend, to the extravagant vicissitudes of the younger Swann's passion and obsession. And this is a very good way to learn or read such a story. It obviates the weakness native to nineteenth-century fiction, which proceeds through the unknown to the known, through unforeseen vicissitudes to a foreseen end – I mean, the temptation to lapse into the childish and the trite.

We touch here on a theme of Frank Kermode's *The Sense of an Ending*, *viz.* that the fictional imagination, with its insistence on beginnings and endings, resembles the apocalyptic or chiliastic one in real life. It springs from an inborn desire to make sense of things and to find 'consonances' in them – in defiance of the 'reality-principle' (or in Freud's terms, repression) which would deny this satisfaction to one. A treaty is signed between the two powers, which is described by Kermode thus:

> 'Now peripateia depends on our confidence of the end; it is a disconfirmation followed by a consonance; the interest of having our ex-

> pectations falsified is obviously related to our wish to reach the discovery of recognition by an unexpected and instructive route. It has nothing whatever to do with any reluctance on our part to get there at all.'[10]

This is persuasively put. Nevertheless there is a trouble for me with Kermode's book in that, sometimes, he seems to give too much endorsement to getting what we *want* from fiction (and especially the wanting that everything should fit). So much play with the 'need' for fictions and their power to 'console' begins to make them seem weak-minded. One asks oneself if the imagination cannot be more positive and active, a tougher customer than that. There is something preferable, in a way, in Barthes' unsentimental language about Narrative as 'merchandise' and about 'the relation of the contract of which it is the object'. But perhaps (yes, I am inclined to think so) it is wrong after all to class the Swann-Odette episode as a 'marriage-novel'. It is truer to life, and Proust has subdued it more to the 'reality-principle', so that the equivalence between marriage and death (our 'likeness-across-a-difference') is proportionately less felt. Truth to life has diminished 'likeness to life'.

We come back to 'likeness'. I cling to a belief in 'expressive form' in literature, and to that extent to the somewhat blown-upon doctrine of *mimesis*. It seems to me obvious that the form of, say, certain couplets by Pope or lines by Milton is expressive and imposes an important kind of mimicry on the reader. And the more complex and subtle the effect, the more one is made aware of the remoteness of the medium from the thing expressed. This gulf of difference goes without saying, in poetry. But when we come to fiction and its own kind of 'expressive form', the difference seems to call for more comment. In general, one can't do better when considering the difference of novels from life than to remember Proust's words on the subject:

> 'A "real person", profoundly as we may sympathise with him, is in a great measure perceptible only through our senses, that is to say, he remains opaque, offers a dead weight which our sensibilities have not the strength to lift. If some misfortune comes to him, it is only in one small section of the complete idea we have of him, that we are capable of feeling an emotion; indeed it is only in one small section of the complete idea he has of himself that he is capable of feeling any emotion either.

> The novelist's happy discovery was to think of substituting for those opaque sections, impenetrable by the human spirit, their equivalent in immaterial sections, things, that is, which the spirit can assimilate to itself.'[11]

In novels the difference from life is more interesting than the likeness. And it goes with this that, if you are looking for the 'likeness' between novels and life you will find it, not in the novels' supposed 'subject-matter', but in their *devices*. Let's think of that favourite device of nineteenth-century novelists by which we are made to observe a character, apparently a stranger, for a few moments before it is revealed that this is someone we already know quite well. Here is Hardy in *Jude the Obscure*:

> 'It was the spring fair at Kennetbridge, and though this ancient trade-meeting had much dwindled from its dimensions of former times, the long straight street of the borough presented a lively scene about midday. At this hour a light trap, among other vehicles, was driven into the town by the north road, and up to the door of a temperance inn. There alighted two women, one the driver, an ordinary country person, the other a finely built figure in the deep mourning of a widow. Her sombre suit, of pronounced cut, caused her to appear a little out of place in the medley and bustle of a provincial fair.'[12]

And who is this handsome-looking widow? Well, of course, it's our old friend Arabella. This device of re-introduction works, you might say, in the opposite fashion to 'recognition-scenes' in classical tragedy, part of its function being to suggest how much *other* life, never knowable to us, is led by even the people we know closest. (Flaubert is drawing on emotions not so very different in that famous actual, and not pretended, recognition-scene in *L'Education sentimentale*, where in the murderous policeman Frédéric recognizes his old associate Sénécal.[13]) And in some ways, pretended 're-introductions' such as the Hardy one are 'like' the occasions in real life when, in real life, we catch sight of people we know very well and for a moment or two do not recognize them and see them as strangers. But as a device, offering a whole set of relationships between narrator and reader, this trick of 're-introduction' has a different destiny in fiction from what it has in real life, and a richer one. It is an 'improved suggestion' from life, hardly more closely tied to its origin that pastoral is to rural life or an *andante* is to walking. There is a 'likeness to life' involved, but one that we do not need to ponder too earnestly.

Notes

1 J. Fitzjames Stephens, 'The Relation of Novels to Life', *Cambridge Essays, Contributed by Member of the University* (1855), pp. 154, 156.
2 George Eliot *Middlemarch*, Book 4, Ch. 35.
3 David Lodge *The Modes of Modern Writing* (1979), p. 112.
4 P. N. Furbank *Reflections on the Word 'Image'* (1970), p. 71.
5 Roland Barthes *S/Z* (transl. Richard Miller, 1975), pp. 88–90.
6 *Op. cit.*, pp. 54–5 (my translation).
7 *Op. cit.*, p. 61 (my translation).
8 Stephens, *op. cit.*, p. 171.
9 Henry James, Preface to *Roderick Hudson* (1907), in *The Art of the Novel* (1953), New York, p. 5.
10 Frank Kermode, *The Sense of an Ending* (1967), p. 18.
11 Marcel Proust, *Swann's Way*, Part 1, pp. 112–13 (Chatto and Windus Paperback Edition).
12 Thomas Hardy, *Jude the Obscure* (1895), Part Five, Chapter 7.
13 Gustave Flaubert, *L'Education sentimentale* (1869), Part III, Chapter 5.

The Uses of Fiction
Edited by
Douglas Jefferson
and Graham Martin

3

Individuality and Characterization in the Modernist Novel

Jeremy Hawthorn

Things in the world are not portrayed directly in art. All art is artificial. Another way of expressing it is to say that before something in the world can be incorporated in a work of art it must be adapted in accordance with certain conventions which the artist may modify, but which he or she cannot altogether ignore. Thus speech, when represented in the novel, is adapted in certain ways so that although it represents real speech, it is not identical to it. The ways in which human individuality is presented in the novel are likewise subject to the operations of certain conventions, conventions which we can refer to as notions of literary character. But just as fictional conversations are dependent on actual forms of verbal intercourse in real life even if they are not identical with them, so too an author's – or an age's – conception of literary character is related to the actual, historical development of human individuality. Thus we are likely to find that there is a relationship, although not a mechanical one, between historical changes in the nature of human individuality and alterations in the literary conventions regulating the presentation of character.

The argument of this essay is that in the present century increasingly sharp contradictions in our society have been more and more internalized in human beings, and that this has, in important ways, created a different sort of human individual. It will be further argued that the new sort of literary character which we find in the modernist novel is reflective of this development – and thus in certain important ways helps us to perceive and understand it. I will thus be led to express disagreement with those Marxist critics who have seen literary modernism as a negative development. The term 'modernism' is, as Peter Faulkner points out in his useful little book *Modernism*,[1] one which has assumed wide currency only in the last decade or so. It is somewhat more all-embracing than a term like 'experimental', and suggests the whole family of formal and other revolutions in art which involve a rejection of what Faulkner calls 'nineteenth-century assumptions'. 'The modernist novel' in this essay should be taken to refer to writers such as Virginia Woolf, James Joyce, Franz Kafka, and Albert Camus.

It is by no means an original claim that the development of the novel is implicated in changes in the nature of human individuality. Georg Lukács has argued that

> 'With the growing social division of labour and the complication of social relations in class societies, a division between the public and private occurs in life itself. Literature as the reflection of life cannot help reproducing this process. But this does not only affect the themes of literature which deal with the human problems arising out of this development. The forms of literature, too, as generalized forms reflecting constant and recurring features of life, which grow more pronounced with time, cannot remain untouched by this process.'[2]

A number of critics have drawn attention to the difference between the epic and the novel to illustrate how such changes in the nature of human experience and human individuality lead to changes in artistic and literary form and genre. Ralph Fox, for instance, refers to the general development of society to explain why it is that the epic pays little attention to the individual character:

> 'There was a balance between the characters of the epic and the society in which they lived which has since been lost. Indeed, the *Iliad* is more a picture of society than of any one of its characters, a society in which the individual does not feel himself in opposition to the collective, any more than he feels himself in conflict with nature.'[3]

Erich Auerbach, writing about the *Odyssey* in his book *Mimesis*, comments of a passage from it that

> 'Clearly outlined, brightly and uniformly illuminated, men and things stand out in a realm where everything is visible; and not less clear –

wholly expressed, orderly even in their ardor – are the feelings and thoughts of the persons involved.'[4]

Putting it another way, one can say that in a society where there is no fundamental tension between people, there will be no realm of the private within people, and such people will require a different form of artistic portrayal from those whose lives are less visible and open. Arnold Kettle has commented of the Icelandic Saga that it was produced by a very public society,[5] one where the distinctions between public and private life with which we are familiar were not current. The artist of such a society will not, we can surmise, be interested in 'going inside' characters for the simple reason that not much of interest is liable to be discovered there.

Again commenting on the epic and the novel, Lukács has argued that they

> 'differ from one another not by their authors' fundamental intentions but by the given historico-philosophical realities with which the authors were confronted. The novel is the epic of an age in which the extensive totality of life is no longer directly given, in which the immanence of meaning in life has become a problem, yet which still thinks in terms of totality.'[6]

This is, I feel, a brilliant and suggestive view of the tensions of which the novel is, in part, born. Of all literary forms the novel most urgently seeks to encompass totalities, both social and historical. And yet no literary form finds the exposure of the complete more fraught with difficulties, more problematic. This is as much true of the totality of the individual human being as it is true of the totality of a human society (not that the two can be separated). Pinning precise dates to such changes is always a risky business. One can say with assurance, however, that by the end of the eighteenth century there is a felt need to explore the complex, historically new interlinkings of public and private, part and whole, objective and subjective, and that the development of the novel is thoroughly implicated in this need.

A literary concern with the apparently autonomous, self-directing character, then, cannot be detached from the growth of a society in which real changes in the nature of human individuality are taking place. Indeed, in some ways it is perhaps more accurate to speak not of a change in human individuality, but of the emergence of human individuality at the time when, as Lukács expresses it, a division between the public and the private occurs in life itself. Society is no longer simply public but is also a collection of privacies. Such a change involves a concealment of connections, the apparent loss of that totality which the novel attempts to rediscover. Paradoxically, however – and this is crucial for the rise of the novel as a literary form – although human individuals in early capitalism are more self-contained, self-motivated, 'privatized', socially and intellectually mobile, this development is contingent upon enormous changes in society which are the product of human cooperation and of collective activity. The 'self-contained' individual is, ironically, less able to survive on his or her own than was the feudal peasant, who seemed – and was – anchored in a much more intensely communal way of life. Robinson Crusoe represents one of the most powerful of bourgeois myths precisely because he stands for something – complete material self-sufficiency – that the bourgeois is dimly but insistently aware that he or she can never achieve.

This paradox is mirrored both in the typical form of the novel, which allows assorted privacies and secrecies to be revealed in their interconnections and in their relationship with a determining social context, and also in the novel's larger sociology: the novel is 'consumed' in private, silently, even introspectively, whilst remaining dependent upon the growth of a collective, industrialized society which produces books – and literate individuals – in their hundreds of thousands.

Harley C. Shands, in an essay to which a number of references will be made in the pages that follow, draws a revealing contrast between a present-day undeveloped society and an industrialized Western society. In the course of this comparison he makes a number of points about the 'construction of individuality' in these differing contexts which have points of contact with some of the comments already quoted concerning the differences between the societies which produced the epic and the novel.

The approach of Shands, and of those writers quoted earlier, appears more rewarding than recent neo-Freudian approaches to the 'construction of the self', which are generally asocial and ahistorical, and which thus fail to make what is to me the essential point, that human 'selves' are not all the same. Taking Lévi-Strauss's distinction between 'concrete' and 'abstract' thinking, Shands suggests that the 'concrete savage' (Lévi-Strauss's term), 'is "embedded" in his group, and . . . *does not need* internalized thoughts or feelings.'[7] He further notes that 'modern man', in contrast 'is *abstracted* man, *disembedded* man, who lives not in a world of immediate meaningful sensory experiences but in a world of remote indirect conceptual structures (p. 195). Shands argues that 'embeddedness' is a positive barrier to the development of an industrial society, which requires self-determining individuals who can move beyond traditional, socially conventional modes of behaviour. (Whether such mobility constitutes genuine self-determination is, of course, a moot point.)

Is the notion of 'embeddedness' a useful tool in discussing the development of human individuality? Clearly there are different sorts and levels of embeddedness: the pre-literate 'concrete savage' can be seen to be embedded in concrete sensations, while the modern industrial worker who, in Shands's terms, is clearly 'disembedded' in some ways, is also deeply embedded in certain ideological assumptions. Thus a person in the modern world can combine levels of embeddedness and disembeddedness. Nevertheless, the term allows us conveniently to talk of the extent to which an individual has a conception of him or herself as separate from society in some way or another. Shands argues, interestingly, that to achieve disembeddedness a measure of self-objectification is necessary, and that this can only be achieved where a written technology exists.

> 'Until and unless human beings find a written technology, it is impossible to perform certain intellectual operations – although, on the other hand, once the implications of the written technology are developed and internalized, it becomes possible to carry out many intellectual operations "in the head" . . .' (p. 198)

Even more interesting: this process of self-objectification can produce a complex rather than a simple, unitary self; a self in which different identities are subsumed and combined, identities which can even discourse with one another:

> 'The process by which a human being learns how to split himself so as to become his own primary respondent is best described as one of *inner speech*, in which "I" talk (as it were) to "me"; then, suddenly shifting places, often quite without realizing that the "subject" is now different . . . a different "I" hears a different message.' (p. 198)

The crucial question this raises, and to which I will return in discussing characterization in modernist novels, is whether these different personae are complementary or contradictory – in tension or in agreement. A temporary answer to this question is that that will depend upon the social origins of these internalized identities: if the different identities represent different, and conflicting, social forces then we can expect to find a conflict-ridden individual.

Shands's observations may be usefully complemented by mention of the work of the Soviet psychologist Lev Vygotsky on the child's acquisition of 'inner speech'. In *Thought and Language* Vygotsky argues that as the human being matures, thought and language develop a complex, dialectical relationship whereby advances in the one are made possible by, and encourage, advances in the other.[8] Thus Vygotsky, to simplify his argument, plots a path from social speech, through egocentric speech, to inner speech and, finally, thought. The crucial aspect of such a model of the acquisition of language and thought is that it privileges the social, which is seen as primary, and thus gives us a way of understanding the precise mechanism whereby the dominant relationships in social life can become, in modified form, those of thought and of the inner psyche. The individual's subjectivity and identity are, according to such a model, constructed in a social mould. Shands's article is primarily concerned with those in modern industrial societies who have somehow failed to build themselves a consistent inner self, a failure which Shands seeks to explain by reference to a lack of formal education. Such an explanation certainly ties in with the findings of Vygotsky's pupil and colleague, A. R. Luria.[9] But a further possibility demands consideration: what if the social reality upon and within which an inner self has to be constructed is too contradictory for some people coherently to internalize it? Certainly Shands's terms 'embedded' and 'disembedded' seem to have some force when applied to the epic and the novel. The epic is the art form of men and women embedded in the values and activities of a group; the novel in contrast concerns itself with 'characters', with human individuals who normally have a distinct sense of self that is far less dependent upon day-to-day construction via 'immediate meaningful sensory experiences'.

Let me summarize at this point, and stress that in the construction of human individuality in the modern age there seem to me to be two crucial elements to bear in mind. Firstly the spread of literacy and formal education, which allows for an awareness of alternative realities and the development of techniques of self-scrutiny. A. R. Luria's interviews with illiterate peasants in his book *Cognitive Development* give striking and convincing evidence that people who cannot read or write and who have received no formal education cannot project themselves imaginatively into situations not based on immediate personal experience, cannot scrutinize themselves from outside, and, in brief, in important ways do not have a private self in the way that a typical, literate individual in an industrial society does. But secondly, the larger social and productive relations in society will have a crucial determining effect on the construction of individuality within that society. Where people are ranged in antagonistic classes, then to a greater or lesser extent they will tend to be possessed of internally contradictory and antagonistic selves.

In the early days of the development of a class-divided society such contradictions may not appear too immediate or pressing. Certainly in the early days of the development of the novel the novelist seems primarily concerned to bring the concealed part of life to light rather than to explore the conflicts between the public and the private. Thus E. M. Forster is quite right in suggesting (although he is not consciously making a historical point) that the major difference between a fictional character such as Moll Flanders and a 'real person' is that Moll 'belongs to a world where the secret life is visible, to a world that is not and cannot be ours.'[10] He further notes that when a novelist knows everything that there is to know about a character then we get from this a reality of a kind that we never get in daily life (p. 70). Behind Forster's (and Defoe's) approach to the novel lies, one suspects, the essentially pre-modernist view that life in any age is complicated only to the extent that much of it is hidden. Once reveal this submerged reality and what is made visible will all fit neatly together like a jigsaw; it may be complex, but it will make sense. For the modernist writer, in contrast, the uncovering of what Forster calls 'the secret life' is necessary, but he or she has no corresponding confidence in the production of coherence out of this process. Many pieces of the jigsaw will not fit, and many different pictures can be made from those that do.

Dostoyevsky is a novelist whose work falls interestingly between these contrasting forms and periods, and in his treatment of character we can see an early response to the pressures that were to become crucial in the modernist novel. His creative adaptation of the murder mystery allows him to work within a popular formal framework which focusses attention upon the need to 'discover' something, to expose a secret. But unlike the reader of the popular murder mystery, the reader of Dostoyevsky's work cannot feel that everything has been rendered clear and non-problematic when that something has been discovered. Somehow we have more questions to answer when we know who killed old Karamazov that we had before. One explanation of this may be that Dostoyevsky recognizes the 'lowest common denominator' of privacy in his society to be not the individual action, or consciousness, but something within the individual of which that person is unaware. Human subjectivity, in other words, had become not just private, but the site of contradictions. In *The Brothers Karamazov* the Elder Zossima, in his valedictory message, characterizes his age as one in which

> 'all men are separated into self-contained units, everyone crawls into his own hole, everyone separates himself from his neighbour, hides himself away and hides away everything he possesses, and ends up by keeping himself at a distance from other people and keeping other people at a distance from him. He accumulates riches by himself and thinks how strong he is now and how secure, and does not realize, madman that he is, that the more he accumulates the more deeply does he sink into self-destroying impotence. For he is used to relying on himself alone and has separated himself as a self-contained unit from the whole. He has trained his mind not to believe in the help of other people, in men and mankind, and is in constant fear of losing his money and the rights he has won for himself. Everywhere today the mind of man has ceased, ironically, to understand that true security of the individual does not lie in isolated personal efforts but in general human solidarity.'[11]

The new element here is the perception of the self-destructive nature of 'privatization' in a divided society, and this element is prophetic of many later developments in the modernist novel. It is of course important to recognize that complexity in character, even contradiction and inner conflict, is not born only with the novel. Auerbach, in *Mimesis*, points out that there is another tradition from that which can be illustrated by reference to the Homeric epic. Taking the biblical account of Abraham's journey to sacrifice his son Isaac, Auerbach comments that

> 'the most important thing is the "multilayeredness" of the individual character; this is hardly to be met with in Homer, or at most in the form of a conscious hesitation between two possible courses of action; otherwise, in Homer, the complexity of the psychological life is shown only in the succession and alternation of emotions; whereas the Jewish writers are able to express the simultaneous existence of various layers of consciousness *and the conflict between them.*' (p. 13, my italics)

It is surely no accident that it should be within the work of Jewish writers that this tradition of portraying a character's inner thoughts and feelings and their contradictions should arise: a context which is not only highly literate, but which is also that of an oppressed group, where individual subjectivities are formed in the mould of larger social conflicts and tensions. This also explains, perhaps, why aspects of the Jewish-Christian tradition should find such a ready acceptance within capitalist societies, for in both contexts social conflicts are involved in the production of contradictory, multi-layered individuals.

The recognition of conflict is central to Dostoyevsky's view of humanity in his own time, both for the individual and for humanity at large. At one point in *The Brothers Karamazov* it is almost as if he is anticipating and answering the claims of Marshall McLuhan that technological development, 'better communications', will end all conflict – all 'breakdowns in communication' – and create a serene, integrated global village.

> 'We are assured that the world is getting more and more united and growing into a brotherly community by the reduction of distances and the transmission of ideas through the air. Alas, put no faith in such a union of peoples. By interpreting freedom as the multiplication and the rapid satisfaction of needs, they do violence to their own nature, for such an interpretation merely gives rise to many senseless and foolish desires, habits and the most absurd inventions.' (p. 369)

To return to my starting point, however, it is worth reminding ourselves that when reality changes then art has to develop new conventions to cope with such changes. The novelist has to learn new ways of representing the sort of inner conflict that is increasingly important in the present century. Auerbach pointed out, in a passage already quoted, that Homer might imply inner conflict by showing a character hesitating between two courses of action, in other words by objectifying a possible subjective tension. To present the reader with the inner conflicts and tensions of Ivan Karamazov Dostoyevsky gives us Ivan, in the early stages of a nervous breakdown, talking to a hallucinated version of one part of himself. Such a technique cannot but appear rather contrived and mechanical, and it is interesting to see how, in different novels, Dostoyevsky progressively refines a more sophisticated technique involving the use of social eccentrics.

This fondness for the depiction of eccentrics can be explained by noting how the portrayal of the eccentric allows Dostoyevsky to make public and manifest what is more normally concealed within a character's inner psyche, but without making the reader feel that he or she is somehow being subjected to a rather mechanical contrivance. Eccentrics exist in real life; they are also treated in Dostoyevsky's novels by other characters much as real eccentrics might be treated by other people, but the difference is that Dostoyevsky's eccentrics are revealing in socially significant ways. In his address 'To the Reader' at the start of *The Brothers Karamazov* Dostoyevsky suggests that

> 'far from "always" being a personality and an exception, an eccentric sometimes, on the contrary, expresses the very sum and substance of a certain period while the other people of the same period for some reason or other do not seem to belong to it.' (p. xxv)

It is because Dostoyevsky so clearly perceives the link between inner contradiction in his characters and larger contradictions in society (as the speech of the Public Prosecutor in *The Brothers Karamazov* demonstrates) that his work represents such an important staging point in the development of the novel. Compare, for instance, the unmasking of the murderer in *The Brothers Karamazov* with the unmasking of the murderer in Dickens's *Martin Chuzzlewit*: in the latter novel it is hard to feel that much *mystery* is left for the reader after this event.

Dickens's portrayals of inner conflict are, like those of his Russian contemporary, still seeking for adequate conventional expression. Wemmick, in *Great Expectations*, is revealing for the social historian, but perhaps rather less satisfying for the literary critic. His portrayal indicates that Dickens was very well aware that social institutions created conflicts of interest and identity for human beings, but it is not a portrayal that we can feel is altogether satisfactory in capturing the confused and complicated ways in which such contradictions are internalized. Making the contradictions so public makes them appear simpler, more accessible than they in fact are.

Wemmick is, at the same time, one of the first examples in literature of the divisions a job can as it were 'insert' in an individual, and also one of the last examples in which such divisions can be portrayed as wholly on the surface, wholly public. From this time on the novel tends to portray an individual's contradictions as less obvious, more complex, more concealed, and if we search the novel form for examples of undivided, non-contradictory heroes, we discover in general that they are fools, dropouts, failures, lunatics: Stevie in Conrad's *The Secret Agent*, Septimus in Virginia Woolf's *Mrs Dalloway*, Meursault in Camus's *The Outsider*. Such a development may not be wholly a literary one. If we consider Willy Loman in Arthur Miller's *The Death of a Salesman*, we realize that the reason the contradictions in his life destroy him while the contradictions in Wemmick's life can be neatly compartmentalized and tolerated is that there is, in Loman's society, a powerful ideological pressure to deny that such contradictions exist. In Dickens's day, for various complex reasons, this appears not to have been the case – partly because the full extent of the contradictions was not so fully perceived. Again, Wemmick knows he lives two lives, Loman does not. Loman's attempt to lead a single, coherently ordered life incorporating public and private values is as destructive for him as it is, revealingly, for Stevie, Septimus and Meursault.

Georg Lukács, of all Marxist literary critics, is best known for his lack of sympathy with modernist literature. On the topic of modernist characterization he has criticized many writers. Some of these criticisms have considerable force, but even so it seems ironic that the critic who saw most clearly the connection between socio-historical changes and the rise of the novel should fail to appreciate that further socio-historical development might demand new modes of literary characterization. In particular it is Lukács's demand that characters be possessed of historical *consciousness* that causes problems. Thus he praises Walter Scott's

> ' "necessary anachronism" [which] consists, therefore, simply in allowing his characters to express feelings and thoughts about real, historical relationships in a much clearer way than the actual men and women of the time could have done.'[12]

Given such a predilection it is understandable that Lukács should fail to sympathize with the work of, for instance, Kafka. But had Kafka made his characters historically self-conscious in the way that Scott's characters are, would his readers have recognized their own historical predicaments in the portrayals? Kafka's work can rightly be criticized for suggesting that life is meaningless, but it does have the great virtue of capturing the truth that for many people in our century it has seemed meaningless. To this extent it has at least started a process of coming to terms with this truth and attempting to explain it. Lukács's own admiration for *Don Quixote*[13] might, one feels, have shown him that uncomprehending characters could have a role in producing comprehending readers. Jack Lindsay has commented of Lukács that in dealing with modernist works he forgets his own doctrine of mediations[14] – in other words that the writer does not give the reader reality, but reality which is as it were transformed through the operation of codes and conventions. The modernist character may not be 'like life' in an obvious sense, any more than Dostoyevsky's eccentrics were conspicuously in evidence in contemporary Russia, but it may enable us better to understand life nonetheless.

Lukács would doubtless argue that a full consciousness of the world is a feature of the development of socialism in the present century, and should be reflected in the novel. But the portrayal of the unconscious character may well be an element in the social attainment of such knowledge. Lukács, correctly in my view, writes of 'a great social need', 'the desire for the contradictory but inseparable unity . . . of individuality and sociality, whose fulfilment is the role of art.'[15] For Lukács,

> 'The more developed a human being is, the more he is an individual, but this can only be realized truly, seriously and deeply in him if this individual is more, and qualitatively different from the random combination of accidental individual features; if therefore what is manifested in him is not merely the deaf and dumb purely natural endowments of the human species, but if the species' truly human articulation gains an intelligent voice in his deeds and words.' (p. 54)

This is a fine statement, and one not summarily to be dismissed. But unfortunately, in moving from the highly abstract and general level of this statement to the question of the subject matter of art, Lukács seems to me to make the mistake of assuming that this human ideal must be fully represented in the individual artistic character.

> 'The aesthetic type, therefore, in which particularity is most artistically manifested signifies the road of the concrete fulfilment of human existence as a species. It is the central category of artistic creation because it is through it that artistic creation becomes the sensually unfolded and united concrete reflection of the embodying of a stage in the great road of the human species seeking and finding itself.' (p. 54)

Lindsay's comment seems to me to be particularly apt here. It is as if Lukács is ignoring the whole problem of artistic mediation – the complex ways in which art works are received, interpreted, used by different people. If a work of art is to help the human species to seek and find itself then, for Lukács, the seeking and the finding must be present, visible, in the work. Lukács never seems to consider that a work which shows the seeking may encourage readers to accomplish the finding.

So far as our discussion of character is concerned, Lukács seems to insist that the novel show the supersession of human divisions and contradictions in its presentation of character, rather than presenting these divisions and contradictions bluntly and implying the need to overcome them. Engels pointed out a long while ago that socialist writers needed to remember who they were writing for, drawing attention to the fact that as novels 'under our conditions' are 'mostly addressed to readers from bourgeois circles',

> 'The socialist problem novel in my opinion fully carries out its mission if by a faithful portrayal of the real conditions it dispels the dominant conventional illusions concerning them, shakes the optimism of the bourgeois world, and inevitably instils doubt as to that which exists, without itself offering a direct solution of the problem involved, even without at times ostensibly taking sides.'[16]

Engels certainly understood the point reiterated by a recent critic of Lukács's,[17] that the individual novel was only a part—often a small part—of the forces that changed the consciousness of an individual reader, and that the single novel does not have the responsibility of presenting all reality, giving all the answers, within its pages. So far as characterization is concerned, Engels also clearly understood that as human beings changed historically (a change that Lukács's use of a term like 'the human species' may conceal from him on occasions), characterization too needed to change. Writing to Ferdinand Lassalle about Lassalle's play *Franz von Sickingen*, Engels commented that

> 'The characterization of the *ancients* no longer suffices nowadays, and here, I think, it would have done no harm to have taken a little more account of the significance of Shakespeare . . .'[18]

Interestingly enough, Marx himself, also writing to Lassalle about the same play, commented that 'the characters are lacking in character', arguing that they were used as 'mere mouthpieces' and were 'too abstractly depicted'.[19] One fears that he might have felt the same way about Lukács's comments on the aesthetic type.

Let me return, finally, to a consideration of characterization in modernist novels. My argument is that this often illuminates (because, in complex ways, it reflects) aspects of the development of human individuality in our society. Consider, as a starting point, Shands's description of a typical psychosomatic patient of his who

> 'may be highly intelligent and cognitively well trained, but show a major defect in affective function. He seems literally to know nothing about his own feelings and so little "consciously" about his relations to even his closest relatives. In [an earlier article] I suggested that losses of close relatives were often significant in the precipitation of psychosomatic disorders; now it is possible to add the suggestion that these losses are important because their affective implications cannot be taken into account.' (p. 177)

Shands suggests that such individuals have failed to construct themselves a consistent inner self, and have defined themselves purely in terms of external factors, so that when these factors change the individual is left 'selfless'. Such an experience is, arguably, peculiarly representative of a modern crisis in the establishment of consistent selfhood, and can be explained by reference to the contradictory values which the individual in our society is supposed coherently to internalize to construct a self.

Consider Meursault in Camus's *The Outsider*, and Septimus Smith in Virginia Woolf's *Mrs Dalloway*. For both characters the loss of a loved one (Meursault's mother, Smith's friend Evans) precipitates a crisis. They both believe that they can no longer feel, and they clearly cannot take into account what Shands calls the 'affective implications' of the death. In Meursault's case perhaps we have an 'embedded' man in a society where there is nothing consistent or coherent enough in which to be embedded. His society is doubly divided: he lives in the Arab quarter of an Algerian town in the period of French colonial rule. All his commitment is to concrete experience: swimming, eating, love-making. These, however, cannot give him the knowledge of the world that he needs to survive within it. His embeddedness takes the form of a blankness in the face of anything that is not a physical sensation:

> 'I answered that in recent years I'd rather lost the habit of noting my feelings, and hardly knew what to answer. I could truthfully say I'd been quite fond of Mother – but really that didn't mean much.'[20]

His grasp of abstract concepts such as 'guilt' is purely mechanical, achieved at second-hand through the adoption of socially current attitudes rather than by appealing to a consistent set of internalized values.

> 'It was then I felt a sort of wave of indignation spreading through the courtroom, and for the first time I understood that I was guilty.' (p. 91)

Like Rhoda in Virginia Woolf's *The Waves* (another classically 'self-less' character), he had to 'look first and see what other people do'[21] in situations requiring the display of emotion.

While in prison Meursault discovers a scrap of newspaper containing a story about the murder of a Czech villager. Murder seems to fascinate Camus as it fascinates Dostoyevsky because it serves as a revealing objective correlative for a set of incipiently destructive relationships between the members of a single society.

> 'One of the villagers had left his home to try his luck abroad. After twenty-five years, having made a fortune, he returned to his country with his wife and child. Meanwhile his mother and sister had been running a small hotel in the village where he was born. He decided to give them a surprise and, leaving his wife and child in another inn, he went to stay at his mother's place, booking a room under an assumed name. At dinner that evening he showed them a large amount of money he had on him, and in the course of the night they slaughtered him with a hammer. After taking the money they flung the body into the river. Next morning his wife came and, without thinking, betrayed the guest's identity. His mother hanged herself. His sister threw herself into a well. I must have read that story thousands of times. In one way it sounded most unlikely; in another, it was plausible enough.' (p. 82)

The idea of the mother destroying her son has a special force in the context of *The Outsider*, in which Meursault's social collapse seems – as with many of Shands's patients – to have been precipitated by his mother's death. But the story also gives us an indication of why Meursault cannot become a disembedded man, cannot successfully conceptualize his world and unite an abstract understanding with a set of confirming, concrete-sensual experiences. His world, like that of the Czech villager, is one riddled with contradictory elements, with relationships based on both cash, and human, values.

Lukács claims of the work of the leading modernist novelists that it presents an image of man as one who is 'by nature solitary, asocial, unable to enter into relationships with other human beings.'[22] It is not difficult to see how a novel such as *The Outsider* can be used to underwrite such a view. And yet even in this novel it is far from the whole truth. Meursault is solitary, he is asocial in many ways, and he is unable to enter into relationships with other people. But there is ample evidence in the novel that this is not 'his nature', that indeed his whole nature cries out against this life. What the novel reveals to a sympathetic reader is a man forced against his nature to be solitary and asocial. Or consider Kafka's 'K', a character who never ceases trying to break out of his increasingly desperate isolation. It is true that Kafka gives us no clear indication of the escape route, but like the greatest modernist writers he testifies to the human need to search for it, and this affirmation of human solidarity in a world in which social contradictions have permeated to the very centre of human beings' inner selves may be worth more for some readers than artificially self-conscious or 'positive' heroes.

At its best the modernist portrayal of character allows us to see things in art that habit conceals from us in life. In particular, it can remind us that the divisions in our society are not all 'out there', but that many of them have found their way 'in here', into the very stuff of human subjectivity. We cannot expect the writer to portray our supersession of such problems prior to their general recognition, and if writers such as Kafka and Camus do nothing else, they perform the time-honoured artistic role of holding a mirror up to nature. If we do not like what we see then that may well prove to be the first stage of changing what there is to be mirrored.

Writing of Shaw, Arnold Kettle has observed that

> 'One of the most helpful ways of looking at much "Modernist" literature of the early twentieth century is, I think, to recognise its role as puncturing or undermining the *sort* of seriousness, the sort of consciousness and therefore the sort of art which nineteenth-century capitalist society all the time tended to generate and encourage.'[23]

One of the most crucial of such myths is that of the inner consistency of the 'free' individual, the view that however confused and divided the external world may be, human beings are born whole, with a set of coherent inner values to appeal to. Novels such as *The Outsider* and *The Castle* may not give us a view of a better world or even of a route by which a better world may be reached. But read with sympathy they do undermine the sort of consciousness generated and encouraged by capitalist society. In particular, through the development of a new sort of literary character they raise questions about the relationship between our inner selves and the contradictory aspects of the society in which we live.

Notes

1 Peter Faulkner *Modernism* (1977).
2 G. Lukács *The Historical Novel*, translated by H. and S. Mitchell (Penguin edition, 1977), p. 156.
3 Ralph Fox *The Novel and the People* (1937, reprinted 1979), p. 43.
4 Erich Auerbach *Mimesis* (Princeton, N.J., 1971), p. 3.
5 Arnold Kettle *The Late Nineteenth Century Novel*. Unit 23 of Open University Course A302 (Milton Keynes: The Open University Press, 1973), p. 10.
6 G. Lukács *The Theory of the Novel* (1971), p. 56.
7 Harley C. Shands 'Verbal Patterns and Medical Disease: Prophylactic Implications of Learning', in *Sight, Sound and Sense*, edited by T. A. Sebeok (Bloomington, Ind. and London: Indiana University Press, 1978), p. 194.
8 L. S. Vygotsky *Thought and Language* (Cambridge, Mass: MIT Press, 1971), p. 197.
9 See especially, A. R. Luria *Cognitive Development* (Cambridge, Mass. and London: Harvard University Press, 1976).
10 E. M. Forster *Aspects of the Novel* (1927; Penguin edition, 1970), p. 69.
11 Fyodor Dostoyevsky *The Brothers Karamazov*. Translated by D. Magarshack (Penguin edition, 1976), Vol. I, p. 357.
12 G. Lukács *The Historical Novel*, p. 69.
13 In his essay 'The Intellectual Physiognomy in Characterisation', Lukács argues that 'Don Quixote is one of the most typical characters in world literature', and that typicality in character and situation implies departure from everyday reality'. *'Writer and Critic' and Other Essays* (London, 1970), p. 158.
14 Jack Lindsay *Decay and Renewal* (1977), p. 41.
15 G. Lukács 'Art and Society', *The New Hungarian Quarterly*, Vol. XIII, pp. 47, 53.
16 Letter to Minna Kautsky, London, 26 November 1885. In Karl Marx and Frederick Engels, *On Literature and Art*. Moscow: Progress Publishers, p. 88.
17 John O Thompson 'Up Aporia Creek', *Screen Education*, Vol. 31, Summer, 1979, p. 29.
18 Letter to Ferdinand Lassalle, Manchester, 18 May 1859, in *On Literature and Art*, p. 140.
19 Letter to Ferdinand Lassalle, London, 19 April 1859, in *On Literature and Art*, p. 100.
20 Albert Camus *The Outsider*. Translated by Stuart Gilbert (Penguin edition, 1974), p. 68.
21 Virginia Woolf *The Waves* (1931; reprinted 1972), p. 31.

22 G. Lukács *The Meaning of Contemporary Realism*. Translated by J. and N. Mander (London: Merlin Press, 1969), p. 20.
23 Arnold Kettle 'Bernard Shaw and the New Spirit', in *Rebels and their Causes: Essays in Honour of A. L. Morton* (1978), p. 220.

The Uses of Fiction
Edited by
Douglas Jefferson
and Graham Martin

4

Region and Class in the Novel

Raymond Williams

I am not sure when certain novels, or kinds of novel, began to be called 'regional'. My estimate is that the distinction began to be significant only in the late nineteenth century, and to be confident only in the twentieth century. At first sight it seems a simple distinction; it indicates a novel 'set in' or 'about' such regions as the Lake District or South Devon or mid-Wales. But then as distinct from what? There are three possible answers, each ideologically significant. First, that certain places are 'regions', with a recognized local or provincial character, while certain other places are not. Second, that certain novels are 'regional' in the sense that they tell us primarily, or solely, about such places and the life lived in them, rather than about any more general life. Third, that one kind of novel is 'regional' because it is 'about' or 'set in' some specific social life, as distinct from novels which address broader and more permanent kinds of human experience.

We can look more closely at each of these answers. The first has direct political significance. A 'region' was once a realm or kingdom or a country, in the sense of *regere* (to rule), but it was also, with a characteristic political ambiguity of such divisions of the earth, a specific part of a larger ruled area: a diocese, a district, a bounded tract, in the sense of *regere* (to direct). The latter sense became common in English, from the sixteenth century in church government, though the former, more absolute, sense persisted in natural and metaphorical descriptions. It was then obviously as a function of increasingly centralized states, with a newly formalized centralization of government and administration continuously 'delegating' and 'devolving' limited kinds of authority, that 'region' came to take on its modern meaning of 'a subordinate area', a sense which is of course compatible with recognition of its now 'local' – 'regional' – characteristics.

And then which is striking, in matters of cultural description, is the steady discrimination of certain regions as in this limited sense 'regional', which can only hold if certain other regions are not seen in this way. This is in its turn a function of cultural centralization; a modern form of the 'city-country' discrimination. It is closely connected to the distinction between a 'metropolitan' and 'provincial' culture, which became significant from the eighteenth century. Yet this is no longer a distinction of areas and kinds of life; it is what is politely called a value-judgement but more accurately an expression of centralized cultural dominance.

One entertaining form of this cultural description is the expression 'Home Counties' – distinct from the assize circuit (the 'Home Circuit') – centred on London, and taking on wider significance in the nineteenth century. The point can be tested by asking whether a novel 'set in' or 'about' the Home Counties, or 'set in' or 'about' London or some district of London – Chelsea, Hampstead, or Bloomsbury – would be described as 'regional' in a way comparable to descriptions of similar novels 'set in' or 'about' the Lake District or South Devon or mid-Wales – or, shall we say, Dorset or 'Wessex'? At this level, the description is plainly ideological. The life and people of certain favoured regions are seen as essentially general, even perhaps normal, while the life and people of certain other regions, however interestingly and affectionately presented, are, well, regional.

The second possible answer is obviously, in many mouths, a mere variant of this, and because less explicit more pretentious. Experience is not, *a priori*, more general or more significant because it occurs in London or Paris or New York rather than in Gwynedd or the Carse of Gowrie or Anatolia. Yet, at a different level, there is a real point here: a distinction which, as we shall see, is important also in considerations about 'class' in fiction. For there is indeed a kind of novel which is not only set in its own place but set in it as if there were no others. As a matter of fact this is at least as likely to be true of a New York or California or Home Counties novel as of the more readily perceived type, in which what happens in, say, the Lake District (compare the novels of Constance Holme) is seen as happening, even in the twentieth century, as if this were indeed an essentially self-subsistent life, which in none of its major characteristics is influenced or determined by social relations extending beyond it and penetrating into it. To be sure, the most important cases of this kind are particular types of late bourgeois fiction – the *rentier* novel, the corporation novel, the university novel – in which absorption in the details of an essentially local life depends, ultimately, on not seeing its relations with a more general life: the work which is at the source of the *rentier* income; the market and power relations which are the true substance of the corporation's internal operations and manoeuvres; the wider processes of learning and resources and access which constitute a particular kind of university.

Yet that there is a form of encapsulation which is distinctly 'regional' cannot be doubted. It is indeed a popular form. Much twentieth-century rural fiction has this fly-in-amber quality. Its essential strategy is one of showing a warm and charming, or natural and even passionate, life, internally divided by its own rhythms, as if rural Britain, even in its most remote and 'unspoiled' parts, had not been shot through and through by a dominent urban industrial economy. Or, as a variant of this, the 'region' is so established, in autonomous ways, that pressures on it can be seen as wholly external: that other life against this region.

I suppose I am particularly conscious of this because I can see that it catches up certain actual social processes; much of the pressure has indeed been that way. But the truly regional novel, in this limiting sense, has initially so isolated its region, and thus projected it as internally whole – 'organic' – that it is unable to recognize the complex internal processes, including internal divisions and conflicts, which factually connect with those wider pressures. I know that I wrote *Border Country* seven times to find that alternative form in which these internal processes and divisions have their real weight, and in *The Fight for Manod* I found that form very continuously and explicitly, though it is still, deliberately, a novel about a particular region. To put the matter more generally, the fiction in which to explore and clarify the problems of 'regionalism' is, of course, pre-eminently Hardy's. Some metropolitan idiots still think of Hardy as a regional novelist because he wrote about Wessex – that strange, particular place – rather than about London or the Home Counties. But at a more serious level, the distinction is very clear inside Hardy's work, as between, on the one hand, *Under the Greenwood Tree* and even *Far From the Madding Crowd*, which can be seen as regional in an encapsulating and enclosing sense, and *The Woodlanders* or *Tess of the D'Urbervilles*, which are set even more deeply in their region but which are not in any limiting sense 'regional': what happens in them, internally and externally – those two abstractions in a connected process – involves a very wide and complex, a fully extended and extensive, set of relationships.

The third answer, at its only serious level, can be connected with this point. At its trivial conventional level it is merely a late bourgeois prejudice: that novels are not 'about' or 'set in' kinds of social life; novels are about people – individuals – living sexually, spiritually, and above all privately. The very idea of a novel which recognizes a wider social life is pushed away. Indeed it is lucky – though 'luck' now is ambiguous – if it is not put on a different shelf as Sociology. Yet at the same time, not in those late bourgeois terms but more generally, we do have to distinguish one reasonable sense of regionalism in fiction: a sense which indicates that a novel is indeed more about a region or a way of life than about those people in relationships who inhabit or constitute it.

It is not a matter of simple categorization. The question of people in relationships – their degree of realization, individuation, space and time for development – is of course historically and socially variable, and the only relevant distinctions are in turn historical and social. The late-bourgeois isolation of private individuals, whose lives can be closely and intimately explored as if there were no wider social life, is evidently dependent on the social existence of individuals for whom power or money has created the possibility of *practical* distancing or displacement. In other communities and classes there is no such firm distancing or displacement, but of course it can then happen that a novel so concentrates on the most general features that it is unable to recognize – a recognition involving the simultaneous existence of real pressures and some space – the individual people who inescapably embody and enact these general features. More significantly it can fail to recognize those real areas of experience and relationship which, while they must coexist will and are usually influenced or are at times determined by the most general and common situations and processes, are still not reducible to the most general and common terms: for example, sexual and spiritual experiences (to retain these conventional descriptions), which are not only or 'merely' functions of the social situation. 'Regional' is not the most obvious word for those many novels which effect such reductions, but the factor of subordination of certain kinds of experience to the most general 'way of life' is common between certain directly regional types and the more recognizable 'documentary' or in a genuinely specifying sense 'sociological' novels.

It is at this point that we can make a useful transition from the concept of 'region' to the concept of 'class' in fiction. It is particularly relevant to the idea of 'the working-class novel'. There are, evidently, uses of this description which are strictly comparable with uses of the 'regional' description: assigning certain novels to a deliberately limited area; indicating their limited status by this kind of 'narrowness' or by their limiting priority of 'social' over 'general human' experience. On the other hand, yet in some overlapping ways, such novels have been valued in the labour and socialist movements, just because they declare their identity in such ways. The undoubted neglect of majority working experience, and of the majority of working-class people, within the bourgeois fictional tradition, seems to justify the simple counter-emphasis. A whole class, like whole regions, can be seen as neglected. The implication of its marginality or, as often, its inferiority of status or interest, is rejected by deliberate selection and emphasis. A programme in defence of working-class fiction is then proposed in terms which in effect accept elements of the 'regional' definition, but with some of its value transposed.

The issue has again to be considered historically. The 'working-class novel', in the broadest sense of fiction which includes substantial elements of working-class experience, has to be seen as from the beginning different in kind from the regional novel. Thus the earliest novels of this type – the English industrial novels of the 1840s – were not written from within these class regions. On the contrary they were written by visitors to them, by sympathetic observers, or by people with some special though still external mode of access. This is very unlike the regional novel, which is from the beginning characteristically written by natives. It is a major fact of nineteenth-century cultural history that the many talented working-class writers did not, with only the occasional exception, include novelists. This had primarily to do with the available *forms* of the novel, centred predominantly on problems of the inheritance of property and of propertied marriage, and beyond these on relatively exotic adventure and romance. These offered few points of entry for working-class writers, unless they left their class and pursued individual careers through conventional themes. Where most working-class writers turned, instead, was (apart from essays, pamphlets, and journalism, directly related to class causes) to autobiography and memoirs, or to popular verse.

However, one paradoxical effect of the social base of the first industrial novelists was that *class relations* were at issue from the beginning. Through all the observable ideological manoeuvres and shifts, Elizabeth Gaskell, Dickens, Kingsley, Disraeli, George Eliot and the others were continuously and intensely concerned with the active relations between as well as within classes. A problem in the definition of 'class' is then especially relevant. A class can indeed be seen as a region: a social area inhabited by people of a certain kind, living in certain ways. That is indeed its ordinary descriptive sense. But a Marxist sense of class, while indeed and inevitably recognizing social regions of this kind, carries the inescapable and finally constitutive sense of class as a formation of social relationships within a whole social order, and thus of alternative and typically conflicting (in any case inevitably *relating*) formations.

Thus to see a class on its own, however closely and intimately, is subject to the same limitations as seeing a region on its own, and then to some further limitations in that certain of the crucial elements of class – that it is formed in and by certain definite relations with other classes – may then be missed altogether. We can find examples of this in the late nineteenth-century 'Cockney School' of fiction, with some precedents in Gissing, where much of the real life of the East End of London is effectively within, but characteristically in isolating – and then often in externally 'colourful' or 'melodramatic' – ways. For one of the essential constituents of East End life was the existence – pressing and exploiting but of course by definition not locally and immediately visible – of the *West End*. Without that relation, the most vigorous depiction of specific localities and characters lacks a decisive dimension. This is relatively easy to see, theoretically, but that is not – as in structuralist analysis – the end of the matter. For what is really in question is practice, and the conditions of practice. These can be observed, in their actual and complex development, in the twentieth century.

In England there are the very different examples of Tressall and D. H. Lawrence. What is distinctive about Tressall is that *The Ragged-Trousered Philanthropists* is founded, from the beginning, on a view of class *relations*. All his obversations and fictionalizations of working-class life are determined by that, to the extent of the deliberate adoption of caricatured and rhetorical modes. In one sense this connects with the older mode of the sympathetic observer – and the link with Dickens is clear – but the observational mood has changed. This is a participating and exposed observer, seeking transformation rather than reconciliation.

Yet the element of externality persists, as can be seen by the strictly literary contrast with Lawrence, who has turned out to be typical of at least two generations of 'working-class writers' in the specific conditions of his practice. For Lawrence was *born into* at once a working-class family and a specific locality (in both respects, it seems, unlike Tressall/Noonan). 'Working-class life' is then from the beginning mediated by the experiences of family and locality, with their particular and powerful immediacies. Thus Lawrence is never in any danger of writing a reductive novel about working-class life, since what first materialized was not the class but family, neighbours, friends, places. Of course he eventually saw some of the true class relations, but significantly only when he was already moving away from them – as in *The Rainbow* and *Women in Love*. And by that time he was already primarily interested – from a determination in the conditions of his practice quite as much as from his personal and ideological predilections – in individuals who were moving out and away from their origins. Thus, in his later fiction, both the working-class and the general complex of class relationships are displaced: the former to childhood and adolescent experience, without significant attention to the continuing conditions of adult working-class life; the latter, almost wholly, to generalities of an ideological kind, often fictionalized by a kind of back-formation, in ideologically 'representative' figures, such as Gerald Crich.

This is an analysis, not a criticism. These particular conditions of practice have continued to be powerfully determining, and especially in the matter of fictional form. Thus the direct inheritance from Lawrence is a series of fictions of escape and flight, or at best of retrospect. Yet much of this is still represented as 'working-class fiction' *tout court*. Yet some other moves were possible, within these conditions. They are well exemplified in the Welsh industrial novel. This began with the work of Thomas Keeting (see *The Flower of the Dark*, 1917), but with all the marks of the nineteenth-century difficulties. Keeting was a working miner who later became a journalist. His novels include some of the finest direct descriptions of colliery work that we have, but as in *The Flower of the Dark* these are inserted in, and in effect overwhelmed by, a bourgeois romance of a familiar nineteenth-century kind. It was really not until the 1930s that the best form of the 'working-class family' novel was found, in Gwyn Jones's

Times Like These (1936). This is remarkably close and convincing, and it is free of the (largely ideological) distances between the class and the particular family which disfigures Lawrence. On the other hand, as Gwyn Jones came to recognize, the limitation to a single family has a certain effect of closure, even where the action is that under economic pressures the family is broken up and dispersed. However, that this general social action can be shown, as again and very powerfully in T. Rowland Hughes's *Chevalfa* (1946), is a significant advance on the fiction of individual (individual writer's) escape or flight.

In the 1930s there are two Welsh examples of quite different directions, each attempting to move beyond the class as (family and locality) region. There is the work of Jack Jones, socially panoramic as in *Rhondda Roundabout* (1934), family-based but through generations and therefore through history as in *Black Parade* (1935). There is also the world of Lewis Jones, in *Cromardy* (1937) and *We Live* (1939), again family-based but with the difference that the class element, and indeed the class struggles, now have explicit presence in the experience of the Miners' Federation and the Communist Party. It is significant that each of these new directions was found by an adult working-class writer, as distinct from writers who had been born in the working-class but had moved out of it.

The common view of these Welsh novels as regional – indeed as doubly regional: Welsh and working-class – is to a large extent simple prejudice. Yet there are still basic obstacles, even in these new forms, to any full realization of class relations. For any actual working class, within its locality, other classes are very selectively and often quite misleadingly represented. The local class enemy is usually the manager, or more broadly the local petty bourgeoisie. The dominant bourgeoisie is less visible and indeed is often, at this stage of capitalist development, physically absent. Thus class relations materialize either in very local (internal or working-class and petty-bourgeois relations) or in very general and fully ideological ways. The short-cut to full class relations via the political party, as in Lewis Jones, thus has its (in factual terms) substantial as well as local historical and political difficulties. Even with the fine perspectives of history, as in *Black Parade*, the very strength of class and locality cuts off certain moving forces, in its very constitution, because they are distant and alien, in the fiction as often in the fact. It is ironic that the best historical fiction about the Welsh working-class has been written (though with its own kinds of fault and limitation) by a sympathetic outside observer, who could *read* as well as experience the history: Alexander Cordell (see

The Rape of the Fair Country, 1959). The form does much, but with still significant and weakening connections to the historical romance. The way in which the form avoids some of the local difficulties as well as some of the hardest local recognitions can be seen in a comparison with the most important novel of this whole phase, Gwyn Thomas's *All Things Betray Thee* (1949), which significantly is centrally concerned with the problems of writing – speaking, singing – this complex experience: the clear objective reality as subjectively – but by a collective subject – experienced.

Given the generations of neglect, there is more than enough room for hundreds of working-class novels which are still, in effect, regional novels: of a district, of an industry, of an enclosed class. But the central creative problem is still that of finding forms for a working-class fiction of fully developed class relations. The problem has in some ways become more objectively difficult. Further tendencies in monopoly capitalism have removed to an even greater distance the decisive individuals and functions and institutions by which most working-class life is formed. To realize such relations substantially – as distinct from the alternative modes of projection and extrapolation, as characteristically now in science fiction – is then especially difficult. Changes inside the working-class, in types of community and in both general and individual mobility, provide both problems and opportunities. It is becoming virtually impossible, wherever the writer stands, to write serious enclosed fiction, except in retrospection and residual modes. Thus just as the limited 'regional' novel is passing out of serious consideration and possibility, in advanced capitalist societies (though it is still being effectively written in post-colonial and intermediate societies), so the limited 'working-class' novel shows its limits ever more clearly.

But then there is still great need for those words, rooted in region or in class, which can at once achieve that close living substance (in marked contrast to what is now happening, through etiolation, in metropolitan and international bourgeois fiction) and yet seek the substance of those finer-drawn, often occluded, relations and relationships which in their pressures and interventions at once challenge, threaten, change and yet, in the intricacies of history, contribute to the formation of that class or region in self-realization and in struggle, including especially new forms of self-realization and struggle. The formal and technical problems, for the novelist, are very severe, but if we are looking for a direction – and not to be doing so, in the present state of fiction, is incomprehensible – this is our best road, or, more probably, our best set of connecting paths. Historically, in any case, regions and classes are only fully constituted when they fully declare themselves. There is still much for novelists to contribute to those decisive declarations.

The Uses of Fiction
Edited by
Douglas Jefferson
and Graham Martin

5

Revelation and Repression in Conrad's *Nostromo*

Kiernan Ryan

The inner truth is hidden – luckily, luckily.
Heart of Darkness[1]

No really satisfactory account of *Nostromo* can, I think, begin to emerge without recognizing how the whole novel is produced and informed by a radical contradictory dynamic pulsing at the core of all Conrad's major fiction. Arnold Kettle raised the problem of the text's conflicting impulses some thirty years ago in *An Introduction to the English Novel.* On the one hand, as he points out, *Nostromo* powerfully and clearly pursues its uncompromising 'moral discovery' of corruption and dehumanization in a society developing within the matrix of imperialism. Yet, at the same time, there is 'a certain mistiness . . . buried deep in the language and symbolism of the book' and 'there are moments in the novel when a sense of "the cruel futility of things" does seem to overcome Conrad', a sense 'that something in the very nature of things, something beyond human control (yet never defined), is responsible for the tragedy of *Nostromo*'.[2]

This perception of a fundamental contradictory tension troubling *Nostromo* has not, however, been confronted and thought through. Instead, criticism has oscillated between interpretations centred on only one main tendency of the novel at the expense of the other.

Nostromo is construed as an essentially straightforward realist novel providing a solid representation and critique of a transparently intelligible social reality: 'the essence of the novel's meaning [is] that progress, leashed to faith in material interests, is inhuman, without rectitude, continuity, or force.'[3] And from within this critical perspective it can be affirmed that 'there is nothing nihilistic about *this* "Tale of the Seaboard" '.[4] An opposing critical tendency, however, is concerned precisely to stress the nihilistic nature of *Nostromo*, its despairing, ironic vision of life as a meaningless illusion. This is the metaphysical version of Conrad epitomized by J. Hillis Miller's account,[5] a version whose most recent avatars have produced an ultra-modernist *Nostromo* for which the impossibility of rendering reality at all, the problem of writing as such, is the real concern of an intensely reflexive text:

> 'Instead of mimetically authoring a new world, *Nostromo* turns back to its beginning as a novel, to the fictional, illusory assumption of reality; in thus overturning the confident edifice that novels normally construct *Nostromo* reveals itself to be no more than a *record* of novelistic self-reflection . . . a revulsion from the novelist's whole procreative enterprise and an intensification of his *scriptive* fate.'[6]

What is the exact nature of the text capable of producing such radically divergent interpretations? Conrad himself, significantly, can be cited in support of either critical emphasis. There is the strong, confident Conrad who sees his art as 'a single-minded attempt to render the highest kind of justice to the visible universe by bringing to light the truth, manifold and one, underlying its every aspect'; whose task is 'by the power of the written word to make you hear, to make you feel – it is, before all, to make you see' (Preface to *The Nigger of the 'Narcissus'*, pp. vii, x). But then too there is the artistically paralyzed, agonizing Conrad before whom that 'visible universe' dissolves into a meaningless void, its truth utterly beyond hope of communication:

> 'Even writing to a friend – to a person one has heard, touched, drank with, quarrelled with – does not give me a sense of reality. All is illusion – the words written, the mind at which they are aimed, the truth they are intended to express, the hands that will hold the paper, the eyes that will glance along the lines. Every image floats vaguely in a sea of doubt – and the doubt itself is lost in an unexplored universe of incertitudes.'[7]

We need to face the fact of a *constitutional* contradiction at the heart of Conrad's artistic vision and production of meaning. Criticism which suppresses this recognition in the recuperative quest for a unitary, harmonized version of Conrad severely distorts the contradictory character of his texts. Thus the unperturbed, straightforward 'realist' readings of *Nostromo* are compelled to evade, or marginalize as mere 'obliquities of presentation',[8] the novel's rebarbative strategies of narrative disorientation, its sabotaging of conventional fictional expectations. But equally misleading are the reductive 'modernist' versions of the text which shrivel its mimetic range and depth to a mere reflexive writhing, dismissing the massive, objective concretion of the social reality it deliberately constructs.

Neither perspective can accommodate the actual scope of a novel whose structure of meaning might best be described as a double spiral of simultaneous revelation *and* repression, critical exfoliation *and* legitimizing obfuscation. Driving through *Nostromo* is the compulsion to open up social-historical reality, to lay bare the concealed conjunction of corrupt motives and 'material interests' producing a private and public history overtly condemned by Conrad as false and inhuman. But *at the same time* there is an equal counter-thrust towards the opposite effect: the representation of reality as inherently unintelligible, as beyond objective cognition and moral evaluation. And the implicit ideological import of this counterperspective is clear. For instead of unmasking the prevailing social order as the all too explicable product of a changing human history, it tacitly underwrites and consolidates that order by ascribing to it the unfathomable, metaphysical status of an eternal human condition.

This tension between aperture and closure, cognitive penetration and blurring obstruction – writing as it were *sous rature* – is generated by the contradictory pressures under which Conrad narrates. Politically conservative, indeed reactionary as he is, when Conrad takes up his pen to work his fiction he enters a psychologically excruciating situation to which his anguished letters bear constant witness. For to fulfil the artistic pledge set forth in the Preface to *The Nigger of the 'Narcissus'*, to make the reader see the truth of reality and thereby rouse him to that 'subtle but invincible conviction of solidarity' (p. viii), leads Conrad necessarily to expose and indict the prevailing imperialist society which he otherwise endorses, and on whose validity, indeed, he stakes his social identity. 'A single-minded attempt to render the highest kind of justice' to reality means an interrogation of the entire structure of presuppositions and values on which his ideological allegiance rests, an erosion of the very foundations of his subjectivity.

Writing is such an agony for Conrad because it involves this threat of psychological self-destruction, of reality and identity dissolving into 'an unexplored universe of incertitudes'. That striking phrase in *Lord Jim* where Marlow concedes that 'enlightenment' had been brought into the Archipelago 'for the sake of better morality and – and – well – the greater profit too' (p. 219) graphically articulates the pressure under which Conrad forces out the truths which cut against the grain of the ruling consciousness to which he subscribes. But to transcend his divided self, to break completely with that false consciousness and emerge into a new, oppositional vision of reality, is beyond Conrad. Therefore he must contrive instead to write the truth of reality in such a way as to extinguish it *in the very moment* of its articulation. His narration must proceed in such a way as to engineer the coincident release and blockage of its otherwise insupportable revelations.

This, I think it could be argued, is the central dynamic of all Conrad's major fiction. We can see it most clearly at work if we turn for a moment to *Heart of Darkness*, whose title condenses in a phrase the cognitive tension between blindness and insight structuring this paradigmatic Conradian text. The narrative of Marlow – Conrad's recurrent means of internally distancing and so controlling his potentially self-destructive conflict as a writer – penetrates to the rotten heart of contemporary imperialist 'civilisation', exposing and explaining its inhuman essence; and in the same breath it floods that recognition in metaphysical darkness, transforming the knowable heart of this historically produced reality into an enigmatic, impenetrable void. This deadlocking strategy of revelation and repression organizes the text from beginning to end.

Thus on the one hand the narrative cuts clean through all the lies and cosmetic rhetoric – through the ideology – to lay bare the rapacious and murderous barbarity of colonialism in Africa. The Company's office is recognized at once as 'a house in the city of the dead' (p. 56) whose door is the door to hell. From the beginning, having intimated to his enthusing aunt that 'the Company was run for profit' not philanthropy, Marlow feels himself 'an imposter' (pp. 59, 60) alienated from his own humanity, contaminated by the moral fraudulence of the whole enterprise. When he arrives at the Company's station he denounces it as run by the 'flabby, pretending, weak-eyed devil of a rapacious folly' (p. 65) and discerns its achievements all too clearly in the infernal grove of dying blacks reduced to mere 'bundles of acute angles' (p. 67). The colonialist exploiters and parasites, the sarcastically dubbed 'pilgrims', are excoriated throughout as the predatory walking dead, the *papier-mâché* hollow men with 'nothing inside but a little loose dirt' (p. 81).

Nor, even before Marlow reaches Kurtz, is there any doubt as to the sordid rationale of 'the horror'. Kurtz 'had collected, bartered, swindled, or stolen more ivory than all the other agents together' (p. 113) and 'evidently the appetite for more ivory had got the better of the – what shall I say? – less material aspirations' (p. 130). And, when at last reached, Kurtz is identified as the dreadful epitome of the dehumanization and reification (he seems 'carved out of old ivory', his very skull an 'ivory ball': pp. 135, 115) at the heart of an all-devouring imperialism: 'I saw him open his mouth wide – it gave him a weirdly voracious aspect, as though he had wanted to swallow all the air, all the earth, all the men before him' (p. 135). This ruthless drive to strip all pretence away climaxes in Marlow's recognition that with his decision to remain 'loyal' (p. 151) to Kurtz, to tell the lie and so preserve the ruling false consciousness, he himself is now 'numbered with the dead' (p. 147). For he thereby conspires in concealing the very imperialist barbarity he has indicted throughout and thus sustains the smug citizens of the 'sepulchral city', who blindly feed off the inhuman horror deliberately perpetrated on their behalf.

But although he exposes the lie *as* a lie, Conrad must simultaneously legitimize that lie as the only way to maintain 'that great and saving illusion' (p. 159), to destroy which 'would have been too dark – too dark altogether' (p. 162). The lie is thus a paradigm of the self-cancelling strategy central to the whole novel. For in the face of its own clear-sighted articulation of the social nature and cause of 'the horror', the text insists on the irredeemably cryptic nature of the reality Marlow experiences, rewriting 'the horror' as the inherent quality of a now metaphysically conceived 'human condition' of meaningless futility, implicitly beyond man's choice and control. Within this perspective the novel simultaneously reworks Marlow's objective experience of colonial actuality, transmuting it into a mystical *voyage intérieur* 'within the toil of a mournful and senseless delusion' (p. 61). The brutal exploitation is dehistoricized and desubstantialized, reconstrued now as a nightmarish phantom world, as 'an unfathomable enigma' (p. 105) defying cognition by the density of its darkness or its blinding whiteness, by its absolute emptiness and utter, inscrutable silence. The deliberate dissection of the heart of imperialism can only proceed, so to speak, under the anaesthetic mystification of life as 'that mysterious arrangement of merciless logic for a futile purpose' (p. 150).

The same splicing of critique and legitimation, the drive to display the true historical construction of the changing world inextricably cross-woven with the counter-drive to *ontologize* the historical in the service of the status quo, determines the form and meaning of *Nostromo*. For, in relating the history of the founding of the Sulacan Republic as a modern capitalist state within the controlling matrix of American imperialism, Conrad again inflicts on himself the narrative exploration of a social order he instinctively endorses, but whose unjust, dehumanizing rationale and alienating consequences he apprehends with painful clarity.

Indeed the creative anguish, the mind-snapping tension between the subversive unmasking and the occlusive confirmation of the prevailing social order, is more acute than ever with *Nostromo*, 'the most anxiously meditated of [my] longer novels' (*Nostromo*, p. xv). The razor's edge sense of his dilemma is conveyed with nightmare precision in a letter of 1903 to Wells soon after beginning the novel: 'I . . . am absolutely out of my mind with the worry and apprehension of my work. I go as one would cycle over a precipice along a 14-inch plank. If I falter I am lost.'[9] It is also, significantly, the closing stages of the ordeal of *Nostromo* that generate Conrad's trenchant definition of himself as 'a *homo duplex*, in more than one sense.'[10] For in *Nostromo* Conrad must once again both clearly see and yet be blind to 'the visible universe', ever disclosing yet veiling the actual composition and movement of reality in a truly 'duplex' tension whereby the novel is at once propelled and paralyzed.

Thus on the one hand, in order to penetrate the ideological facade concealing the full historical and human truth, *Nostromo* deploys a range of strategies designed to deconstruct the bourgeois version of history and the whole 'adventure novel' genre tendentially disposed to embody it. The text ruthlessly subverts all expectations of the kind of realist novel of epic action and exotic escapade which the title, subtitle and opening chapter deceptively arouse. In so doing it embodies an aggressive refusal of the hegemonic 'providential' conception of history which finds ready mediation in the heroic and 'colourful' historical 'yarn'. That conception is, indeed, ironically salienced within the novel in the pompous, complacent discourse of Captain Mitchell. And in a sense the whole novel can be understood as a dislocation and fracturing of the Captain Mitchell version of Sulaco's history: a labyrinthine excavation of the truth buried beneath the glib public lie distilled in Mitchell's 'stereotyped relation of the "historical events" ' (p. 473), his mythologized official account of how Sulaco became the 'Treasure House of the World' (p. 480).

What *Nostromo* refuses to deliver is an orthodox, chronologically coherent narrative which, by culminating in a climactic struggle for and founding of the Sulacan Republic, would implicitly consecrate that culmination as the realized 'aim' of a dovetailing historical process: the legitimizing point at which all the particular and general human fates would converge and find their purposive rationale, their retrospective *sense*. This whole structure of thinking, with its tacit teleological assumption of the modern capitalist state within imperialism as the natural 'end' of history, is exploded by *Nostromo*'s violations of conventional narrative expectations.

Thus what would otherwise be the epic historical consummation of the fight for Sulaco is defused at once, robbed of its sense and teleological impact as Mitchell's 'memorable occasion' (p. 11) by being prematurely broached and stranded right at the opening in Chapter 2. This anticlimactic effect is multiplied throughout by similar deconstructive prolepses, most notably in Part Three, when the action builds towards a momentous climax in Chapter 9 – will Nostromo make the impossible ride to Cayta and save Sulaco? – and the next chapter brusquely deflates that expectation, along with its sense of an imminent historical ending, by refusing to relate Nostromo's 'famous ride to Cayta' (p. 473) and instead displacing the entire account of the winning of Sulaco into the stale retrospective of Mitchell. 'The history of that ride, sir,' says the Captain in a resonantly ironic remark, 'would make a most exciting book' (p. 482). Indeed: precisely the kind of book Conrad's integrity cannot permit *Nostromo* to be.

This puncturing elision of the heroic ride foregrounds another crucial deconstructive strategy: the contradictory tension between the title and the actual *absence* of Nostromo from the centre of the 'historical' action. The recurrent myth, vital to the Mitchellesque strand within bourgeois ideology, is that of history being made by the colourful Garibaldian 'Man of the People' – a myth calculated to conceal the ruling economic and class interests actually constructing history. A monument to the Separation, says Mitchell, 'could not do better than begin with the name of Nostromo' (p. 482), and that of course is exactly what Conrad's novel does *begin* with. But, having seen and understood that history is in fact made in the 'material interests' and at the discretion of the Goulds, the Sir Johns and the

Holroyds, Conrad can no longer write as if it were made by the Nostromos – by 'our man' on behalf of all of us. And Conrad articulates this recognition, that Nostromo cannot be 'the hero of the Tale of the Seaboard' because in reality 'silver is the pivot of the moral and material events',[11] by writing a novel whose putative hero can never become its hero, a novel which stubbornly refuses to acknowledge its own protagonist.

This demythologizing of the 'illustrious Capataz de Cargadores', of the Nostromo flagrantly indulged for a moment in that 'exotic' scene with the Morenita (pp. 126–30), proceeds through his conspicuous relegation to the periphery of his own story. The whole of Part One and most of Part Two are haunted by a Nostromo glimpsed repeatedly on the margins, in the mere interstices of the main narrative concerns. In his fleeting appearance at the endangered Casa Viola (pp. 22–3) or as Sir John's escort – 'a most useful fellow' – at the edge of the firelight (pp. 42–3); as the 'phantom-like horseman' (p. 95) materializing to solve the Company's labour problems or passing mysteriously beneath Antonia and Decoud on Gould's balcony (pp. 185–6), Nostromo always seems *about to* endorse the novel's title and snatch up the reins of the narrative. But he remains doomed to its verges by Conrad's uncompromising recognition of his real objective status as a blind tool of the ruling classes. And when Nostromo does at last move to the seeming centre in the Placido Gulf sequence it is only to discover that his 'legendary' act of saving the silver is in fact of no vital consequence and that he himself is thoroughly dispensable. Likewise his momentous ride to Cayta cannot be represented as a climactic feat of unalloyed heroism because, as Conrad brings Nostromo himself to see, his daring courage served but to save 'the lives and fortunes of the Blancos, the taskmasters of the people' (p. 492). His heroism is polluted by its complicity in securing the continuance of an oppressive social order, whose historical course is actually dictated by the propertied minority. Hence, insofar as his own personal tragedy as slave of the silver is allowed at last to occupy the close of the novel, it is as the mere postscript to a history callously indifferent to him.

The same demythologizing drive, moreover, powers Conrad's tunnelling beneath the facades of all the major characters. Narrative progression is repeatedly surrendered to extended retrospective probings beneath the mythical official selves preserved in Mitchell's pantheon and encoded in the characters' recurrent epithets (the vestiges, so to speak, of the identities they would have preserved unchallenged in the 'straight' adventure novel Conrad could not write). Thus

Conrad peels back the public versions of the Goulds – 'El Rey' and 'the First Lady' of Sulaco – to reveal a man spiritually congealed and utterly alienated from his wife, 'alone within a circumvallation of precious metal' (p. 222); and a woman, the universally revered 'Doña Emilia', disillusioned, lonely and guilt-ridden, 'in the grip of a merciless nightmare' (p. 522) from which she cannot awake. In the Goulds Conrad exposes the self-deluding hollowness of the liberal rhetoric of progress and philanthropy legitimizing private enterprise: the soul-destroying contradiction between the cosmetic ideology and the dehumanizing reality of exploitation and corruption it conceals.[12] And of course the pressure to demythologize exerts itself no less on the historically superseded figures of Don José Avellanos and 'the heroic Giorgio Viola', as also on the romantic Mitchellesque version of Decoud, 'the brilliant Costaguanero of the boulevards', who in fact ends as the mere alienated ghost of himself, literally sinking in despair beneath the weight of the all-powerful silver, the capital which, as Conrad intimated, is the real protagonist of this inhuman history.

This irrepressible compulsion to tear the ideological veil from historical reality issues towards the end in increasingly explicit, apodictic statements of the truths the text cannot evade. Thus the disabused Nostromo discovers through his own experience that 'Kings, ministers, aristocrats, the rich in general, kept the people in poverty and subjection; they kept them as they kept dogs, to fight and hunt for their service' (p. 415). Monygham pronounces his devastating critique and prophecy:

> 'There is no peace and no rest in the development of material interests. They have their law and their justice. But it is founded on expediency, and is inhuman . . . Mrs Gould, the time approaches when all that the Gould Concession stands for shall weigh as heavily upon the people as the barbarism, cruelty and misrule of a few years back.' (p. 511)

And as for Mrs Gould herself:

> 'She saw the San Tomé mountain hanging over the Campo, over the whole land, feared, hated, wealthy; more soulless than any tyrant, more pitiless and aristocratic than the worst government, ready to crush innumerable lives in the expansion of its greatness.' (p. 521)

Given this order of recognition, moreover, the novel is further able to glimpse the emergence of those oppositional forces destined to challenge the whole social structure of which the mine is a function.

Mitchell himself is alert to 'these socialistic Italians' now drawing even the natives towards their new Democratic party (pp. 478–9); and, 'by a stroke of astonishing intuition',[13] as Arnold Kettle observes, alone at Nostromo's deathbed is placed the Communist, at whom Conrad has the 'Man of the People' direct 'a glance of enigmatic and profound enquiry' (pp. 562–3). In short, the whole deconstructive trajectory of *Nostromo* embodies a genuinely *historicizing* dynamic, illuminating the real formation and motion of society in history – history being grasped as a humanly produced, changing and changeable process whose rationale, laws and consequences are not only fully intelligible but susceptible of definite moral evaluation.

But this historicizing impulse is simultaneously cancelled by the pervasive ontologizing pressure exerted within and across the deconstructed sectors of the text by *Nostromo*'s basic *descriptive* style. What is opened up on one plane as intelligibly developing history made by men is written out on another intersecting plane as an opaque, unchanging condition devoid of meaning and beyond evaluation. That his fundamental style of writing serves a deep need to evade or repress forbidden dimensions of cognition is suggested by Conrad himself in a striking remark whose full measure we can now begin to take: 'It is evident that my fate is to be descriptive and descriptive only. There are things I *must* leave alone.'[14] Exactly how 'description' supplies Conrad with the means of forestalling, blocking or neutralizing his own sure critical penetration of historical reality becomes clear if we look at Lukács' critique of the 'naturalistic' style in his classic essay 'Narrate or Describe?'

Focusing on Zola and Flaubert (Conrad's acknowledged master, of course), Lukács shows how the reductive and deforming 'descriptive' method is produced by, and itself reflects, the intensely alienated experience of life in the imperialist era, 'the domination of capitalist prose over the inner poetry of human experience, the continuous dehumanization of social life, the general debasement of humanity'.[15] For in its painfully honest endeavour to mirror reality 'as it really is', with scrupulously detailed, comprehensive objectivity, naturalistic writing in fact ends up with an essentially static, two dimensional, surface *description* of its subject instead of a dynamic, three-dimensional and processive *narration* of it grasped both from within and without. The descriptive approach hypostatizes the current imperialist order, investing its degrading but transient reality with an absolute and universal status. It robs human life of all sense of being made out of the transformative interaction of men and women with each other and with their natural and social world.

The descriptive strategy of *Nostromo* is most immediately evident in its meandering mode of advance through set-piece tableaux rendered with a lingering profusion of detailed circumstance. One thinks of the opening friezes of life at the Casa Viola; of the O.S.N. *convité* on the *Juno*; of the Goulds frozen silent in their house; the troops' embarkation under Barrios; the Goulds' party, with Decoud and Antonia on the balcony; Decoud alone at night in the Casa Viola; the hypnotic Placido Gulf scene; Nostromo and Monygham spell-bound before the grotesque suspended corpse of Hirsch; Decoud lost out of time in the infinite solitude of the island. The novel delivers no sense of developing action emerging through the vital interplay of the characters with each other and their world. Quite the reverse. The narration does not flow, it coils and eddies through a configuration of still centres, congealed *settings for* action which, if recounted at all, is not fully narrated from the 'inside' as well – through the evolving subjectivity of active participants – but statically depicted as a ready-made phenomenon, a finished product. The essential 'action' of *Nostromo* is treated as something that, in an absolute sense, *has already happened*, that was, as it were, over and sealed off before the author arrived; not as a *process* to be represented in its full dialectical composition and movement.

Instead of writer and reader actively collaborating in the exploration of an unfolding human experience, both are reduced by description to passive observers of a dead world, fixed and frozen in advance. The characters in *Nostromo* are presented either as given and fixed thus or, insofar as they exhibit change, as subsequently *having become* thus: they are presented, in other words, as *results*. There transpires no inwardly illuminated, conflictive drama of becoming, for 'description provides no true poetry of things but transforms people into conditions, into components of still lives . . . The result is a series of static pictures . . . The so-called action is only a thread on which the still lives are disposed in a superficial, ineffective, fortuitous sequence of isolated, static pictures'.[16]

In *Nostromo* there is no real *exchange* either of language or experience. The pervasive sense of stasis, of almost lifeless reification, is immediately evident in the descriptions of the characters. Giorgio's face has 'the immobility of a carving' (p. 28) and to the end he remains 'unstirring, like a statue of an old man' (p. 554). The Sulaco ladies 'looked like white plaster casts with beautiful living eyes' (p. 49). Mrs

Gould, 'her face powdered white like a plaster cast', confronts a people 'suffering and mute, waiting for the future in a pathetic immobility of patience' (pp. 86, 88). She is repeatedly depicted in withdrawn poses, and the conclusion leaves her frozen in 'her still and sad immobility', displaying 'the charm of an attitude caught and interpreted for ever' (pp. 520, 521). Nostromo likewise appears typically waiting, 'silent on a motionless horse' (p. 96) or transfixed in 'silence and immobility' (p. 418). Don José 'appeared almost inanimate, sitting rigidly by the side of Mrs Gould', his face 'as if modelled in yellow wax' (p. 149). Father Corbelan 'remained quite motionless . . . with that something vengeful in his immobility' (p. 197). Pedrito Montero 'became motionless and silent as if turned into stone' (p. 445). The characters' state of paralysis and petrifaction is intensified throughout, moreover, by the quality of the surrounding world: 'outside the house there was a great silence' (p. 244); everything is 'steeped in a clear stillness as in an imponderable liquid' (p. 40).

This vision of an inherently dehumanized world of stone and statue, reified beyond all hope of human transformation, finds condensed symbolic expression in various haunting focal images: the mountain Higuerota, periodically looming forth over Sulaco 'like a frozen bubble under the moon' (p. 41); the enigmatic corpse of Hirsch, 'suspended in his awful immobility' (p. 436); above all the image of Decoud and Nostromo motionless in the viscous blackness of the Placido Gulf (pp. 260 ff.). For there the occlusive, metaphysical counter-vision of the novel finds its supreme imaginative realization in an apocalyptic anti-climax of absolute stillness, silence, emptiness and deathlike darkness. Reality dissolves within 'the thick veil of obscurity that felt warm and hopeless all about them' (p. 263). It is one of Conrad's most compelling sustained images of nihilistic despair in the face of an utterly illusory and unknowable reality: 'No intelligence could penetrate the darkness of the Placid Gulf' (p. 275).

This dehistoricizing, coagulative impulsion crystallizes out in authorial pronouncements in direct conflict with the trenchant critical recognitions articulated through Nostromo, Mrs Gould and Monygham. Thus, although the text reveals only too clearly why the Sulacan people suffer, and will continue to suffer, under the '*imperium in imperio*' of Gould and the whole social order he represents, Conrad can nevertheless conclude from the scene in which Gould observes a woman kneeling by the side of a dying *cargador*, mortally wounded while defending the interests of the mine: 'The cruel futility of things stood unveiled in the levity and sufferings of that incorrigible people;

the cruel futility of lives and deaths thrown away in the vain endeavour to attain an enduring solution of the problem' (p. 364). This metaphysical blurring climaxes in the categorical generalizations proliferating around Decoud's suicide: 'In our activity alone do we find the sustaining illusion of an independent existence as against the whole scheme of things of which we form a helpless part' (p. 497). Decoud disappears 'without trace, swallowed up in the immense indifference of things' (p. 501).

Nostromo's convergence of critical revelation and mystifying closure has the effect of a continuous suppressed explosion. Within the deconstructive perspective the dispersive drive of the narrative forces the reader to respond in an intensely critical way – analysing, discriminating, inferring and synthesizing, reconstructing an authentic, oppositional version of the private and public history of Sulaco. In this sense *Nostromo* indeed 'succeeds most wonderfully in capturing the truth of social movement', its achievement being 'nothing less than the presentation . . . of society in motion, history in the making'.[17] But the dispersed, tesselated sectors of *Nostromo* are concurrently subdued to a stylistic pressure which thickens and reifies the deconstructively disclosed world, which freezes character and paralyzes action, ontologizing and thus evacuating the historical, which nevertheless survives as a pervasive, insistent *absence* swelling beneath the surface of the text. It is this dimension of the novel which accounts for Leavis's troubled intuition that 'for all the rich variety of the interest and the tightness of the pattern, the reverberation of *Nostromo* has something hollow about it; with the colour and life there is a suggestion of a certain emptiness'.[18] It is what accounts, in short, for that sense one has with Conrad that 'in working his fiction . . . the writer is shaping a vacuum, sculpting a void'.[19]

'So foul a sky clears not without a storm': as the novel's epigraph confirms in its presiding image of congestion and explosive tension, the central structure of feeling organizing *Nostromo* is that of radical impasse, of deadlocking self-cancellation. It's surely just this profound sense of blockage stemming the clear flow through of the fictive vision that explains Conrad's own intriguing judgement of the novel in a letter to Gide in 1912: 'But it doesn't work; that is true. There is something that prevents it from working. I don't know what. All in all, even with all my tenderness, I myself cannot stand to read it.'[20] Conrad is here circling once again round the cryptic heart of his own productive impulse. In grasping *Nostromo*'s constitutive double dynamic of revelation and repression we can, I think, move closer to a full understanding of the nature of that impulse and thus a clearer comprehension of the quality and value of his fiction as a whole.

Notes

1 p. 93: all page references to Conrad's work are to the Dent *Collected Edition of the Works of Joseph Conrad* (London, 1946–55).
2 Arnold Kettle, *Introduction to the English Novel*, 2 vols, second edition (London: Hutchinson, 1967), II, pp. 71–2.
3 Eloise Knapp Hay, *The Political Novels of Joseph Conrad* (Chicago and London, 1963), p. 170.
4 Jacques Berthoud, *Joseph Conrad. The Major phase* (Cambridge, 1978), p. 130.
5 See J. Hillis Miller, *Poets of Reality: Six Twentieth-Century Writers* (Cambridge, Mass., 1965).
6 Edward Said, *Beginnings. Intention and Method* (New York, 1975), p. 137.
7 *Letters from Conrad 1895–1924*, ed. Edward Garnett (London, 1928), pp. 152–3.
8 Berthoud, *op. cit.*, p. 99.
9 Gerard Jean-Aubry, *Joseph Conrad: Life and Letters* (New York, 1927), I, p. 311.
10 Conrad, *Lettres françaises*, ed. Gerard Jean-Aubry (Paris, 1930), p. 60.
11 Jean-Aubry, *Joseph Conrad: Life and Letters*, *op. cit.*, II, p. 296.
12 On *Nostromo*'s critical exploration of the relations between ideology and the material reality of social life see the chapter '*Nostromo*: Materialism and Idealism' in Jeremy Hawthorn's excellent *Joseph Conrad: Language and Fictional Self-Consciousness* (London, 1979), pp. 56–71.
13 Kettle, *op. cit.*, II, p. 74.
14 Garnett, *Letters from Conrad, op. cit.*, p. 94.
15 Georg Lukács, 'Narrate or Describe?', in *Writer and Critic* (London, 1978), pp. 110–48 (p. 127).
16 Ibid., pp. 139, 144.
17 Kettle, *op. cit.*, II, pp. 69–70.
18 F. R. Leavis, *The Great Tradition* (London, 1948), p. 200.
19 Terry Eagleton, *Criticism and Ideology* (London, 1976), p. 137.
20 Conrad, *Lettres françaises*, *op. cit.*, p. 120.

The Uses of Fiction
Edited by
Douglas Jefferson
and Graham Martin

6

D H Lawrence and Class

Graham Martin

In the extensive secondary literature that now clusters round Lawrence's fiction, the topic of 'class' scarcely receives a mention, and from one point of view this is welcome. Early commentators who noticed Lawrence's awareness of class-distinction in English life either judged it unhealthy, even tinged with snobbishness (some memoirists, T. S. Eliot); or believed that it showed Lawrence settling for the petit-bourgeois proto-fascist route of escape from his working-class origins (Caudwell). Evidence for the first view was at best sparse and ambiguous, but for the second drew mainly on Lawrence's non-fictional writings, *Movements in European History* (1921), *Reflections on the Death of a Porcupine* (1925), some essays posthumously assembled in *Assorted Articles* (1931) and in *Phoenix* (1936), though also upon simplified readings of the 'political' novels, *Kangaroo* (1923) and *The Plumed Serpent* (1926).

But what of the fiction as a whole? As is well-known, it was by pressing this question that F. R. Leavis intervened so decisively in the history of Lawrence's reputation. The *Scrutiny* essays (1950–53) and *D. H. Lawrence: Novelist* (1955) shifted attention from Lawrence's express polemicizing, from what he himself would have called his preachy Salvator Mundi side, towards a proper consideration of his fictional art. Yet in so doing, Leavis may also be said to have removed 'class' from the agenda of relevant discussion of Lawrence's work. There was a general reason for this. The anti- or a-political nature of Leavis's conception of culture in itself entailed a refusal to explore the relevance of 'class' to literary-critical practice, except in the narrow sense of strictures on aspects of Bloomsbury and 'the metropolitan centre'. More immediately in Lawrence's case, Leavis's canonization of *The Rainbow, Women in Love*, certain *nouvelles* and short stories, as constituting the novelist's major achievement, had the implicit result of setting side such novels as *Sons and Lovers* and *Lady Chatterley's Lover* in which 'class' is evidently an issue. And where Leavis led, Lawrence critics have, by and large, followed.[1]

But explicitly too, Leavis's own treatment of the issue had this effect as in 'Lawrence and Class', the chapter in *D. H. Lawrence: Novelist* (pp. 73–95), whose title I have adopted for this essay. There Leavis dismisses the charge of snobbery by means of an analysis of a previously unregarded *nouvelle* in *The Prussian Officer* (1914) collection of Lawrence's earliest short fiction, 'Daughters of the Vicar', which turns on a conflict of class values. Lawrence's handling of the issue (argues Leavis) shows not just that he was a close observer of a lamentable fact about English society, but that he perceived it from the vantage ground of 'classless truth', avoiding both sentimental idealization of the working-class and animus against the middle-class. The sterile and repressed Lindley family, obsessed by 'proud class-superiority', push one daughter into a marriage whose sole recommendations are money and position. But the other daughter rebels by choosing 'life', her relationship with a young collier of the district, overcoming both the cold hostility of her family and the subtler barriers within her own and her lover's class-influenced feelings. For Leavis, this outcome contains the essence of Lawrence's view of 'class'. Class-division, class-feeling exist as poisonous facts about English society, and Lawrence hates them. But they can be overcome by 'life', that is to say, by individual men and women sufficiently courageous, tender, and fiery, to establish human relationships beyond 'class'.

The general application of this account to other of Lawrence's writings will, of course, be clear. Yet formulated in this way, it omits the crucial fact that the 'classless truth' affirmed by these lovers is not permitted to find an English home. Unable to prevent their daughter's scandalous *mésalliance*, the Lindleys insist that the young couple leave the district. They offer no resistance and plan to emigrate to Canada, where their offence will no longer retain the force of a direct challenge to the Lindleys' social position. Leavis is surely correct in identifying

Lawrence's *authorial* view of this as a victory over 'class' at the personal level. But what we need to add is that the tale speaks more complexly, more interestingly, than the artist. The conclusion which so emphatically robs the Lindley ethos of its last vestiges of moral authority is equally emphatic in confirming its social *power*. Such a triumph of 'life' over 'class', however un-idealized at the personal level, bears an uncomfortable resemblance to defeat – certain individuals escape but the objective determinations of 'class' persist, scarcely recognised as such.[2] In this essay, I want to claim paradigmatic status for such narrative structures within Lawrence's work as a whole, and to propose that his perception of 'class', realized in these ways, gives us a measure of his achievement, both of its strength and its limitations.

A paradigm takes concrete form only in its variants, so some of these must now be considered. Amongst the early fiction, 'Daughters of the Vicar' broaches the 'class' issue with a clarity hardly to be repeated before *Lady Chatterley's Lover*. The question is more characteristically present as a contradiction, or counter-current, subverting the narrative authority of the main story. In *Sons and Lovers*, we meet this:

> ' "You know," [Paul] said to his mother, "I don't want to belong to the well-to-do middle class. I like my common people best. I belong to the common people."
>
> "But if anybody else said so, my son, wouldn't you be in a tear. *You* know you consider yourself equal to any gentleman."
>
> "In myself," he answered, "not in my class or my education or my manners. But in myself I am."
>
> "Very well, then. Then why talk about the common people?"
>
> "Because – the difference between people isn't in their class, but in themselves. Only from the middle classes one gets ideas, and from the common people – life itself, warmth. You feel their hates and loves."
>
> "It's all very well, my boy. But, then, why don't you go and talk to your father's pals?"
>
> "But they're rather different."
>
> "Not at all. They're the common people. After all, whom do you mix with now – among the common people? Those that exchange ideas, like the middle class. The rest don't interest you." ' pp. 314–15[3]

H. M. Daleski uses this exchange (amongst other evidence) to argue for Paul's unconscious identification with his father, more generally, for a conflict between his overt and his suppressed feelings about each parent, and few critics would wish to deny some such sub-text in the novel's articulation of Paul's attitudes.[4] Yet the argument, characteristically psychological in emphasis, needs its complement. Lawrence has constructed Paul's thinking about 'class', by means of a binary opposition (middle-class = ideas/working-class = warmth) that persists throughout his work. Moreover, if we turn to the presentation of Morel's positive qualities, we can see that 'warmth, life itself' is further defined. The rare occasions when Morel is at one with his family occur 'when he worked and was happy at work . . . Then he always wanted several attendants, and the children enjoyed it. They united with him in the work, in the actual doing of something, when he was his real self again': mending boots, patching his pit-trousers as too dirty for his wife to mend, or making fuses with wheat-straws and gunpowder, a detail followed by one of the few direct glimpses of Morel's life in the mine, when he tells stories about the pit-pony and the mouse up his sleeve (pp. 102–4).

Indeed, critical foregrounding of the relationships *within* the Morel family lead one to forget how thoroughly Part I of the novel is imbued with the working rhythm of the colliers' lives, the trooping back and forth to the pit, the early returning when work is slack, the many references to Morel in his 'pit-dirt', in effect the uniform of his job, which holds the attention of the children in exactly the degree to which it repels them. Or again, when Paul and his mother first walk to the Leivers' farm they see Minton pit in the distance. Paul stops to sketch the pit-hill and the line of waiting trucks, saying 'I like the feel of *men* on things while they're alive. There's a feel of men about trucks, because they've been handled with men's hands, all of them.' (p. 167) Paul's contradictory feelings about his father have, that is, their social dimension; and though the 'class' issue remains unformulated in narrative terms, the over-all rejection of Miriam, not of course middle-class but central to Paul's response to 'ideas', takes on an unexpected implication in the light of the conversation quoted above. Unlike his brother William, whose career involves becoming 'a gentleman' (p. 132), Paul remains in his own class, amongst 'the common people' whom he likes best.

Women in Love, however, is the first full-length novel in which class opposition is discernible, though occluded in form. Countering Leavis's emphasis on the contrast between the fates of Ursula and Birkin and Gudrun and Gerald, Raymond Williams has called the novel 'the tragedy of a single action' where all four protagonists combine, to register a root-and-branch negation, not just of the available social formation of pre-1914 England, but 'of humanity itself'.[5] Yet the question needs to be asked: does the novel present a *single* action? Modern criticism is so deeply (silently) committed to the notion that the significance of a text derives from its unity, that perhaps one shouldn't be surprised at the practice of discounting the novel's internal contradictions. Yet surely these are emphatic. Birkin himself is as much the site of unresolved debates as the semi-official spokesman he is usually taken to be. The residual obscurity of his final relationship with Ursula (does it or does it not realize the conception of marriage he has argued for? is the desired further friendship with Gerald necessary to the permanent realization of true marriage, and if so, why didn't we hear about it much sooner?) which *has* been debated, is only one aspect of this.

Birkin's attitude towards English society is equally unresolved. For Williams, the over-riding note is the radical misanthropy of Birkin's final meditation over the death of Gerald. Here, he supposes that the human species may be an evolutionary mistake, which the ultimate 'creative mystery' will replace, as the horse replaced the mastodon. This ultimate negation constitutes the 'single action' of the novel. Yet this expression of it is interestingly qualified with 'it was very consoling to Birkin to think this' (p. 580) – consoling, that is, to Birkin's grief at the death of his friend. And just as emphatic is Birkin's inner conflict of love and hate for his native country, his admission of which prompts the more profoundly cynical Gudrun to gibe at him as 'a patriot' (p. 488). Nor does Birkin refuse this term. A similar ambivalence has already appeared when Birkin and Ursula decide to cut all their connections with society and together 'just wander about on the face of the earth', words which Birkin immediately counters when he confesses to 'a hankering after a further sort of fellowship . . . I always imagine our being really happy with some few other people – a little freedom with people' (pp. 451–2). This 'further fellowship' directly relates to Birkin's desired friendship with Gerald. It is usual to notice the personal, quasi-homosexual element in this, yet as with Paul's attitude towards his father, its social dimension is also clear. Gerald is the man of action, of effective social and political power, and Birkin's defeated hope that their friendship might have rescued Gerald from his self-destructive love for Gudrun, gestures towards a more creative future than the death in the Alps. The conflict in Birkin's mind can be summed up in this way. Do he and Ursula belong, with everybody else, in 'the river of corruption' which Loerke, the supreme nihilist, is exploring ahead of them all (p. 523)? Or have he and Ursula opened up a different possibility? The sense of an ineluctable process of history drawing pre-1914 English society towards a final destruction is one of the memorable features of *Women in Love*, and Birkin, a kind of latter-day Jeremiah, is its explicit voice. But whether he is part of the process, or opposed to it, is never finally settled.

Where does 'class' enter into this uncertainty? The important point to make is that *Women in Love* recognizes the objective existence of class determinations as no earlier work of Lawrence had done. In Chapter 17, we learn of the critical change in the relationship between the paternal late-Victorian capitalist Sir Thomas Crich and his miners, brought about by a major strike. This event reveals to Sir Thomas that his Christian ethic is 'an illusion . . . and this really broke his heart. He must have the illusion and now the illusion was destroyed. The men were not against *him*, but they were against the masters.' (p. 298) In this struggle, says Lawrence, the miners were driven by two hopelessly entangled emotions, democratic aspiration and 'cupidity'. But the first was only a mask for 'the desire for chaos', that is to say, the destruction of all hierarchic relationships, and therefore of relationship itself. Gerald then resolves the conflict by embroiling master, management and men in over-riding loyalty to 'the great productive machine' (p. 301). He initiates a thorough-going mechanization of every aspect of the mining process. At first bitterly resentful of the change, eventually 'the men were satisfied to belong to the great and wonderful machine, even whilst it destroyed them. *It was what they wanted.*' (p. 304, my italics.) Now as David Craig has pointed out, we need to recognize the tendentiousness in Lawrence's account of this phase of English history, how little justice it does to the complex development of industrial trade-unionism and spreading Socialist struggle of the years 1880–1914.[6] Yet it is also true that the underlying fact of 'class' opposition is clearly registered, together with a Lawrentian version of the process some historians have described as the bourgeoisification of the working-class during the later Victorian period. Moreover, not only is the process of historical change seen as a product of a contest over the means of material production, the novelist's attitude is detached, analytic. Gerald, the new-style capitalist, is in his personal life as much a victim of mechanization as the miners, as his relationship with Gudrun reveals. Except in his purely mechanical role as the creator of the Machine, he becomes irrelevant to the productive process. The personal condition for his success as a mine-owner is the human emptiness which leads finally to his death.

On balance, certainly, Lawrence's concern is with the individual careers of his four protagonists. The particular social formation with which they finally break is, for Lawrence, irredeemably tainted, the history set in motion by Gerald and his like irreversible. Yet we have to add that its working-class members are nevertheless a significant presence, possessing an ambiguous attraction. In the scene where Ursula and Birkin give the antique chair to the young working-class couple, the man is seen as both repulsive and beautiful 'somewhere indomitable and separate, like a quick vital rat.' (p. 450) Birkin calls them 'the children of men, they like market-places and street corners best', and says they will inherit the earth. The notion of a powerful subterranean life, both 'glamorous' and horrifying is more extensively conveyed in Gudrun's feelings about Beldover, following upon the episode in which the Brangwen girls watch Gerald master his horse.

> 'There were always miners about. They moved with their strange, distorted dignity, a certain beauty, and unnatural stillness in their bearing, a look of abstraction and half-resignation in their pale, often gaunt faces. They belonged to another world, they had a strange glamour, their voices were full of an intolerable deep resonance, like a machine's burring, a music more maddening than the sirens' long ago.' (pp. 175)

These are the same people later said to be completely in the grip of the great Machine established by Gerald. Gudrun feels their attraction as physical and sexual, threatening her precariously achieved individual identity. They are 'the common people', yet she cannot resist joining them on market-nights 'like any other common girl of the district.' (p. 176) When, later, she is tutoring Winifred Crich, she and Gerald walk out one evening and pass under a railway bridge where 'she knew that . . . the young colliers stood in the darkness with their sweethearts, in rainy weather. And so she wanted to stand under the bridge with *her* sweetheart, and be kissed under the bridge in the invisible darkness.' (p. 414) And so it turns out.

Gudrun's temporary sense of identification with the people of Beldover is in contrast with Paul's mere statement that he 'likes the common people best'. In Gudrun we are presented with her conflict of feelings, and for people clearly identified as a class formation in a world dominated by industrial capitalist production. That the mining village is seen 'as through a glass, darkly' may be conceded. But the fact remains that its inhabitants *are* seen. We are reminded of that suppressed passion and energy when in the final discussion about England in which Gudrun calls Birkin a patriot, he says 'when the English really begin to go off *en masse*, it'll be time to shut your ears and run.' (p. 385)

Finally, we should notice the more elaborate use of the binary opposition used by Paul Morel to distinguish the common people from the middle-class: 'life'/'ideas'. The Beldover miners and the young working-class man embody a distorted and subterranean vitality, while Ursula's peculiar attraction for Birkin derives from her special quality of 'life' (p. 270). 'Ideas', on the other hand, are associated with Birkin's world, a bohemian demi-monde of artists and intellectuals, with an upper-class dimension. 'Ideas', too, are no longer straightforwardly admirable. Sometimes, they amount to a falsifying 'idealism' which masks a ruthless will-to-power (Hermione, Sir Thomas Crich, Gerald). Their bohemian manifestation in Halliday and his set, is presented as vapid or (obscurely) corrupt. Birkin, a principal source of 'ideas' and with a foot in each camp, is characteristically a site of contradictions. Ursula discerns in his theorizing about marriage a mere attempt to bully her. Part of Birkin's self-disgust arises from the suspicion that he *has* been dangerously complicit with Hermione's style of 'idealism'. Yet Birkin's own 'ideas' are also accorded respect, as he struggles to find the right formulation for his relationships with Ursula and Gerald. Gudrun's conscious rejection of the class position which marriage to Gerald would bring has a certain parallel in Birkin's rejection of 'ideas' in their false manifestations, whether located in the upper-class settings of Breadalby and Shortlands, or in the intellectual bohemia of Halliday's set. With this in mind, we can read the Birkin-narrative as a transition from 'ideas' (false form) to 'life', leaving the reader with a significantly unanswered question. What is the connection between the 'life' of the Beldover miners which attracts Gudrun and which Birkin recognizes, and the 'life' in Ursula which Birkin consciously desires? Lawrence's novels are, of course, famous for avoiding resolution, and at the personal level (not altogether 'personal' in Ursula's and Birkin's unresolved debate about Gerald) *Women in Love* is a signal case. But the radical contradiction lies at a less conscious level, articulated through the opposition between 'ideas' and 'life' and their shadowy adumbration in terms of opposed classes. Here is the clearest index of a counter-movement opposing the dominant narrative authority which Williams proposes in his conception of the novel's 'single action'.

We have seen that in 'Daughters of the Vicar' the escape from 'class' into 'life', unproblematic from the narrator's point of view, is differently signalled in the narrative. In *Women in Love*, though again it is the narrative that articulates the deepest sense of unresolved contradiction, a dim consciousness of inner turmoil may be said to affect the narrator's sense of the issues at stake. The simplest illustration of this development lies in the conclusions of each narrative. In 'Daughters of the Vicar', the narrator confidently adopts what might be called the 'colonial solution': the fugitives from 'class' will emigrate to Canada. No such solution is available to Birkin and Ursula. They exultantly choose a life of wandering (Chapter 26), but they end back in England, in a sort of limbo, with nowhere to go. We shall see that in *Lady Chatterley's Lover*, the narrator's consciousness of the issues wholly accords with that of the narrative. But first, it will be useful to glance at two post-war *nouvelles* characterized by a movement of 'internal' exile, in contrast with the literal and explicit exile present in the earlier narratives.

'The Ladybird' and 'The Captain's Doll' are distinct tales, but they share a number of traits. Located respectively in an aristocratic and upper-middle class milieu, each turns upon a marital deadlock finally broken by a representative of that familiar Lawrentian type, the mysteriously potent 'dark' male figure. Both marriages are characterized, in Lawrence's analysis, by the imposition of 'ideas' upon the reality of passional 'life', a romanticization of sexual difference, which by trying to obliterate 'otherness' leads to mutual destruction (Gerald and Gudrun represent the fullest analysis of this condition). Both stories also register the impact upon English and European society of the 1914–18 war. The 'dark' hero is defined in opposition to the old social order, effectively cancelled by the war. The narrative structure in both cases involves the 'dark' hero's successful wooing of a woman initially a member of the old order. The heroes are, or become, exiles in the sense that their criticism of the pre-war social order is almost as radical as Birkin's in *Women in Love*. But the exile is 'internal'. The hero's success in persuading the woman to join him establishes a relationship of unresolved mystery, his 'darkness' being a coded allusion to this state of affairs. The wealth of biographical and psychological commentary on this symbolism has had the effect of obscuring its social dimension. Yet the tales' insistent location of the deadlocked marriages within specific class *milieux* makes this dimension inescapable. Moreover, the sense of unresolved contradiction within each class *milieu* arises primarily from the balanced pairing of the characters. In 'The Ladybird', the aristocratic English Major Apsley, the romantic day-time husband, is doubled against the aristocratic European Count Psanek (the name, we are told, means *outlaw*), victim of near-fatal war wounds, who becomes the night-time husband (and lord) of Lady Diana of English aristocratic lineage. The story ends with these two relationships in counter-poise, so that Lady Diana is in effect doubled into conflicting day-time and night-time identities. Apsley represents the mere survival of the old, but superannuated, aristocratic class; Psanek voices some of Lawrence's proto-fascist social theorizing, a prominent feature of the later 'leadership' novels. But the tale ends in the mystery of Psanek's symbolic underworld, where he is lord of a reconstituted hierarchical order, a 'dark' mirror image of the dead day-time aristocratic world in which Lady Diana grew up.

This doubling is more intricate in 'The Captain's Doll'. Captain Hepburn is both the husband of Mrs Hepburn, married on 'romantic' terms of adoring worship, and Countess Hannelle's lover, the 'dark' Hepburn, with whom she nevertheless wants a 'romantic' marriage. Like Lady Diana, the Countess moves from one marriage-idea to another. Whereas she is of European aristocratic family displaced by the war, Hepburn is English upper-middle class, but neither is exactly a 'class' fugitive. Hepburn, moreover, evolves from his initially divided condition into a new 'dark' identity, and the conclusion even hints at a version of the 'colonial' solution: they might go and farm in Kenya. Yet this counts for less than the symbolic statement of Hepburn's new identity, which culminates in the tale's concluding sentence: 'He pulled back quickly into the darkness.' p. 251 We are left with an unresolved contradiction between this mysterious promise and the daytime world of postwar Europe represented in the socially formless and pleasure-seeking life of the Alps and Austrian sequences.

From the angle of 'class', we can read these tales as re-workings of the ambivalent ending of *Women in Love*. The impact of the war on the authority of the old upper-class is registered, yet the shadowy alternatives glimpsed in the novel are absent, the social relationship of the 'dark' hero and his bride to the altered class structure left unresolved. Sources of the new 'life', neither wanderers nor bohemian fugitives, they remain as socially-undeclared challengers of the post-war European order.

Of Lawrence's subsequent fiction, *Kangaroo* and *The Plumed Serpent* are too substantial to be discussed here, though their relevance to the argument may be briefly indicated. In *Kangaroo* the 'dark' hero's rejection of both proto-fascist and socialist responses to the aftermath of the war is justified in terms of 'life' as against falsifying political 'idealism'. But it is 'life' without social content, evoked only in the mysterious landscapes of Australia. *The Plumed Serpent* then represents Lawrence's struggle to clothe this 'life' with political and social form, sketching a kind of fascism without material 'base'. Only in *Lady Chatterley's Lover* do we find a substantial extrapolation of the 'life'/'ideas' opposition in terms of social class. The task of analysis is complicated by the existence of the three versions, the 'class' issue emerging in interestingly different ways from one to the next. Here, it will be necessary to concentrate on the third with only glancing reference to the earlier texts. A general point, though, may be made about all three. That disjunction between narratorial and narrative emphasis, between teller and tale, noticeable in Lawrence's earlier fiction has disappeared. The narrator is now entirely explicit that 'class' is a central issue in the novel, and unambiguously locates 'ideas' and 'life' within opposing class formations.

Clifford and his friends are the site of 'ideas' (Platonism, aestheticism), of an absence of warmth and tenderness characteristic of Clifford's 'class and race' (p. 74), and also of an underlying will-to-power transforming Clifford from dilettante writer into the post-war industrial capitalist who successfully revives the profitability of the Chatterley mines. The opposing cluster of values signified by 'life' is to be located, though not without severe qualification, within the mining populations of the district. On the positive side, we can cite Mrs Bolton's surviving passion for her dead collier-husband, source of her secret antagonism towards the Chatterley family as of her decision to side with Connie when, having guessed that Mellors is her lover, she provides a protective alibi by starting the rumour that Connie might yet have Clifford's child (pp. 153–4). Mellors's origins place him in the same camp, though here the situation is more complicated. His opposition to the industrial machine is, of course, unambiguous; the spirit of 'life' which he sustains in his work and in himself is Clifford's determined enemy. The Connie-narrative recounts her journey from the site of 'ideas' (her own youthful enthusiasms, as well as initial complicity with Clifford's position) to that of 'life', and underscores the emphatic break with his class when she tells Clifford that if, lacking a divorce, she can't marry Mellors, she would rather their child were illegitimate than remain the Chatterley heir (Ch. 19). What of the people of the mining villages (Tevershall, Stacks Gate)? The duality of attitude mutely present in *Women in Love* is now fully articulate, though the emphasis falls more on the negative side. In the often-cited Chapter 11, describing Connie's drive through the district surrounding Wragsby, its people are seen as ugly, culturally impoverished, radically infected with a grasping materialism expressed in shallow leisure activities and an obsession with the money needed to pursue them. The miners seem to Connie subterranean 'animas of coal and iron and clay' (p. 166). Yet also, as victims of the 'leaders of men' (p. 159) who have brought this about, they are possessed of a 'weird inhuman beauty', product of the conditions imposed upon them. Considered in their human aspect, they are 'patient and good men', and Connie both laments the impotence of their virtue and fears its opposite: 'supposing the dead in them ever rose up! but no, it was too terrible to think of. Connie was absolutely afraid of the industrial masses.' (p. 166) The 'life' in the mining populations is thus suppressed, underground, and only Mellors, a child of these people, succeeds in affirming it in a new manifestation. In his final letter to Connie, he re-iterates the criticisms voiced by the narrator in Chapter 11, and concludes:

> 'There's a bad time coming, boys, there's a bad time coming! If things go on as they are, there's nothing lies in the future but death and destruction for these industrial masses. I feel my inside turn to water sometimes, and there you are, going to have a child by me.' (pp. 315–6)

Connie and Mellors, then, are fugitives from their respective classes, hoping (somewhat desperately) to bring to birth the 'life' which in different ways each class denies, with the final responsibility for its denial being laid at the door of the upper-class represented in Clifford. Mellors' alienation from his class is conscious from the start, a frozen withdrawal from which he is revived by Connie, while the process of *her* alienation from her class is the story of the novel.

So, as with 'Daughters of the Vicar' though now with full narratorial consciousness, the question the novel leaves us with is: where will this 'classless' life find a *home*? We can see from the earlier versions that Lawrence struggled with this question. In *The First Lady Chatterley*, Parkin rules out both Canada and farming (Ch. 18), determines to stick to his job at the Sheffield steelworks partly because he had become branch secretary of the Communist League, leaving us with the possibility that he and Connie might marry and live near his work (Ch. 22). 'Class', moreover, is an issue which enters into their relationship. Connie is much more '*Lady* Chatterley' and he is bristlingly sensitive to possible patronage. 'Life' in this version of the novel prompts Lawrence to conscious, if inconclusive, exploration of its probable social and political manifestations in the English Midlands in the 1920s.[7] There is also a cautious *rapprochement* between 'life' and 'ideas', signalled in the character of Connie's intellectual friend Duncan Forbes, entirely on the lovers' side, and not unsympathetic to radical political change (Ch. 23). In *John Thomas and Lady Jane*, however, where again Parkin is distinctly a working-man whose social and economic vulnerability are unmistakable, the political dimension has gone and the conclusion is indeterminate. Connie vetoes the Canada solution voiced by Parkin (Ch. 13), though only for the vague alternatives of Italy, or farming – no place specified (Ch. 25). 'Class', moreover, is held to be an anachronism (Ch. 13) to be set aside by a few select individuals courageous enough to seek a full human relationship, while the sexual relationship is now more heavily stressed.

This second version shows Lawrence withdrawing from the complex formulations tentatively proposed in the first, a movement completed in the third where Parkin has become Mellors, working-class in origin, yet as has often been noticed, sufficiently de-classed by his war-years to feel entirely on terms with Connie's father. This enables Lawrence to dispense with the working-class *milieu* of the earlier versions (Sheffield, the Tewson family) entailed by the characterization of Parkin as unambiguously working-class. 'Class' is no longer an issue which Connie and Mellors have to face in personal terms. It remains as a structure of the world which they are about to leave. 'Life' in their terms is only conceivable *outside* the social and economic conditions which the novel has presented. The evolution of the novel towards this final version strikingly demonstrates the structuring power of the 'life'/'ideas' opposition in Lawrence's thinking. Starting from the more complex first version, which implicitly challenges the terms of that opposition, Lawrence simplifies and abstracts, reworking the material till it is more consonant with the basic formula. Yet at the same time, the full narratorial consciousness that 'class' is a central issue has its effect. As Mellors' letter indicates, there is as much despair as hope in the conception of 'life' which he and Connie represent. The power of the structures they are determined to escape has been too strongly stated to be easily forgotten.

In summary, we can identify three stages in Lawrence's work, seen from the angle of 'class'. The first notices 'class' as a state of affairs from which certain individuals can disengage, culminating with *Women in Love* in which disengagement leads nowhere and the notion that 'class' constitutes a set of determining social structures begins to press for narratorial recognition. The second stage, from about 1918 and evidently in response to the war, shows a clear narratorial consciousness about 'class', but of a limited kind. The social and economic structures glimpsed in the first phase are no longer present. There is an attempt to dissolve 'class' into imaginary political structures based on a resurrected, but also dematerialized aristocratic principle. This phase culminates in *The Plumed Serpent*. The third phase, probably initiated by Lawrence's visit to Eastwood in September 1926, a key event in the production of the *Lady Chatterley* novels,[8] combines a full consciousness about 'class' with an explicit grasp of its social and economic conditions, yet also renews the concern with disengagement, differing in this respect from the first phase in a greater sense of its difficulty. Dominating all three phases are the assumptions that 'life' can only be sought outside these determining structures, and that 'ideas' are often evidence of a sterile pretence to have escaped them. These assumptions have such a hold on Lawrence that they block the development of his more complex thinking about 'class'.

This aspect of Lawrence's work should surely figure prominently in our estimate of his achievement. For most novelists, 'class' is a matter of the social minutiae which signal sub-divisions within that amorphous and shifting category of 'the middle-class', a condition which it is supposed that narrator and reader can jointly view from a non-aligned position of 'classlessness'. Of some of Lawrence's work, and especially some of the tales and short stories, this can also be said. But as I have tried to outline here, several major texts register a deeper and more complex sense of 'class', and considered as a succession, show a pressing into consciousness, which is also a response to a changing history, that no other novelist of his time can equal. Lawrence's struggle both to articulate this new consciousness, and at the same time to resist it, opens up a perspective on his work that deserves wider and more detailed recognition.[9]

Notes

1 Arnold Kettle's discussion of *The Rainbow* is a notable exception. He defines its theme as 'what bourgeois society does to personal relationship' (*Introduction to the English Novel*, Volume II, 1953, p. 129). 'Class' as such, however, is a good deal less prominent in *The Rainbow*, than in the texts I discuss here. Ursula and Skrebensky talk about 'class', but it is hardly registered as a structure of the world Ursula inhabits. For some discussion of 'class' see John Goode's chapter on Lawrence in *The Twen-*

tieth Century, 1970 (edited by Bernard Berganzi, *Sphere History of Literature*, Volume 7); and Graham Holderness *D. H. Lawrence: History, Ideology and Fiction*, 1982.

2 As Graham Hough points out in *The Dark Sun* (1956) p. 43, the handling of 'class' in 'Daughters of the Vicar' is not unlike traditional 19th century treatment of the theme.

3 Page references are to the Penguin version of this and subsequent Lawrence novels.

4 In *The Forked Flame*, 1965, p. 113.

5 Raymond Williams, *Modern Tragedy*, 1966, p. 135.

6 David Craig, *The Real Foundations*, 1973, pp. 143–67.

7 Geoffrey Strickland proposes that for this and other reasons, the first version is very much better than its successors. See A. H. Gomme (ed.) *D. H. Lawrence: A Critical Study of the Major Novels and Other Writings*, 1978, pp. 159–171.

8 See 'Return to Bestwood' in *D. H. Lawrence: A Selection from Phoenix*, ed. A. A. H. Inglis (Penguin, 1971), recounting Lawrence's impressions of the General Strike in the Erewash Valley, especially pp. 152–7.

9 For a characteristically psychological reduction of Lawrence's sense of class difference, see his 'Autobiographical Sketch' (1929), in *A Selection from Phoenix* (ed. Inglis), p. 17.

The Uses of Fiction
Edited by
Douglas Jefferson
and Graham Martin

7

A Mania for Self-Reliance: Grassic Gibbon's *Scots Quair*

Angus Calder

'When I read or hear of our new leaders and their plans for making of Scotland a great peasant nation, a land of little farms and little farming communities, I am moved to a bored disgust with those pseudo-literary romantics playing at politics, those refugees from the warm parlours and lights and policemen and theatre stalls of the Scots cities. They are promising the New Scotland a purgatory that would decimate it. They are promising it narrowness and bitterness and heart-breaking toil in one of the most unkindly agricultural lands in the world . . . This life is for no modern man or woman – even the finest of these.'

Lewis Grassic Gibbon, in *Scottish Scene*[1]

I

Lewis Grassic Gibbon's trilogy about life in the Mearns has the status in Scotland of a modern classic. Elsewhere its reputation is not wide, though critics on the Marxist left commonly respect it as one of the most remarkable of 'proletarian' novels.

The three books of the *Quair*, published individually from 1932 to 1934, take the story of Chris Guthrie from childhood to death. *Sunset*

Song (1932) projects the life of a peasant community from 1911 through the First World War. The Guthrie family have moved from Aberdeenshire to a peasant croft at 'Kinraddie' in the Mearns. Here John Guthrie's wife, finding herself pregnant again and fearing the pain of another childbirth, poisons her young twins and herself. His son Will revolts against him and emigrates. Guthrie himself soon dies after a stroke, leaving his highly intelligent daughter, Chris, with a choice between going elsewhere to complete her education or turning peasant farmer in her own right. She decides on crofting, then marries a labourer, Ewan Tavendale. They produce a son, also named Ewan.

Their idyll is barely touched at first by the outbreak of war, which indeed brings unwonted prosperity to the area. But eventually Ewan enlists. His death in France, shot as a deserter, and those of Chae Strachan the Socialist crofter and Long Rob the freethinking miller represent the end of a peasant tradition.

Chris marries Kinraddie's new minister, Robert Colquohoun, who was gassed at the front and has come home a socialist. In *Cloud Howe* (1933), which spans the 1920s, Colquohoun transfers to the manse of 'Segget', a small Mearns town where shopkeepers and craftsmen stand disdainfully apart from the workers in the local jute mills. Gibbon's evocation of this place is as remarkable as his handling of peasant life in *Sunset Song*. The General Strike of 1926 is central to the second novel. Robert commits himself to the workers' side, and the loss of his child, which Chris is carrying, just as the cause founders, betrayed by its leaders, matches the destruction of his revolutionary hopes. He slumps into sentimental Christian mysticism, and when he rallies at last, to preach radically again, his gassed lungs give way and he dies in his pulpit.

His stepson, Young Ewan, brought up an English-speaking, middle class child of the manse decides, at the opening of *Grey Granite* (1934) not to live off his mother but to become an apprentice in a steel works in 'Duncairn', a city on the Mearns coast. Moving there with him, Chris becomes part-owner and manager of a lodging house. Young Ewan, despite his initial contempt for working class 'keelies', is drawn, at the height of the slump, into left-wing agitation, and suffers at the hands of the Duncairn police. Chris is married for a third time, to Ake Ogilvie, a joiner from Segget who has migrated to the city. But Ake soon decides to go further, to seek work in Canada. Young Ewan leaves at the head of a hunger march to work for the Communist Party in London, and Chris goes back to farm alone the croft in Aberdeenshire where she was born.

Few characters in fiction have endured such a series of calamities as Chris. Yet her personality seems to survive unmutilated. She is courageous but not domineering, warmly human yet strong in detached reflection. 'Chris Caledonia', as Robert calls her, could be taken to symbolize Scotland in a most attractive way. She is so alive in a credible modern world that her eventual retreat to solitude on the land is disappointing, and she is so appealing that readers do not want to believe that Gibbon kills her off, still barely forty, on the last page of the trilogy where, meditating on a hill top, she slips from consciousness into death. By contrast, even left-wing readers tend to recoil from the callous, arrogant militancy of her son. The common opinion is that *Grey Granite*, despite some brilliant writing, fails. Those who want it to be a Scottish nationalist text can hardly be happy with a conclusion which might suggest that Scotland, personified by Chris, is dead, while those in search of the Great British Proletarian Novel may be uneasy about the inhumane crudity of Young Ewan's commitment.[2]

I aim in this essay to explore the *Quair*, in relation to Gibbon's life and times, so as to promote a way of reading the text which will permit us to say that *Grey Granite*, despite flaws in execution, does complete the trilogy adequately. My main argument is that in it Gibbon completes a critique of peasant 'independence' which he began in *Sunset Song*. His fictional methods exclude direct authorial comment. If we identify him too closely with either Chris or Young Ewan we misread the trilogy and are liable to underestimate its achievement.

The action of the *Quair* is conveyed to us by a flow of voices. Even when it isn't clear that Gibbon's prose is dialogue or internal monologue, it remains intimately within the point of view of a character or characters. Here Young Ewan is falling in love with Ellen Grant:

> 'And she tripped beside him, sweet, slim and demure in act and look, dark cool kitten, and inside was frightened at the wildness there. So up Windmill Steps through the sheet of the snow, a corner with a mirror, here the snow failed, Ewan halted panting while she made to run on.
>
> But he caught her arm and drew her down, she wriggled a little, the light on her face, startled, eyes like stars and yet drowsy, he drew her close to him and they suddenly gasped, with wonder and fear and as though their hearts broke and were shattered in the kiss, sweet, terrible, as their lips met at last.'[3]

Could 'omniscient' prose be more inward? The procedure through comma after comma, characteristic of Gibbon, suggests the unpunctuated nature of human thought and speech, as well as, in this case, the breathlessness of two youngsters hurrying home from a dance, excited by love. 'Dark, cool kitten' is Ewan's appraisal, foreshadowing, in its more-than-hint of a sneer, his eventual discarding of Ellen. The latter part of the same sentence gives us Ellen's feelings.

Every sentence in the *Quair* is creating character, evoking experience; there is no room for detached comment. Though Gibbon gives special prominence to the voice and consciousness of Chris, he cannot be implicated in her views of life – still less in those of Young Ewan. And as Gibbon adapts his technique, through the trilogy, to the social worlds which he projects, his separation from Chris becomes more obvious.

In *Sunset Song*, the narrative voice of Chris is not far from the gossip voices of Kinraddie, where, although they have a habit of sneering, folk exhibit strong communal feeling in moments of celebration and crisis, till the war brings economic success and social disaster. Gibbon, it has been pointed out, uses the pronoun *you* in moments when Chris, narrating, addresses herself:

> 'So mother had worked and ran the parks those days, she was blithe and sweet, you knew, you saw her against the sun as though you peered far down a tunnel of the years.'

Here the effect of the *you* is to bring the reader into special intimacy with Chris. But the previous page (we are close to the *Quair*'s beginning) has established another usage for *you*, even within Chris' narrative voice:

> 'You could go never a road but farmer billies were leaning over the gates, glowering away at the weather, and road-menders, poor stocks, chapping away at their hillocks with the sweat fair dripping off them . . .'

Chris is using 'generic *you*', implying that everyone in Kinraddie has shared, or could have shared, her observation. The 'overlap' between Chris's voice and the 'gossip' narrative voice which also employs generic *you*, helps Gibbon to draw us into the whole community of which Chris herself is so much a part.[4]

But city life did not allow the novelist, still committed to narration through characterized voices, the same ease of continuity. In *Grey Granite*, the passages of narrative-monologue employing *you*, whether 'self-referring' or 'generic' *you*, are distributed between sharply different voices. Four are given to Chris, three to the Anglicized Ewan, seven to a 'keelie' worker named Bob (briefly a Socialist, and as important a centre of consciousness in the novel as Ewan or Chris), four by unidentified workers, and one by a draper's clerk, John Cushnie, overheard, comically and yet movingly, as he begins to revolt against lower middle-class proprieties.[5]

In *Sunset Song*, all voices converge towards one, and Chris dominates. In *Grey Granite*, social distances keep the voices apart, and Chris's relative stature is diminished by the prominence given to centres of consciousness very different from hers; we cannot be enthralled by her view of the world. The diminution of her role makes sense if we see Chris as inheriting a tradition of peasant self-reliance, and her end as figuring the exhaustion of that tradition in the Scotland which Gibbon surveyed in the early thirties.

II

In 1933, James Leslie Mitchell, who had recently begun publishing fiction in Scotticized English, or Anglicized Scots, under the pseudonym of 'Lewis Grassic Gibbon', proposed a collaboration to C. M. Grieve, whose poetry in 'Synthetic Scots' had already enjoyed a certain fame. They had been introduced to each other by John Strachey,[6] and an interest in revolutionary Marxism was one of several things which these leaders of 'Scottish Renaissance' had in common.

Each was an autodidact, reared in an anachronistic community on the periphery of industrial 'civilization'. Gibbon, the son of a peasant farmer from north-eastern Scotland, viewed that civilization with as little reverence as Grieve, whose father had been a rural postman in a small mill-town near the English border, and who was currently praising the 'immense genius' of Major Douglas on the significant grounds that Social Credit would 'establish the economic independence of the individual.'[7] The scalding contempt for gentility which flavours Gibbon's writings matched the class-conscious radicalism passed on to Grieve by his father, but both men felt separate from the urban 'masses', about whom both wrote scornfully on occasion.

Their collaboration produced a mischievous volume called *Scottish Scene*. Gibbon's essays and short stories were written amid the creature comforts of Welwyn Garden City. Grieve's (or to use his pen-name,

Hugh MacDiarmid's) poems and essays arrived from the Shetlands, where he endured a more strenuous kind of exile. The book makes it hard to accommodate either writer in the mainstream of Marxism. While Gibbon jeers at his colleague's panacea, Social Credit, as 'that ingenious scheme for childbirth without pain and – even more intriguing – without a child', he unveils his own 'Diffusionist' view of history (which leaves many traces in the *Quair*). As a self-taught archaeologist, he believed that in a distant Golden Age the naked hunters in Scotland's forests had been free and happy. Agriculture, civilization, rule by lairds, had been imposed by alien seafarers. Though Gibbon admired William Wallace, who had briefly roused and led the 'Pictish' poor, he despised Robert Bruce – a nobleman. The Industrial Revolution had eventually brought complete disaster.[8]

One might see Gibbon and MacDiarmid quite plausibly as brilliant provincial eccentrics whose main obsessions were essentially religious. MacDiarmid was writing 'Hymns' to the Messianic figure of Lenin. In his masterpiece, 'On a Raised Beach' (1934), he addresses an audience of stones – 'I would scorn to cry to any easier audience' – and other people are for him 'human stones'. Towards the end of Gibbon's trilogy, in that novel significantly entitled *Grey Granite*, Young Ewan, long associated with granite in his mother's mind, is at work as a labourer for a granite mason, 'getting interested in granite'. Not to be outdone in stoneyness, Chris herself dies surrounded by stones.

This obsession with stones of two writers who were currently influencing each other might be explained in terms of what both drew from Scottish Calvinism, which had made God as alien as his universe, of which Scotland is one of the stonier portions. While neither is in the least a mystic, their evocations of the vastness of time and space, which mocks the puny lives of individuals, might seem to give each man's materialism an impractical appearance. And Gibbon did write very consciously in a Scottish tradition shaped, for better and worse, by the most intellectual and least ingratiating variant of Christianity. When he died in 1935, he was working on a novel about the Covenanters, whose grim and gentry-hated lives are a point of reference in *Sunset Song*, and in whose traditions of martyrdom Young Ewan is tortured by the politico-legal establishment. But I think that in the context of the early thirties, his stony views, and those of MacDiarmid, had as much to do with existing conditions in Scotland as with inherited cultural factors.

The 'Scottish Scene' was very ugly. After the First World War the country's characteristic heavy industries – coal, iron, shipbuilding –

had lost export markets, but although new consumer-goods industries maintained prosperity for many in southern England, Scotland neither created nor attracted such industries. Mass unemployment led to mass emigration. In the ten years leading up to 1931, nearly 400,000 Scots (say about one person in twelve), left Scotland, and despite high natural increase population actually declined. Politically, Scotland had swung precociously to the left. In 1922 Labour had returned the largest bloc of Scottish MPs and the eccentric constituency of Motherwell had actually elected a Communist. But the abortion of the General Strike was followed by further disillusionment in 1931 when a Scottish premier, Ramsay MacDonald, defected from the Labour party to head a 'National' government, and his former party, which had held over half Scotland's seats, was reduced from 37 to a mere 7.

In 1932, when *Sunset Song* was published, over a quarter of all Scottish workers were unemployed; in the worst hit areas well over half; in Greenock, three-quarters even two years later when the slump had abated somewhat.[9] Though Gibbon lived in an 'affluent' part of England, he frequently revisited his homeland, and the 'granite' ruthlessness of Young Ewan must be understood in terms of what he saw there. Gibbon was not escaping into religious fantasies about Lenin-like young heroes, so much as asking himself how an educated young Scot might react to social disaster. He did not *invent* the corruption, where they had local power, of some Labour politicians, nor the battles between workers and police, nor the hunger marches. As MacDiarmid harangued pebbles in the Shetlands, the political and cultural situation in Scotland was desperate, and Gibbon's would-be 'granite' hero makes a plausibly drastic response to a horrific crisis.

One aspect of the crisis was the destruction of a proud Scottish tradition: the 'independence' of several classes of literate, disputacious manual workers. This is marked in *Grey Granite* by the emigration of Chris's third husband, Ake, a small-town joiner and vernacular poet unable to find a job in the city to which the collapse of his rural trade consigns him. Burns, so often mentioned in the *Quair*, had been these classes' representative hero. The Lowland peasant culture for which Burns spoke had been wrung by capitalist agriculture since the eighteenth century. The related culture of handloom weavers had peaked and declined in the nineteenth. But the lead miners of Wanlockhead maintained the remarkable library which their forebears had started in the eighteenth century, right up to the closure of the mines in 1934.[10]

The worst shock Scotland suffered after 1918 was the collapse of the Clyde shipbuilding and engineering industry. Skilled engineers had attitudes closely comparable to those of the archaic 'independent' classes.[11] David Kirkwood, a leader of the Clyde Workers' Committee during the First World War, looked back admiringly to the 'mania for self-reliance' of his father, a labourer in a weaving mill, yet a devoted Calvinist who idolized the Covenanters and Burns. But Kirkwood himself by the 1930s epitomized one kind of Labour MP whom Gibbon mistrusted – sentimental, conceited, reformist, collaborationist at heart – and the fact that Kirkwood's autobiography appeared with a foreword by Winston Churchill, praising its author and the 'strong type he represents', might prompt us to question the real virtue, in twentieth century society, of that kind of 'self reliance'.[12]

Hammered by post-war slump, the Scottish working-man's tradition which had produced Burns and Carlyle, Carnegie and Livingstone, was at last deprived of a social basis. This might help to explain the prominence of Scots in British Marxist organizations. The tradition which said 'A man's a man for a' that' might well mutate into self-identification with the workers of the world, and a grounding in Calvinist theology was not the worst basis for a delight in dialectics. If we took Grassic Gibbon in *Grey Granite* to be simply endorsing Young Ewan's view, we could see him as exemplifying the process whereby the cult of self-reliance gave way to one of self-obliteration in the impersonal forces of history.

But there is strong evidence that Gibbon stands apart from Young Ewan. 'A hell of a thing to be History, Ewan!' his mentor in Communism, Jim Trease, tells him – at which Young Ewan thinks, enraptured, 'not a student, a historian, a tinkling reformer, but LIVING HISTORY ONESELF, being it, making it, eyes for the eyeless, hands for the maimed!' Masochistically, he supposes that the Party, historically speaking, *are* the workers, yet when the proletariat finally rise, 'most likely' he and Trease will be 'flung aside or trampled under', and, racing on through the commas with which Gibbon punctuates interior monologue, 'it didn't matter, nothing to them, THEY THEMSELVES WERE THE WORKERS and they'd no more protest than a man's fingers complain of a foolish muscle.' (*Grey Granite*, pp. 160–1, 195)

Trease gives History only an initial capital. The slogan-like capitalizations which follow belong to Young Ewan and serve to characterize him. He is very young. Beneath his composure, he is sentimental in his extreme anti-sentimentality. It must finally seem a weakness in *Grey Granite* that Gibbon cannot persuade his readers that Young Ewan, despite the truly heroic aspects of his role, is not a spokesman for his creator. But he could only have done this at the high cost of lapsing from that closeness with his characters which makes the *Quair*, though it has its faults, such a powerful work overall.

Young Ewan despises 'bunk symbolism'. But his mother is made to think symbolically. The titles of the three novels are, as it were, provided by Chris's symbolizing proclivities. The first isn't called 'Twilight of the Peasants'. Nor is it called 'Gloaming Sang', as nationalistic critics might wish. It is *Sunset Song*, and its shape and force depend on symbolic linkings 'made by' the part-Anglicized Chris. She *sings* the old lament over Flodden, 'Flowers of the Forest', during the celebration of her marriage to the first Ewan. At the end of the book, clearly at her suggestion, it is played by a piper at the ceremony where her next husband, the minister, unveils a monument to Ewan and the three other Kinraddie men killed in the war. The symbolism of this monument must likewise be of Chris's devising. Above her own croft, on one of a circle of standing stones, the names have been cut after the style of a tribute to persecuted Covenanters at Dunnottar Castle where 'the Covenanting folk had screamed and died while the gentry dined and danced in their lithe, warm halls.' (*Sunset Song*, p. 126) Chris and Ewan had seen it on a jaunt in the early days of their love. Chris inherits her peasant father's class feeling against the gentry, but she does not make an intellectual connection (e.g., that the ruling class had been responsible for the carnage of the war). Like her theatrical deployment of bagpipes, an easy way to induce tears which blur over the historic conflict between Highland and Lowland, this suggests that her vision of Scotland and of history is inadequate. The end of *Sunset Song* could not be so moving if Gibbon did not expect his readers to implicate themselves in temporary acceptance of the sentiment. But this does not mean that in *Cloud Howe* and *Grey Granite* we are to regard Chris as an oracle rather than a character, to accept her mythology and to attribute it to her creator.

One critic makes this mistake when he claims that Gibbon's point is 'All is change, nothing endures but the land, while the forms of social organisation are blown away like chaff.'[13] This is, in fact, what Chris thinks. But despite a certain obvious truth in her notion, we should not attribute Chris's fatalism to Gibbon himself.

The contrast between Chris's view and her son's has prompted the suggestion that Gibbon sees history in terms of struggle between 'the masculine' and 'the feminine'.[14] Not continually, but in significant crises, Chris does indeed struggle with the men in her life. Her confrontation with her son gives us the last conversation in the trilogy. Chris denies the validity of all creeds:

> '*Yours is just another dark cloud to me – or a great rock you're trying to push up a hill.*
>
> He said it was the rock was pushing him: and sat dreaming again, who had called Robert dreamer: only for a moment, on the edge of tomorrow,/ all those tomorrows that awaited his feet/by years and tracks Chris would never see,/ dropping the jargons and shields of his creed,/ thinking again as once when a boy,/ openly and honestly, kindly and wise:
>
> *There will always be you and I, I think, Mother. It's the old fight that maybe will never have a finish, whatever the names we give to it – the fight in the end between FREEDOM AND GOD* (*Grey Granite*, p. 20)

The italics are Gibbon's, who thus avoids the conventional separation of speech from the surrounding narrative. The division into verses, of four beats each, is mine. David Craig has objected to Gibbon's 'mechanical metre' in certain passages, to his resort to 'a sort of soaring operatic highnote . . . whenever he wants that sort of kick.'[15] But its function in this particular passage is clear. The flight into rather flatulent 'poetry' is consonant with Ewan's drift into 'dream'. The rhythm characterizes his state of mind, as he blurs over the prospect of his mother's death and looks forward, sentimentally, to moving *back*, past his creed, to childhood candour.

He hankers, for a blink, to regress. His mother has actually regressed and will regress further. This is not because she is a woman, and Gibbon does not typify 'eternal femininity' through her. Gibbon was ahead of his time in his understanding of the legitimate demands of women from life. Contraception is a major issue in all three books. Want of it drives Chris's mother to suicide. Having it enables Ellen Grant to restore Ewan's relationship with his own body after the Duncairn police have tortured him. Ellen, like Maggie Jean Gordon in *Sunset Song*, Cis Brown and Else Queen in *Cloud Howe*, shows us that Gibbon's appreciation of the capacity of women for self-emancipation was not exhausted in his creation of Chris. On the contrary, Chris – though, paradoxically, by an unconventional act of will – throws up the chance of a wider life which her success at school might have given her. The emancipation of other characters shows up her relative conservatism, and their actions contradict her own association of 'creeds' with men. While most of the men in the *Quair* aren't ardent believers in anything, Maggie Jean, going off with her Labour doctor to organize farm workers, obeys the call of a 'creed' long before Young Ewan does. Is the latter talking nonsense perhaps in his last dialogue with his mother? While we may be prepared to associate him with

FREEDOM, does anything we have read in the *Quair* entitle him to identify the atheistical Chris with God? Is he not splurging like some literary critic (most likely Scottish!) projecting some big fanciful theory?*

Cairns Craig is not such a nonsense-talker, when he argues that the absence, since 1707, of a distinctive Scottish political history has given the Scottish novelist special problems of applying narrative patterning to social experience. 'What Scottish novelists have had to do again and again in recent times, is to link their novel to some moment of historical dynamism which intrudes upon the historyless Scottish community: Scotland can only be known through narrative in those moments when narrative possibilities are forced upon a society that has lost all sense of its own narrative.' So the Great War and the General Strike are, in this view, necessary 'intrusions' in the *Quair*. Cairns Craig admires Gibbon's commitment of Young Ewan to 'history', to 'the only possibility there is for transforming an inhumane environment', but argues that Chris's role, balancing his, is to deny history. She is 'identified at the end of the novel with the eternal principles of a landscape that is untouched by human changes, its granite permanence implacably opposed to human transformations.'[16]

This might make sense of what Young Ewan says: if Chris equals landscape and landscape equals eternal principles, then Chris equals God – the stony, impermeable God of Calvinism brooding over the puppet shows presented by humankind with its useless freedom. But if this is so, why is it that when she perishes Gibbon explicitly sits Chris not on *stone*, but on 'a great mass of crumbling cement', left by astronomers who came up the hill to make observations a hundred years before? (*Grey Granite*, p. 174) Chris herself denies the existence of anything 'permanent' in her last reverie. The dreams of men are transient. Intellectually she accepts the tyranny of change, which the cement represents not only in its relative newness, but also because it is already as much an archaeological relic as the 'standing stones' of ancient men. But by going back to the land, Chris has turned from the possibility of constructive change which the city offers.

History has destroyed her family and her childhood community, killing her first two husbands and her second baby, now taking her third husband and her son away from her. She cannot accommodate further her 'wearied body' and her battered self – or selves – to changes

*His remark is actually less absurd if we assume that he equates GOD with HISTORY and sees Chris as aiming for FREEDOM from HISTORY. But I am just not clear what Gibbon could have intended us to make of it.

within history. She regresses to infantile peasanthood, from which she was educated to be a 'second Chris', an intellectual girl, and removed in class terms by her marriage to a minister.

Her relationship with Ake is as significant in the *Quair*'s scheme as those with the elder Ewan and with Robert. 'I'm no body's servant, the Broo folk's, or the bobbies' ' is a saying of his which wins Chris's liking – he'll stand neither with the unemployed nor with the Establishment. Ake, with his 'slow independent walk', gives her, not rapture with marriage, but 'ease'. In his company she slides back to the values of her childhood, those of dour, uncommunicative Mearns folk who think it daft to say goodnight to their wives. He is, she thinks, 'crude and clean as she herself had been before a playing at gentry enslaved her'. He has in her eyes the 'sneering, half-kindly, half-bull-like face, the face of the folk of the Howe throughout, canny and cruel and kind in one facet, face of the bothies and the little touns.' And one of her lodgers muses 'Queer the resemblance between her and Ogilvie-chips, of the same bit of stone in a way.' (*Grey Granite* pp. 70, 137, 157, 178) Unromantic though their relationship has been, Ake's going is not her wish. Defeated by history, but still a skilled man, he can move on to Canada. Skilled in nothing but housework and farm-work she can think only of return to the croft of her origins.

III

Gibbon's politics were heterodox. MacDiarmid alleged that Gibbon was a Communist, but was kept out of the CPGB by his adherence to Trotsky.[17] One awaits further evidence of this 'Trotskyism'. His writing left him no time for activism. In an article published in *Left Review* just before his death, he wrote: 'I hate capitalism; all my books are explicit or implicit propaganda. But because I'm a revolutionary, I see no reason for gainsaying my own critical judgement.'[17] His nationalism was equally reserved. He wrote that he was 'some kind of Nationalist', but only 'temporarily, opportunistically'. He believed that Nationalism was a temporary cultural aberration and must give way to cosmopolitan community, but saw 'a chance that Scotland, especially in its Glasgow, in its bitter straitening of the economic struggle, may win to a freedom preparatory to, and in alignment with, that cosmopolitan freedom long before England.'[18] So his nationalism was not cultural, but strictly political, and was subject to the conviction that politics must be about class.

He thought that Glasgow workers could destroy capitalism. He knew that the old Scottish radicalism of self-reliance could not. Ake – and Chris – vote Liberal in the 1929 General Election. Raymond Williams has argued that in the *Quair* 'the radical independence of the small farmers, the craftsmen and the labourers is seen as transitional to the militancy of the industrial workers.'[19] It is true that Young Ewan is summoned, as a boy in *Cloud Howe*, to the deathbed of Moultrie, Segget's old radical saddler, and receives unspecified instruction from him. But he himself is middle class by upbringing and is converted to Socialism by an English girl schoolteacher. None of the keelies whom he sets out to lead has a rural background or expounds artisan 'independence'. Since Gibbon's plotting has no place for a David Kirkwood, the *Quair* suggests disjuncture more strongly than transition. Gibbon may in this be untrue to history, perhaps because his judgement was affected by bitter consciousness of how peasant independence had furthered its own destruction.

Ian Carter has shown how 'family' farming, on tracts of less than 100 acres, persisted tenaciously in north-eastern Scotland along with, and even symbiotically with, capitalist agriculture. The peasant farmer depended on hired labour to some extent, except when his children were old enough to work but had not yet left to set up on their own. Peasant agriculture had proved more resilient than capitalist farming during the agricultural depression of the late nineteenth century, but as increased demand for small farms forced up rents, the small man needed a higher cash profit – and was driven towards more thorough exploitation of the labour of sons and daughters.[20]

Hence the nightmarish character of John Guthrie in *Sunset Song* is not a melodramatic creation. He typifies the peasantry of his time. The rapidity of his movements, so much emphasized, suggests the ferocious pace of work which maintaining independence now entailed. His bad relations with his son Will, who escapes to Argentina, show the economic pressure on family relationships. So, in part, does his tragic sexual drive. More children will mean more workers. And the ideal of patriarchal self-sufficiency has obvious psychological consonance with incest; Guthrie's lust for Chris while he is mortally ill matches the rest of his peasant mentality.

Increasing numbers of peasant children fled, like Will Guthrie, from a life of bondage. The selective migration of boys and girls with initiative meant that peasant society lost power to resist just as outside factors conspired to sweep it away. The First World War brought a boom in sales of produce, and triggered a move from mixed-farming self-sufficiency into specialized work for urban markets, exemplified by the Munros in *Sunset Song*, who 'clean stopped from farming every park except one to grow their potatoes in, all the rest were covered with runs and rees for the hens, they'd made a fair fortune with their poultry and all.' (*Sunset Song*, 248–9)

Choosing when her father dies to remain on the croft alone Chris, as a girl, makes a momentous, even scandalous, assertion of independence. But, tragically, her decision coincides with the moment when self-reliance meets nemesis. In *Grey Granite*, her peasant values drag her into regression, stasis, and death.

Yet Chris has stood for something positive. Gibbon himself clearly feels at home with her, more than with the notion which he gives to middle-class-reared Young Ewan – that the masses, unthinking yet all-powerful, are sacred. In his *Left Review* article, he insisted on his own 'critical judgement'. Chris's independent thoughtfulness is her most attractive quality.

The opposition of Chris and Young Ewan at the end of the *Quair* suggests a dialectic of thoughtfulness – in itself, without action, useless and even potentially crippling – and militancy, which may, like Young Ewan's, be rash, cruel and opportunistic. Gibbon's trilogy can be related vividly to recent discussion on the left in Britain of the limitations of 'Leninist' militancy and the need to apply within Socialist politics lessons learnt from the success of the women's movement, with its more flexible and responsive methods of organization.[21] The right synthesis of critical spirit and action might produce a mature Socialism.

But Chris's negative aspects are travestied in Ake, her male look-alike, egotistic and complacent in fiction as David Kirkwood was in the Commons. Like countless 'independent' Scots before him, Ake transports himself to the New World, where the success of some such men has its monuments in the foundations of Carnegie and the banks of Toronto.

Notes

1 Lewis Grassic Gibbon and Hugh MacDiarmid, *Scottish Scene* (1934), p. 295.

2 Roy Johnson however approves of Young Ewan telling a 'big lie' for political ends, in his militant essay, 'Lewis Grassic Gibbon and *A Scots Quair*', in *The 1930s: A Challenge to Orthodoxy*, edited by John Lucas (1978), p. 55.

3 *Grey Granite*, Pan paperback (1973), p. 119.
4 See Graham Trengove, 'Who is You? Grammar and Grassic Gibbon', *Scottish Literary Journal*, Vol. 2, No. 1 (1975), pp. 47–61. Quotations from *Sunset Song* (Longman, 1971), pp. 30–1.
5 See J. K. A. Thomaneck, '*A Scots Quair* in East Germany', *Scottish Literary Journal*, Vol. 3, No. 1 (1976), p. 65.
6 Ian S. Munro, *Leslie Mitchell: Lewis Grassic Gibbon* (1966), p. 151.
7 Gibbon and MacDiarmid, *op. cit.*, p. 154.
8 *Ibid.*, pp. 19–36, 139.
9 John Stevenson and Chris Cook, *The Slump* (Quartet 1979), pp. 5 and 286.
10 Peter Keating, 'A Miners' Library', *Times Literary Supplement*, 6 January 1976, pp. 16–17.
11 'Inside every engineering craftsman lay the ideal type, derived from the old millwright, of the man who is hired to do a job, and to do it from start to finish without interference from his employer.' James Hinton, *The First Shop Stewards Movement* (1973), p. 96.
12 Arthur Marwick, *The Deluge* (1965), p. 70, calls Kirkwood 'the prototype of the hard-headed Lowland Scot'. My quotations from Kirkwood and Churchill come from David Kirkwood, *My Life of Revolt* (1935), p. vi, p. 11. On p. 101, writing about the Munitions of War Act of 1915, Kirkwood exclaims, 'I was happy in Beardmore's as a free man. I resented being in Beardmore's as a slave.'
13 Kurt Wittig, *The Scottish Tradition in Literature* (1958), pp. 330–3.
14 Francis R. Hart, *The Scottish Novel* (1978), pp. 233–41.
15 David Craig, *Scottish Literature and the Scottish People* (1961), p. 292; David Craig, 'Novels of Peasant Crisis', *Journal of Peasant Studies* Vol. 2, No. 1 (1974), pp. 52–3.
16 Cairns Craig, 'The Body in the Kitbag: History and the Scottish Novel', *Cencrastus*, No. 1 (1979), pp. 18–22.
17 Munro, *op. cit.*, p. 176.
18 Gibbon and MacDiarmid, *op. cit.*, p. 146.
19 Raymond Williams, *The Country and the City* (1973), pp. 268–71.
20 Ian Carter, 'The Peasantry of Northeast Scotland', *Journal of Peasant Studies*, Vol. 3 (1975–6), pp. 151–91.
21 See Sheila Rowbotham, Lynne Segal and Hilary Wainwright, *Beyond the Fragments: Feminism and the Making of Socialism* (1979).

I must thank A. Jack Aitken, Cairns Craig, David Daiches, Christopher Harvie and Graham Martin for their help towards the shaping of this essay.

The Uses of Fiction
Edited by
Douglas Jefferson
and Graham Martin

8

Two Women Novelists: Carson McCullers and Flannery O'Connor

Cicely Palser Havely

Margaret Drabble has been particularly highly praised by British critics. Because the range of her early work was so narrowly domestic, she was frequently compared with Jane Austen – but those who praised her in those terms were too often only invoking gentle Jane. In effect, Margaret Drabble was being praised for sticking to what women are supposed to know best, *Kinder*, *Küche* and private *Angst*. Then something happened. In *The Realms of Gold* (1975) she made her heroine a successful and famous archaeologist, thus enlarging both the temporal and spatial range of her themes, though it was still clear that she was more at ease loading the dishwasher in Putney, or unearthing family history in the provinces. Then in *The Ice Age* (1977) with an exhilaration which effectively challenges the despair in the novel, she took on the corruption at the heart of the British collusion between capitalism and socialism – a decisive move into the heart of male-dominated territory. But in her latest novel, *The Middle Years* (1980) she has gone back to the old, safe 'female' provinces. I had hoped that a novelist in whom I find so much to admire would go forward to some more progressive mixture of male and female concerns. Virginia Woolf expressed similar hopes for the novels that would be written by then newly emancipated women:

> '. . . her attention is being directed away from the personal centre which engaged it exclusively in the past to the impersonal, and her novels [will]

> naturally become more critical of society, less analytical of individual lives . . . The novel will cease to be the dumping ground for the personal emotions.[1]

But her novels were more, not less directed to 'the personal centre' than those of George Eliot, or Mrs Gaskell, or the author of *Shirley*; and they roused Mrs Leavis to a famous attack:

> One's own kitchen and nursery, and not the drawing-room and dinner table where tired professional men relax among the ladies (thus Mrs Woolf) is the realm where living takes place, and I see no profit in letting our servants live for us.[2]

She adds 'I myself . . . have generally had to produce contributions for this review with one hand, while actually stirring the pot, or something of that kind, with the other.' She might have been writing a manifesto for the Drabbleasian school. Yet how few of its members have really set out a balanced response to the wisdom of Mrs Leavis's point of view. The hand that stirs the pot has got its due, but not the hand that writes the review, or operates a machine or does any of the things that a woman must set her other hand to. While women of all classes (not just the women who have always worked outside the home) have gradually achieved a fuller share in the public life of the community, the reflection of their lives in the novel has tended to narrow, and to concentrate on the domestic and interior aspects to a degree that was actually much less often found in the nineteenth-century novel, when the servants of middle-class women did so much of their living for them. Then so many women novelists, not just the famous, used the novel to participate in all the major public controversies of their time, barred as they were from pulpit and parliament.

This concentration on the inner and private life is sometimes most marked where it appears least likely to be so. Doris Lessing's work is partly valued for the record it contains of the political climate of post-war Britain. But this record is only to be read through thick veils of highly individualized consciousness. In *The Four Gated City* (1972) Martha Quest works for and has an affair with a vaguely political figure who, like Mr Rochester, has a mad wife. But in this novel madness is a welcomed experience rather than the fearful excess that it is in *Jane Eyre*. Unlike Jane, Martha Quest falls in love with the mad wife and it is with her that the richer relationship develops, opening the way to Martha's own incipient insanity. Jane Eyre's subjective point of view looks like the most detached objectivity compared with the view of the world through Martha Quest's tortured and abnormal consciousness. *The Four Gated City* is extremely impressive but it is a mistake to think of it as a political novel simply because its characters attend political rallies. In choosing to elaborate on the familiar subjective formula of *Jane Eyre* Doris Lessing actually draws attention to how deep within the eccentric private self is the source of her point of view.

Some of the most ingrained traditions of the novel have helped to make such narrow concentration on the private self, and especially the sexual aspects of the private self, difficult to escape from. *Pamela* and *Clarissa* have remained powerful models, and the tensions and patterns of sexual behaviour have become inextricably involved with the structures of the novel. A reader without our cultural antecedents might think that the destruction of Le Voreux was climax enough for *Germinal*; it is possible to imagine Pip suffering just as badly from expectations that did not include Estella; and Insarov's biographer would probably relegate Elena to a footnote. The importance of sex in the novel, the sheer amount of novel time it takes up, is blatantly unrealistic – even in the Victorian 'realists'. All kinds of themes are developed through the expression of the protagonists' sexuality. Daniel Deronda looked for 'the blending of a complete personal love in one current with a larger duty' and found Zionism not only through Mirah, but inseparable from her. Hardy was one of the still very few novelists to give any attention to the working lives of his characters, but crises in their working lives are invariably indicative of crises in their inner and sexual lives as well. D. H. Lawrence effectively tied the knot with his insistence that the sexual aspects of the lives of men and women are not only of central importance, but that everything else that might seem to be separate in their lives relates to their sexuality. And because he embodied such ideas in his novels, still heavily influenced by the traditions of nineteenth-century realism, he effectively cemented a bond between the expression of sexuality and the novel form itself which has proved to be almost unbreakable. Nadine Gordimer (like Doris Lessing) is an explicitly 'political' novelist. Yet she too expresses the tensions and conflicts of South African society in terms of very private individual relationships and locates the critical points of these tensions within the ultimate intimacy of sexual love. This is less an undistorted reflection of the ways in which a society works, than a formula proceeding from the traditional novel itself, subsuming in sexual relationships all the various crises of moral behaviour that men and women endure.

The novel as our culture has derived it from Richardson's prototypes is a forum of the emotional, rather than the rational life. The emotions have been supposed to be the province of women, rationality that of men. In so far as there is any value in this distinction, the novel has become a 'feminine' form, predisposed to the inner life; and though by no means only women novelists explore such material for their fiction, there is a more urgent need for them to break from it. Men writing about the inner life must (in a sense) enter a foreign country; but women have no other well-established territory to move into. Like so many of the snares that beset women, the entanglement is complex. One of the things that feminists want to tell the male-dominated world is that being barred from the public world has trapped women within their inner lives. But the available form accommodates the treatment of the inner life so readily that the necessary political perspective is too often lost. There can be nothing wrong with any writer's desire to give the fullest possible account of an exclusively female experience or point of view. But the danger in the situation is that so much women's writing about women tends to consolidate the unhappy status quo, and not to advance the claims of women to a fuller life in every respect.

The better the thing is done, the easier it is to believe that this is the thing that women do best, and from there it is too easy a step to believing that it is the only thing they can do. This is why I want to look at the work of two women writers of the generation before this who have been very much neglected in Britain: Flannery O'Connor and Carson McCullers. Both achieved in their writing a degree of balance between the inner life and the public world which suggests that there is a way forward which has been missed.

Flannery O'Connor's fiction has only recently become available in Britain. But a misleading reputation has preceded her. She is held to be a Christian of the worst kind, more interested in the operations of grace than in progressive or liberal values. A Christian writer often has no worse enemy than the Christian critic. *Greenleaf* (1956) is a trenchant little comedy about Mrs May's struggle to protect her farm against various depredations, and especially the incursions of an irrepressible bull. She has to cope with the rancid indifference of her sons, the sublime indolence of her hired hand (' "I thank Gawd for everthang" Mr Greenleaf drawled. You might as well, she had thought. . . you've never done anything for yourself.' (p. 324)[3]) and the galling success of his industrious boys whose children will one day be 'society'. It is the Greenleaf boys' skittish bull which gets among her stainless herd and finally gores her to death. Everyone and everything is against Mrs May, yet the very name of her prime enemies (Greenleaf) suggests a deep collaboration which she can never perceive. As well as flowering, of course, Mrs May's name suggests something conditional, possible but not certain. The triumph of the Greenleaf bull brings Mrs May to an unlikely and ambiguous flowering only in the last split second of her life.

Until then the whole of Mrs May's inner life consists of frantic rationalization and resistance to what she sees as the forces of unreason beyond her control. One of her sons is a 'policy man' who sells insurance of 'the kind that only negroes buy'. He brings too close to home the exploitative nature of the social system which Mrs May wants to preserve. When the Greenleaf boys' black worker asks 'Is you my policy man's mother?' (p. 326) the question suggests an intimacy she cannot bear to acknowledge between herself and what her class most despises.

A bitter pragmatism protects her from the assaults of the irrational:

> 'Out of nowhere a guttural agonized voice groaned "Jesus! Jesus!" In a second it came again with a terrible urgency, "Jesus! Jesus!" Mrs May stopped still, one hand lifted to her throat. The sound was so piercing that she felt as if some violent unleashed force had broken out of the ground and was charging towards her. Her second thought was more reasonable: somebody had been hurt on the place and would sue her for everything she had.' (p. 316)

In fact the voice is Mrs Greenleaf's in an uninhibited religious ecstasy. This 'violent unleashed force' anticipates the bull's charge, of course; but here Mrs May can still step briskly aside:

> ' "Jesus" she said, drawing herself back, "would be ashamed of you. He would tell you to get up from there this instant and go wash your children's clothes".' (p. 317)

She has long since learnt to cope with such daily assaults on her certainties: 'There's nothing for it but the iron hand!' But how feeble her defence really is, her son brutally exposes:

> ' "Look at Mama's iron hand!" Scofield would yell and grab her arm and hold it up so that her delicate blue-veined little hand would dangle from her wrist like the head of a broken lily. The company always laughed.' (p. 322)

The real meaning of that striking simile is derived from her own earlier observation that Mr and Mrs Greenleaf 'lived like the lilies of the field, off the fat that she struggled to put into the land.' (p. 319)

Mrs May's real enemy is the future, the advancing twentieth century and more generally, the power of evolution. It finally defeats her in the form of the bull, which combines a vague mythological and evangelical symbolism with a quite specific natural bullishness. Outside her bedroom window at night he is both 'like some patient god come down to woo her' as he calmly chews her garden hedge, 'like an uncouth country suitor'. Half Jove, half Jesus, the foliage his horns have ripped from the hedge has slipped down to become a 'menacing prickly crown'. But it is his unruly, irresistible, death-defying pagan spirit that is most stressed. Just as he is being led off to be 'beefed' he escapes and charges the pick-up truck. A little later he 'ambles' onto Mrs May's property 'squirrel-coloured, with jutting hips and long light horns'. 'This gentleman is a sport,' said Mr Greenleaf approvingly. She orders the bull shot to protect her herd from his less than perfect genes – a last, doomed attempt to protect the narrow, unmerited privileges of her class against the mongrel potency of the Greenleaf's generation.

But the bull finds her sitting alone on the bumper of her car. He charged the truck, he charges her. And in the moment of her death Mrs May seems to realize that he is the necessary means of clearing away a fretful impediment to social progress:

> 'She stared at the violent black streak bounding towards her as if she had no sense of distance . . . and the bull had buried his head in her lap like a wild tormented lover, before her expression changed. One of his horns sank until it pierced her heart and the other curved around her side and held her in an unbreakable grip. She continued to stare straight ahead but the entire scene in front of her had changed – the tree line was a dark wound in a world that was nothing but sky – and she had the look of a person whose sight has been suddenly restored but who finds the light unbearable.' (p. 333)

She sees the same unbearable light that she saw in the Greenleaf boys' spotless milking parlour where it was the product of an entirely human energy. What is so admirable about this and some of O'Connor's other stories is the way in which the protagonist's inner life is 'placed'. Everything is seen not quite through Mrs May's eyes, but over her shoulder: her point of view is subjected to constant ironical adjustments which allow her to be seen as O'Connor wants her seen as well as how she sees herself. The continuous realization of Mrs May's inner life – which O'Connor presents till the very instant of her death – never overwhelms the equally strong realization of her immediate world (the farm and her conflict with her sons and neighbours): of the larger social forces that impinge on that small world (social mobility, the relations between blacks and whites); and even the greatest forces of all, in nature and possibly the supernatural too. Though the status of Mrs May's individual consciousness is so effectively placed, it is not diminished. Pig-headed and wrong though her point of view is, it is – almost – all she has; but it is not, O'Connor insists, all there is.

Carson McCullers achieved fame through subtle delineations of eccentric inner landscapes, as in *The Heart is a Lonely Hunter* (1940) and *The Member of the Wedding* (1946). *In Clock Without Hands* (1961) she went beyond her earlier achievement by relating four such inner landscapes to each other and to the complex social and political situation which involves them all. The unwilling desegregation of the South is not mere 'context'. It impinges directly and violently on her characters' lives even though the particular events they are involved in have little historical consequence. The novel achieves a rare and impressive balance between the demands of private feelings and the claims and pressures of the public world.

Clock Without Hands is about the relationships between blacks and whites in a small Georgia town. All the main characters are men. J. T. Malone, the pharmacist, is dying of leukaemia at the age of 40. His friend, Judge Clane, formerly a Congressman and 'fixed star in the galaxy of Southern Statesmanship'[4] is in his eighties, weighs three hundred pounds and is losing his reason; but he is still shockingly vigorous. His present passion is that the Government should redeem the Confederate currency, of which he has ten million dollars' worth, and pay restitution for freed slaves. With dazzling insensitivity he employs as a secretary for this project Sherman Pew, the half-white son of a black man sentenced to death. Sherman refuses to write the letters, and enraged into action, moves into a white neighbourhood. The judge, who misses the 'white sheeted meetings at Pine Mountain' that are now illegal, calls the foremost citizens to the pharmacy where they decide that Sherman Pew's house must be bombed. The lot falls to the mortally sick Malone who is a weak-spirited creature, with prejudices of his own against Germans and Jews as well as blacks. But with more courage than he has ever shown in his life before, he refuses:

> ' "Gentlemen, I am too near death to sin, to murder." He was excruciatingly embarrassed.' (p. 195)

The preacher at the church Malone attends (for purely conventional reasons) likes to preach about 'drawing a bead on death', yet he is as embarrassed about Malone's individual death as Malone. In a direly comic interview the immortality that confronts him is defined by the preacher as 'an extension of earthly life, but more intensified.' (p. 137) Malone is appalled: he 'thought of the drabness of his life and wondered if it could be more intensified'. With no particular excitement or horror he comes to realize that though no-one has noticed, he has already lost his life; which save for one remarkably trouble-free act of adultery, has been undistinguished by either vice or virtue. His refusal to bomb Sherman Pew's house is the most positive act of his drab life. But it is ineffective. The task is joyfully taken on by Sammy Lank, a poor white with a large family, who, as the Judge says, has 'only . . . the Nigra to look down on' (p. 191) The Judge's grandson, Jester Clane takes the assassin up in a plane in order to shoot him. But Lank reveals that his life's ambition is still unfulfilled. He wanted to father quins, and has produced no better than triplets. Grotesquely pathetic though this revelation is, Jester can no longer kill a man who has become by making it more than the impersonal agent of a hateful cause. So he lands Sammy Lank safely 'to brag to his family that he is such a well-known man that even Jester Clane has taken him on an airplane ride'. (p. 202) Thus ironically a small choice against violence comes to be seen as a gesture approving it. The progress of justice is almost invisibly slow. The novel was begun in 1954, the year in which it is set, and at that time a less restrained optimism would not have been realistic.

Nor is Malone consciously fulfilled or redeemed by his action. Instead, he worries that the good-will value of the pharmacy may have been jeopardized. He dies the day the Supreme Court decides that schools must be integrated. The Judge decides to start his resistance with a radio broadcast which will have all the impact of Lincoln's Gettysburg address but 'the other way round'. But he can think of nothing to say: 'vile words, cuss words unsuitable for the radio . . . raged in his mind' (p. 207) and when he gets to the microphone Lincoln's words are the only ones he can get out. The last act of Malone's mind is to understand that what has happened is 'nothing that was not a long time in the making'. Even a dyed-in-the-wool reactionary like the Judge must now march to the music of Lincoln's tune, the last thing in the world he wants to do.

So the progress which Carson McCullers discerns does not reveal itself in dramatic acts of heroism performed by individuals whose heroism will inspire others. It consists of small, half-understood or even involuntary actions which added together suggest an evolution towards justice of geological slowness but of geological sureness too. Near the beginning of his year of dying Malone contemplates the old pestle ('grey and smooth with use') which he bought from his predecessor with the other effects of the pharmacy. Possibly a relic of Indian times, it will outlast him. The prejudice which corrodes the South cannot be ground down in a single life time.

Both Flannery O'Connor and Carson McCullers got beyond what Patricia Stubbs recently called 'the tyranny of the intensely personal'.[5] In *Clock Without Hands* as in O'Connor's short story the vividly realized inner lives of the protagonists are firmly set in a well observed and well analysed social context which is being subjected to great pressures from without. She is able to take a long view of her subject without loss of detail in the foreground. There may still be people who believe that women are constitutionally unable to take a long view and I feel unhappily obliged to concede that women novelists have not recently done much to disabuse them. So many of the generation of writers who have succeeded McCullers and O'Connor seems to have lost or deliberately abandoned their broad perspectives and turned inwards to the private world. Talented women like Mary McCarthy, Doris Lessing, Edna O'Brien, Fay Weldon, Erica Jong, Marilyn French and Lisa Alther write almost exclusively about the private lives of their own sex. Why did Margaret Drabble take a couple of steps into a broader (I do not say better) world and then scuttle back into safe, familiar territory in *The Middle Years*? Their attitude is not so much chauvinistic as nationalistic. They proclaim the pleasures and pains of their own territories, their own cultures, and exclude all the rest. In this respect feminists are not the only isolationists. There is a similar tendency towards the highly particularized private life among Jewish American writers today, and perhaps it is a characteristic of the writing of other minority groups in search of their identity as well.[6]

In an essay of this length one is bound to appear more divisive than one wishes to be. I do not want to attack good novels of any kind, and I have derived much pleasure, instruction and sisterly reassurance from the novelists I have listed. But I think their vein is nearly exhausted. It is not a critic's business to tell novelists what to do next. But these women, whether they call themselves feminists or not, have chosen to write novels which expound a cause, and I think I am as entitled to exhort them about their cause as any woman – and not a few men. The majority of women's novels about women are only a fragment of the truth. They concentrate on the home, and on intimate relationships. They are for the most part about middle-class, highly educated women, professional people, if they work at all. Of course this area of experience is as entitled to its literature as any other, but vast areas of women's experience are still unexplored – and areas where women's experience meets that of men. There is no reason why women today should not be able to combine the impressive humane understanding they undoubtedly possess with the broader political perspectives of – say – Paul Scott or V. S. Naipaul. It cannot be because they still have only limited access to the public world. The only limits to a woman's vision are conventional, not real, but they are much harder to break through if they are self-imposed as well.

Notes

1 Virginia Woolf, *Women & Fiction*, Collected Essays Vol. 2. (The Hogarth Press, London 1966. pps 147–8.)
2 Q. D. Leavis, 'Caterpillars of the Commonwealth Unite!', *Scrutiny*, Vol. 7, No. 3 (September, 1938), p. 210.
3 This, and subsequent quotations, are taken from Flannery O'Connor *The Complete Stories* (New York: Farrer, Strauss and Giroux, 1977).
4 This, and subsequent quotations from *Clock Without Hands*, are taken from the Penguin edition, 1977. It was first published in New York, 1961.
5 Patrick Stubbs, *Women and Fiction*, 1979, p. 233.
6 And yet Toni Morrison's *Song of Solomon* (1978) seems to have achieved the kind of balance between the private and public worlds exemplified in the writings of O'Connor and McCullers.

The Uses of Fiction
Edited by
Douglas Jefferson
and Graham Martin

9

David Storey's Vision of The Working Class

David Craig

> 'Art is the act of personal revolution . . . To create an art out of the débris of our industrial world is as much an afterthought, once the coffin's lowered, as sticking in the cross. We want a tearing and a smashing open, not commiseration and sentiment and tears.'[1]

'Vision' seems the right word for Storey, rather than 'view', because 'view' implies beliefs in the light of which a writer interprets his experience and which supply to his novels and plays a distinct tendency, even a body of arguable issues. David Storey is in no way incoherent or lacking in thought; in his very rare essays he is his own most lucid interpreter. But he is utterly a novelist, and also a painterly one. He seems to want above all to see people very clearly in their environment, he wants to come at the muscle and bone of human nature as directly as possible. In his novels, when there is a drastic change, a rupture in a family or a relationship, the motives are usually much less distinct than the sheer behaviour into which the motives finally erupt. Storey's style *shows*, with the physical salience and exactitude of Conrad, though he is very different from Conrad in that he often works with deep-seated upsets of a psychological kind rather than with dilemmas of work or duty or other social bonds.

The above applies most closely to the phase in his work from *Radcliffe* (1963) through *Pasmore* (1972) to *A Temporary Life* (1973), and *Saville* (1976). His first published novels, *This Sporting*

Life and *Flight Into Camden* (both 1960), are more 'traditional' in that they follow clear trains of behaviour and often attend closely to the business of living in a northern city. What follows is based wholly on these six novels and the film of *This Sporting Life* (1962), which Storey scripted.[2]

Storey sees people as struggling to preserve their vital selves – struggling to escape from bonds which chafe and tear them cruelly. The constricting conditions include material need, the grind and grubbiness of cramped living conditions and monotonous work for a low wage. These are classically imaged in *This Sporting Life*, *Saville*, and a passage or two from *Pasmore*. They also include the grippy emotional narrowness, the grudging intolerance, which can flourish when people are needy. He has a great writer's sense of all that trammels; he is never inclined to turn the negatives of the victim into some sort of spiritual virtues. He works consistently in the spirit of MacDiarmid's uncompromising lyric from 'Second Hymn to Lenin':

Oh, it's nonsense, nonsense, nonsense,
Nonsense at this time o day
That breid-and-butter problens
Sud be in ony man's way.

They sud be like the tails we tint
On leavin the monkey stage;
A' maist folk fash aboot's alike
Primaeval to oor age.

We're grown-up folk that haena yet
Put bairnly things aside
– A' that's material and moral –
And oor new state descried.

Sport, love, and parentage,
Trade, politics, and law
Sud be nae mair to us than braith
We hardly ken we draw.

Freein oor pooers for greater things,
And fegs there's plenty o them,
Tho wha's still trammelt in alow
Canna be tenty o them.[3]

In *This Sporting Life* Arthur Machin, an engineering worker (in the film a miner), takes a second job, he plays Rugby League for the city team, because he wants to 'keep his head above the general level of crap' (p. 19)[4]. A workmate is already a star in the team and Arthur envies him because the men cluster round him at break times, he is singled out, no longer a mere number, as factory workers bitterly feel themselves to be.[5] Once Arthur succeeds, he is on the way to gaining for himself a public identity something like equal to his sense of his own worth, his energy and strength, his ability to overcome the fear, timidity, and small-mindedness which diminish people. He can buy himself a shorty coat in herringbone tweed and a white Jaguar. His name is in block letters in the evening paper. He can buy his landlady a television, a fur coat, and an expensive meal. His kudos as the new star could get him into bed with the wife of the club's main backer, and that might be nice, because she wears *decent underwear* (p. 127). But, as Storey puts it in his own introduction to the novel, 'the society that Machin knows seeks to use people rather than nourish them'.[6] He is still selling his labour power, he has not broken through into a life where a person is a person, not a commodity. The club's main backer, Weaver, is also Arthur's employer at the works. Arthur's place in the team depends, not only on his prowess, but also on whims and power struggles among the Board of Directors. They have bought him, they can scrap him. And whatever *he* buys for Valerie Hammond (she is Margaret in the film, just as Arthur is changed to Frank), it will remain desperately hard for her to break out from under the rock of fearful guilt which sits on her. Her husband had died when a file pierced his stomach, at Weaver's works. She got only token compensation, and she herself is afraid – depressed almost to psychosis – because she worries that she ' "hadn't been proper to him. I hadn't made him feel that he belonged." ' (p. 33). This piece of her past is not detailed or dramatized. What we have is the darkened and downcast atmosphere (wonderfully imaged by the under-lit, under-exposed, and sometimes slowed-motion photography which Lindsay Anderson uses in the film) that arises from a fear of freedom. She'll go to bed with Arthur, from time to time, but she will not admit to enjoyment of it, nor use words like 'love'. Discouraged by lack of money and lack of space, tired out with drudging work in a small low scullery with a Belfast sink, she has settled for deprivation, curled up inside it, because at least if she hopes for nothing she cannot be disappointed. The tragedy of the novel is that the more he flails around and exerts himself to burst through her reserve, the more, finally, she backs off, until she dies of the stress.

It is impossible to analyse the novel on *either* the social or the psycho-moral plane, as though these were separate. The two flow into each other to create a tragedy of frustrated revolt against stultified living. People might flower, they have the potential; but it is deadened and locked up, not only through want of the material means of life (space, rest, variety of stimulus) but also because of the habits – the low expectations and the succumbing to limiting roles – which arise when people 'make the best', i.e. the worst, of cramping conditions.

Most of the people central to Storey's novels revolt in that way. It isn't seen as any sort of crusade but as a fairly grim resistance. Storey has been placed, in terms of geography, class, and time, to witness, and to suffer in his own living, what may well come to be seen as a quintessential difficulty of the later stages of this century. People from the poorly-off classes 'can' change class, they can win through to clean, comfortable, fairly well-paid work via educational tickets of several kinds. Parents want this for their children. The children are conditioned to achieve this for their parents. As a result they speak rather different languages. The parents have lived not for themselves but for others. The children feel constrained – 'being good' has lasted, not just until puberty or leaving home, but way beyond it. They *must* be happy and satisfied, otherwise the whole familial effort will have been 'a waste', they will be 'ungrateful'. The ingrained frictions and fulminating years-long discontents that can arise out of all this are among the stuff of Storey's vision.

It is made special – specially striking, specially oppressive – by the particular circumstances of Storey's own life, which darken his vision. These are described with perfect clarity in his early essay 'Journey Through a Tunnel'.[7] By 1953 he was studying art in London. Each Friday evening he ran from the life class at the Slade, to his digs, to King's Cross, and got on the train for Wakefield, where he was contracted to play Rugby League. He needed the money. In 'Journey Through a Tunnel' he says it was 'not purely for economic reasons', and yet 'By playing this game on Saturdays, and training two evenings a week, I could give myself time during the rest of the week to carry on what I assumed were the activities of an artist: I could paint and draw . . .' So he did need the money, but he also needed to assuage his guilt at doing something 'useless': 'It was very largely, then, out of feelings of guilt and inadequacy that I signed on as a professional rugby league player.'[8]

> 'What else could my father think when, nearing sixty, he came home each day from the pit exhausted, shattered by fatigue, to find me – a young man ideally physically equipped to do the job which now left him

> totally prostrated – painting a picture of flowers, or writing a poem about a cloud? There was, and there is, no hope of reconciliation . . . I won a scholarship to London with my paintings – the same paintings that had incensed my father, of dark, brooding landscapes, and of equally dark and brooding self-portaits.'[9]

When he is chronicling this conflict in a quite straightforward way, Storey is writing the 'essential history' (Leavis's phrase for equivalent parts of Lawrence's *The Rainbow*) of the later twentieth century. This gives the gist of the last stages of *Saville*. But Storey also sees this split between himself and his working-class heritage as typifying certain fundamental polarities, and here he shows a great artist's ability to perceive and symbolize connections. In 'Journey Through a Tunnel' he writes that the West Riding culture, with its deeply ingrown concern with 'very simple, practical things', issued in a 'profound and ironical puritan distrust of the isolated and solitary man', for example the artist, on his own, absorbedly contemplating flowers, clouds, naked bodies. 'In the working class, and in the mining community in particular in which I lived, the code was amended in this way: that physical work is good, and mental work is evil. Invariably mental work implied any activity conducted from a sitting position.' Yet this is what Saville's miner father wants for his son: ' "Do you want him to be like me or like Reagan [the pay clerk], getting paid for sitting on his backside all day? I know what I'd do." ' (p. 92) Physical and mental. Also physical and spiritual, 'with the demand to be effective in both. I went on painting pictures, I went on playing football, but with increasing despair, obsessed with guilt at the one thing and by the futility of the other.'[10]

The weekly journey from London to Wakefield and back, through the tunnels of the railway and the black of the night and the darkness of his anguish, was a purgatorial connection between the two sides of his life and nature. Because Yorkshire now meant Rugby League, 'an extremely hard game, fierce and grinding, and almost a natural extension of the experience that a man undergoes in digging coal underground', Yorkshire/London now took on gender, became male/female. 'The northern terminus of that journey became associated with a masculine temperament; and when I came to write about its southern counterpart – the intuitive, poetic and perhaps precious world to which I felt I had escaped – I immediately associated it with femininity, with a woman's sensibility and reponses.' This many-sided nexus of opposed forces, or polarities, is taken to its extreme in

Radcliffe, where the mental/spiritual/artistic/feminine is conceived also as the syndrome of submissive-homosexual/upper-middle-class (the Radcliffes are gentlefolk, if not aristocrats), and the physical/earthy/working/masculine is conceived also as the syndrome of dominant-heterosexual/working-class – Tolson, the extremely strong man, a labourer, with a wife and family, who also needs to fuck Radcliffe homosexually and make him bleed. In *Radcliffe* Storey's vision is at its most extreme and obscure. Page after page seems to flood straight up from the subconscious, symbolized in the novel itself by the railway tunnel that passes under the gritstone stratum on which the Radcliffes' Jacobean mansion has been built and makes its foundations tremble and give.

Radcliffe starts a vein of writing – broken only recently by *Saville* – in which Storey evidently feels free to turn intuitions straight into narrative, with a remarkably confident ability not to mind if the result looks weird in terms of ordinary or accountable behaviour. The prose narrative mode remains graphic, bodily, but the transitions from episode to episode, the issuing of behaviour from the people as we have seen them characterized, often seem to involve impulses whose roots remain buried out of our sight. For example, there is the extreme episode in *Radcliffe* in which Tolson assaults Radcliffe in a church and kisses him violently:

> 'Suddenly he grasped Leonard's wrist and, as Leonard cried out, covered his mouth with his own. The whole of Tolson's body seemed centred on the wrist, bowed, stooping towards it as his fingers forced open the skin. For a moment he withdrew, listening to Leonard's cry. Then curving his body more leniently, he enclosed Leonard fully, pulling him between his thighs and locking him securely. Together, with Leonard's smothered cries, they swayed hip to hip, swung to and fro like a huge and single pendulum, their mouths pressed against each other's. Their shadows fled across the empty surface beyond their heads.
>
> Tolson paused. He tightened his grip. Between his hips came a fresh suffusion of cries. He gazed into Leonard's face: mouth, eyes, nose, head were flung back in a shriek of pain and, driving home his finger and thumb against the pierced wrist, he tenderly covered with kisses the screaming face.' (pp. 218–9)

This hardly follows on a convincing train of conflict between the two – there has been some rather forced taunting and challenging – nor does it lead, except in the very long run, to much in the way of remorse or revenge. Yet, while it lasts, the episode has the compelling force, created by the strength of the physical imagery, of Leontes' violent break into jealousy in Act I of *A Winter's Tale*. In neither the Shakespeare nor the Storey is the effect arbitrary: it doesn't take much pondering for us to understand the polarities of character that we are being shown. Jealousy does seize us with abrupt, seemingly random force. People do suddenly reach peaks of intensity in their emotions towards each other. To expect of a narrator only the most clearly explicable and accountable developments would blunt his capacity to show human nature in all its layers.

If I seem there to be arguing with myself as much as with you, as though to work out some doubts, that is because I am. My doubts about *Radcliffe* arise from the weariness I experience in getting through its more darkly visionary passages, especially those situated in the old house. Much of its décor seems merely Gothic (in the literary sense), put there to insist on some sort of heritage of family doom or instability which is never distinctly focussed. That part of the novel might have worked better if the building had been less implanted as a symbol and more a real vestige of gentry society. Radcliffe's family are shadowy, not sufficiently there on the page, yet it is they who might have supplied real links with the West Riding city, its clubs and yards and housing estates. As a result, it seems to me, the class aspect of the many-sided nexus of polarities is vitiated, even though Tolson's and Radcliffe's social circumstances are so insisted on in other ways.

This visionary weakness, as we may call it, co-exists in the novel with long sequences in which behaviour is shown with the clarity of great cinema. Our understanding of its bearings or meanings follows from our responding to the sensuously complete and exact presentation. This is particularly true of the scenes where Tolson and Radcliffe are working for the contractor's crew putting up and taking down tents and marquees for the country show (chs. 5–9). What this sequence shows is the way in which the two men become close, especially through Radcliffe's fascination with Tolson's physical mastery, whether riding his motorbike through the grass and mud of the site (at night the bike sleeps in the tent beside them like a metal animal) or dismantling great amounts of tentage at high speed. The social and physical community of these workers is dramatized in extraordinarily strong and fluent detail. For example, when the same crew put up a splendid marquee for a county party and are then annoyed to find, when they go back after a week, that the place is a shambles of broken glassware and ripped muslin (chs. 13 and 16), the point about hard skilled work and lordly squandering is both unmistakable and purely implicit. It is in no way pushed or underlined and doesn't depend on our taking up an ideological position about it. Yet it *is* unmistakable, as much so as the equally graphic, equally implicit theme of hard skilled work and lordly squandering in the wonderful grouse-shooting sequence in Barry Hines's *The Gamekeeper*.[11] Where *Radcliffe* drags or tails off, it is perhaps because Storey could not conceive of other areas of life in which men like Tolson and Radcliffe might naturally meet and interact, so he fell back on the rather unreal and stage-managed business of Radcliffe's dilettante uncle Austin and his friendship with the club comedian Blakeley.

This vein in Storey's work ends, for the time being anyway, with *A Temporary Life* and *Pasmore*. The former is an unusually interesting novel by any standards and I have doubts about it only because I feel it hangs together awkwardly. Is this grudging? The hero, Freestone, an ex-boxer, teaches at art school, and the low-key lack of spirit and conviction in that place, the Principal's rampant eccentricity and lack of trust in his staff, are perfectly done. So are Freestone's efforts to relate normally to his tragically deranged wife. So are the scenes where Freestone takes on the goons who work for the property developer with whose wife he's having an affair. Yet I remain not as convinced as I'd like to be (because my literary expectations are too conventional?) that these are the most apt areas Storey could have brought together to embody his theme, which seems to be that a man of force and integrity will find himself cast out onto the edges of busy, organized society.

A Temporary Life along with *Pasmore* and *Saville* raise in an implacably disturbing way the question: how is such a person, these days, to feel that there is something necessary enough for him or her to do? At the end of *A Temporary Life* Freestone is sweeping the streets for the Council:

> ' "You were pointed out to me," he says, "the other day."
>
> He looks at the brush, the shovel, at the dustbin on its metal trolley, then stamps his feet against the cold.
>
> "Fallen on hard times."
>
> "I believe in the principle that you should pay people," I tell him, "not to work. Then the ones who do work would do it for purely equitable reasons. I believe in a society built upon that principle," I add.
>
> He shakes his head. "You'd find a lot of loafers, then. There'll be nobody in the factories. Nor down the mines. Nor anywhere, if it comes to that."
>
> "I think you'd be surprised."

"At what?"
"The sort of society that that principle might produce," I say.
"I could get you a job, if you like." He gestures at the shovel. "Better than this."
"I don't know of any job," I tell him, "better than this. This is a job I've chosen," I go on, "of my own volition."
"A man like you?" He stamps one foot and then the other.
"Think about it," I tell him, "when you get back home."' (pp. 233–4).

This is very like the interview in which Saville, miner's son, grammar school boy, and now a trained teacher, is being told off by the headmaster for playing jazz to his class:

' "You're above it, then?"
"No," he said, "But I know it could be different."
"Different to what?"
"That people could be different. That the children could be different."
"Nay, they'll still have to work down a pit," he said. "They'll still have to work in a mill: they'll still have to get married because they can't control theirse'ns. They'll still have to make do with nearly nought: what difference will music make, or poetry, or these books you're alus on about? Tha'll have 'em so refined they won't want to work in a pit at all."
"Maybe that's all to the good," he said.
"Aye. *Thy*'d say that stuck in front of an empty fire, or teaching in a frozen school. I've seen all thy idealists, you know, before: put a bit of hardship in the way and they're up top screaming before anybody else."
"I think things can be changed," he said. "Maybe we should all take it in turns to work down a pit."
"In turn?"
"Three months down a year wouldn't do you any harm. It wouldn't do anybody any harm, if it comes to that. It'd probably do us all a lot of good."
"I can see thy daftness growing every minute: you'll have us out theer sweeping the bloody street up next."
"Why not?"
"Why not? Because I'm trained and qualified to do something better. These skills don't come out of the air, tha knows."
"It's not difficult, teaching," he said. "You'd probably even do it better after three months sweeping the street." He looked out of the window now himself. "It could do with sweeping, in any case," he added.' (p. 503)

This is a crux in Saville's estrangement from his community, even from his parents, who have skimped to 'put him through' education beyond the age of fourteen or fifteen but who have always been dubious about the real value of it. His mother says:

> ' "Do you feel above it all?"
> He shook his head. "I suppose I feel apart."
> "Is that the grammar school," she said, "we shall have to thank for that?"
> "You wanted me to go," he said.
> "Yes," she said. "Don't worry, love. I'm not complaining."
> "I don't feel I'm part of anything there, either," he said, "if it comes to that." ' (p. 333)

Saville is something like the complete history of the working-class child who changes class via schooling, told with the detailed lifelike fullness of classic Naturalism. *Pasmore* is a more visionary, intuitive version of the same,[12] and if there seems to be a gap between Pasmore's 'breakdown' and its likely causes, then I suggest we can fill it by supposing that Pasmore must have lived as Saville would have lived after his move to London. When he is on the verge of going, his lover says to him, ' "You make it sound so clear. But all you do is take the destitution with you: of belonging nowhere: of belonging to no one; of knowing that nowhere you stay is very real." ' He answers, ' "Why shouldn't it be real?" ' She affirms tradition: ' "Don't the dead, doesn't the past only make it real?" ' and he replies, ' "The dead just hold it back." ' (pp. 551–2) By the start of *Pasmore*, the man is deeply dissatisfied with everything he is doing, everything he is expected to do. The physical images of unease with which the novel opens plunge us into his malaise; they almost take its causes for granted. He doesn't talk things out with his wife Kay (whom he 'still loves'), he starts not wanting to touch her, he stops playing with the children. When a colleague sympathizes, he is put down (p. 14). Yet Pasmore has done well. He has three healthy children, a nicely converted house in somewhere like Islington, and a job teaching history in a Poly with chances for sabbaticals and research. In all this he feels out of place, and his *angst* at this estrangement (the classic Existentialist terms fit perfectly, and the affinity with Camus's *Outsider* is striking, though Storey is not in the least derivative) is, in a way, explained as clearly as one might wish in Chapter 2:

> 'Of only one thing in his life had he ever been ashamed – at least to the extent of admitting it to himself – and that was his job. He had continued at college, as a teacher, principally to prolong a situation he was used to, in which no definite decisions had to be taken, and in which, initially, he had further time to think things over and decide what he really wanted to do. From the age of five his life had been spent in one educational institution after another, dourly and stubbornly at first – his parents, as he'd indicated to Coles, were relatively poor and his work had been his only credential – then more pleasantly and triumphantly later when his efforts, in one sinecure or another, had begun to pay off. Now, however, he was coming to a point where he'd begun to sense that all his efforts had been in vain. He had applied for a fellowship – and much to his surprise had been awarded it – and had, somewhat belatedly, begun to write a book – his subject was the lives of certain evangelical idealists who had lived in the industrial north of England in the early part of the nineteenth century, a part of the country, if not a temperament, with which from childhood he had been familiar – and yet, before either of these events could in any sense be said to have been consolidated he had begun to realize that the missing elements of his existence were not to be identified in any of these terms, either of his work, that is, or of his private life. Where else he could look, and for what, he had no idea.' (pp. 21–2)

I say 'in a way' because though the causes we are shown for Pasmore's fearful plunge into a bottomless shaft of black helplessness *might* so affect a person, we aren't shown that they *would* so affect *this* person. But once we have accepted that they do, the stages and consequences of Pasmore's plunge are imaged with unerring force. There is none of the gratuitous oddity of *Radcliffe*, and where oddity is present it works marvellously well as a symbolization of the agonies and horrors that Pasmore has brought upon himself; for example, the way the night cleaners in the street outside his dingy down-town room symbolize the shabby, lost life he could so easily fall into; or the way the fat, unattractive Fowler who befriends Kay after Pasmore has left her is a scapegoat for Pasmore's neurotic resentment at her ability to go on living normally. Above all, Storey's guilty sense of his oppressive working-class heritage and then escape from it is dramatized in the perfect scenes where Pasmore revisits his parents and married sisters back in the West Riding. It is like a pilgrimage, almost penitential, from one well-established little house to another. His father is now the opposite pole to him – so sure and blunt in his basic values. Before Pasmore comes out with the bad news, the old man says:

' "When you were at school, and I was working, every bit of coal I dug I used to say to myself that's one bit he won't have to dig. I could have dug that entire pit out by myself. Making sure, you know, of that."

"You shouldn't put so much into me," he [Pasmore] said. "I mean that. Just for yourself."

"Nay," he said. "Do you know how high it is where I'm working? Thirteen inches." He measured out the distance between his hands. "If it shifts as much as an inch I'm done for. I can feel it, riding on my back. Why, you've got to make it add up to something." ' (p. 86)

Afterwards he says:

' "Well. It was all for nothing, then." His body was stiff. He stared down at his mother, then turned rigidly to the fire. "What a waste."

"No," he [Pasmore] said. "I don't think so."

"No?" His father shook his head. He no longer knew what to do with his feelings. "A man that leaves his wife and kiddies. Why, an animal wouldn't do that." Then, after a moment, he said, "What do you think we are? Everybody has a responsibility to their children. A king or a roadsweeper. Do you think you're any different?" ' (p. 88)

The younger people, sisters and brothers-in-law, are sadly understanding, and Eileen, married to a schoolteacher, diagnoses the case in a fated, accustomed tone:

' "I always felt something would happen."

"Yes?" he said.

"The way my dad sent you out, as his private army."

He didn't answer.

"But still. He didn't have much else." She added, "It seems none of us did, either." ' (pp. 93–4)

When Pasmore next goes north, after the reconciliation with Kay, his father, recovered from the first blows and steadied by disgust, can say things which are profound and clear in their analysis:

' "Everything's been made easier for you. Me flat on my belly half my life has been easier for you. Kay looking after your children while you park off with some woman. I see it all, don't worry. Nothing, not even if you had begged for it, could have been easier. Your life's been so easy I'm surprised you're sitting there at all."

. . . A moment later he stubbed out the cigarette and said to his wife, "Don't you think I don't know why he's gone back home?"

"I don't know," she said.

> "His conscience. He can't bear to live with it himself. He comes back here as happy as you please. 'Sorry.' You're as daft as he is if you believe that, for one second . . . You seems to think," his father said, "that you're a race apart. You're not. You're the same as me. I don't know what you've come here for."
>
> "No," he said. "I'm beginning to wonder." ' (pp. 162–4)

Of course Pasmore goes off south again, down the tunnel, and his last image of the people and the work he is leaving behind is starkly final: 'The sun shone down across the wheatfields, yellow, almost orange, laid out between the pits. Somewhere, underneath, was his father, lying down.' (p. 170)

In his introduction to *This Sporting Life* Storey had written:

> 'It is no virtue to feel oneself torn apart, either from the world, or from one's own spirit or soul; neither is it any virtue to be unable to find any resolution. However, although for some there is no choice, for all of us there is, I believe, the obligation to try and bring the pieces together; and if not together, at least in touching distance. As my novels progress, if they do at all, I hope that this resolution in some sense at least will be drawing nearer. (p. 5)

The many qualifications there are all justified. The feelings of being torn and unresolved are at least as strong in *Pasmore* and at the close of *Saville* as they had been sixteen years earlier in *Flight Into Camden*, where Margaret tries and fails to escape from her conventional secretary's life in Yorkshire and her close workaday family through her love relationship with Howarth, only to find that she can't disown her dependent, ageing parents and her love can't settle for the steady, unfulfilling teaching work that would help keep them solvent. Howarth has taught industrial design at a college and has wanted to be an artist but ' "I'm not creative in that way. That part of me was deadened." ' (p. 231) Saville escapes from the mining village to get away south and try to make something of the creativity which the headmaster would not let him use with the children in school. Storey himself did escape, and fulfilled his creativity and became an artist, but this is not to say that he has resolved the torn feelings, only that he has managed to express them.

Notes

1 David Storey, 'When Artists Sell Out', *The Observer*, 30 September, 1963.
2 Plays like *The Changing Room* and *The Contractor* are clearly relevant to my argument, but not having seen them staged, I don't feel qualified to discuss them here.
3 Hugh MacDiarmid, *Selected Poems* (ed. David Craig and John Manson, 1970), pp. 91–2.
4 This and later quotations are taken from the Penguin editions of Storey's novels.
5 Cf. 'You don't achieve anything here. A robot could do it. The line here is made for morons . . . We're just working here, we're numbers.' Huw Benyon, *Working for Ford* (1973), pp. 114, 121.
6 Author's typescript prepared for Longman's Heritage of Literature edition of *This Sporting Life*, p. 4.
7 David Storey, 'Journey through a Tunnel', *The Listener*, 1 August, 1963.
8 Introduction to *This Sporting Life*, p. 2.
9 'Journey through a Tunnel'.
10 'Journey through a Tunnel'.
11 Barry Hines, *The Gamekeeper* (1975; Penguin, 1978), pp. 140–80.
12 The novel is convincingly placed in the context of post-war social changes in Mary Eagleton & David Pierce, *Attitudes to Class in the English Novel* (1979), pp. 140–47.

The Uses of Fiction
Edited by
Douglas Jefferson
and Graham Martin

10

Bone Flute? Or House of Fiction: The Contrary Imaginations of Wilson Harris and V. S. Naipaul

Mark Kinkead-Weekes

'Opposition is true friendship.' (Blake)

'. . . an unfinished critical study in which I am attempting to make certain intuitive connections between apparently irreconcileable imaginative writers.' (Wilson Harris)[1]

Caliban's isle was always full of voices; but now that these have produced a remarkable literature in English, there are questions to be asked about Prospero's forms of fiction. How must these New Worlds affect old-world ways of imagining human being? V. S. Naipaul occupies the traditional English novel and moves the partitions around from inside; but Wilson Harris denounces it as a structure of colonialism and seeks radically new form, for new consciousness. Naipaul exposes with sardonic realism the deprivations and neuroses of West Indian society, the outcome of its history. Harris regards realism as blind petrifaction, and history as a prison; language itself must be re-made, to cleanse the doors of perception; the West Indian writer must pierce through the masks and shadows of superficial appearance to the deeper forces beneath, finding in deprivation the ground of compassionate sensibility. By breaking the bondage of the past he can decolonize himself, his Caribbean readers, and the erstwhile colonizers too. The opposition is apparently extreme, and often regarded extremely. Naipaul has had great metropolitan success, winning literary prizes and securing a reputation as a major writer; but in the Third World he tends to be disliked as a spirit of negation, and students in India and Africa may react like West Indians. Harris is hardly known in England except to a small *avant garde*, but he is a central figure in Caribbean literary consciousness, a profound influence on other writers and critics – though his 'difficulty' limits his readership. The two writers might seem such contraries in attitude, form, imaginative sensibility, perception itself, as to demand from the critic a radical choice – as indeed Harris has done, in several overt attacks upon Naipaul.[2] Yet to write down either in terms of the other is very unlikely to aid imaginative and critical progression, and the opposition is not their's alone.

Indeed, we find similar contraries at the heart of Prospero's literary tradition. *The Tempest* and *Robinson Crusoe*, with just over a century between them, tell the same basic story. A man from Europe is cast away on an 'unknown' Caribbean island, frighteningly isolated, thrown on his own resources; but he not only develops power over nature and native, he also discovers and reveals a new dimension, or reconception of human being. From that basis, the two fictions develop quite differently, in form, in attitude, and in historic significance. One is a poetic play; the other that new thing being invented by a new kind of society in order to take stock of itself, a 'novel'. Each conceives its 'new man', the nature of his power, and his relations to the natural world and to other men, in strikingly different terms; and the difference has much to do also with the relation one work bears to an age of exploration, when colonial problems of religion and ethics were beginning to be posed, and the other to an age whose 'prospering' was already built on colonization and the slave-trade. But behind even these differences lies a different kind of imagination. Both are 'mythic' in the sense that they seek to uncover, beneath the particular 'histories' of Prospero and Crusoe, an archetypal human condition and structure of creation. But one has magic and music at its heart, seeking to strip away the old reality, the old seeing, to bone and socket, and to recreate life into something rich and strange and visionary. The other is concerned with the realistic and circumstantial process by which terrified, lonely, and unaccommodated man creates a cave-dwelling, a house, a castle from which to govern his life.

Now Wilson Harris has cited, as a central metaphor for what he wants his fiction to be and to do, the religious ceremony which gave the Spaniards the idea that the Caribs were cannibals: the ritual consumption of a morsel of the dead adversary and the fashioning from his bone of a magic flute.[3] When this is played, apparitions from the world of spirit manifest themselves in the smoke of the fire. Through the holes in the flute the outside world of appearance and history is drawn into the void within the bone, to become harmony and vision: all is the music while the music lasts. For Naipaul, however, the other person and the outside world are densely there, not to be disposed of; the past has shaped the present and will not disappear by magic; and the inner void is a state of horror. So the achievement of the house, for him, be it sentry-box or book-shaped, becomes a central metaphor of order, integration, identity. Life is not a visionary moment (or phantasy) but a painful process, of accommodation, to what is ineluctably there without and within.

Fictions written from such opposite assumptions, about history, about the nature of reality, and hence about the nature of perception itself, clearly require different modes of criticism. Yet the effort to produce a binocular view, sensitive to both in different ways, may actually help us to see farther.

Palace of the Peacock,[4] Harris's first and arguably still his most intensely poetic and spontaneous fiction, frustrates every normal expectation of novel readers. There may seem to be 'characters', a 'setting', a thread of plot. A boat journeys up a South American river, through jungle and rapids, to a waterfall. The leader, Donne, needs labourers for his estate on the savannah, and sets out with his dreamy brother, the narrator, to recruit Amerindians in the interior. But because of his cruel mistreatment of his Amerindian mistress and his reputation for violence, the aborigines have fled. The boat follows after, further and further upstream . . . Yet all these seemings prove illusory. The crew turn out to be dead men, drowned and buried near Sorrow Hill. They die again on this journey, but continue to the end. They also continually merge into one another. The landscape, so 'real' at first sight, plays weird tricks. People turn into places, places into states of mind. The river will stand on end, become now a mere spider's web across the eye of God, and now a cliff with windows through which one peers to catch miraculous glimpses of divine creativity, beauty, and love. The visible world finally becomes transmuted into vision: of the City of God in the sun, the city of gold, El Dorado, the palace of the peacock. Characters, setting and story have been dissolved in a seven-day decreation by an extraordinary baffling language, whose central habit is to yoke contradictions, suggesting that one thing is also another, or its opposite. The experience is surreal, or like Rimbaud, disordering the senses. It can seem gibberish at first irritation, but it can also develop a remarkably compelling beauty and power.

Actually the major difficulty lies in our expectations, the state of our minds. We would have far less trouble if we had never read any novels at all; or, even better, if we came to Harris with eyes and imaginations habituated to *mediaeval* fiction: the poetry of dream and vision. The book opens with a vivid dream, of a proud horseman toppled from his saddle by a bullet from the bush, and we go on half-emerging from and lapsing back into dreams in which the dreamer's subconscious reveals further implications of his brother's being. Donne is a man of doing, and power, suggesting the Elizabethan world, and ours. He rules a material universe; a conquistador and colonizer exploiting nature and other people; but his violence calls forth violence, his violations are self-destructive, his clear-eyed vision of the world a blindness. The dreamer wakes, talks to his brother in his stilted house overlooking an empty savannah. 'Look at the sun,' Donne cries (19), and he does. A hundred and twenty-five pages (or a moment) later, at the end of the book, he sees what is really there. Like Blake, who told how one man saw the sun as a round bright disc somewhat like a guinea, and another as a host of angels glorifying God, Harris seeks to turn a dead material eye into an eye of divine energy, to turn sight into vision. As the dreamer looks, he begins to daydream. He sees a map in the sun, the familiar map of Guyana; which turns into a sensuous geography of jungle and river, rock and stream. He is also projecting a landscape of his own subconscious, as dreamers do. He dreams up the boat and its legendary crew who are also facets of himself. They move on a journey into his own interior, through the eye/'I'; but this is also a process of opening that eye to insights coming through material appearance from beyond. The fiction extends a flash of vision into a progress happening stage by stage[5] – as we do when we dream 'stories' that are actually momentary flickerings of the subconscious. But as he dreams, the masks of people, of material scene, of the past, are peeled away. Images suffer sea- or, rather, river-changes. The dreamer becomes aware that the 'characters' or 'seers' are shadows of one another and himself. The 'places' of the journey are ways of locating human blindness, alienation, violence, self-violation, that must be got beyond. They are the traumas of history which can only be overcome by re-experiencing their violence, and reaching the humility of identification with the wretched of the earth. That is why the dream is a pursuit of the folk.

Halfway, 'The Second Death' is a threshold between the known and the unknown world, and a crux for Harris's view of history. The crew have captured an ancient Amerindian woman, at the Mission which bears the name of Donne's ill-treated mistress, Mariella, and from which the aborigines have fled. The old woman's face is wrinkled, still, emotionless, unfathomably patient. It is 'pointless', both reflecting a sense of time that knows no beginning, end, or defining point, and also because its lack of expression includes (and hence negates) all points of opposition,

> 'every threat of conquest and of fear – every shade of persecution wherein was drawn and mingled the pursued and the pursuer alike, separate and yet one and the same person . . .
>
> Before the sun was much higher we were in the grip of the straits of memory. The sudden dreaming fury of the stream was naught else but the ancient spit of all flying insolence in the voiceless and terrible humility of the folk. Tiny embroideries resembling the handwork on the Arawak woman's kerchief and the wrinkles on her brow turned to incredible and fast breakers of foam. Her crumpled bosom and river grew agitated with desire, bottling and shaking every fear and inhibition and outcry. The ruffles in the water were her dress rolling and rising to embrace the crew. This sudden insolence of soul rose and caught them from the powder of her eyes and the age of her smile and the dust in her hair all flowing back upon them with silent streaming majesty and abnormal youth and in a wave of freedom and strength.
>
> The crew were transformed by the awesome spectacle of a voiceless soundless motion, the purest appearance of vision in the chaos of emotional sense. Earthquake and volcanic water appeared to seize them and stop their ears dashing the scales only from their eyes. They saw the naked unequivocal flowing peril and beauty and soul of the pursuer and the pursued all together, and they knew they would perish if they dreamed to turn back.
>
> "Is War Office," Schomburgh screamed but his voice was silent and dead in his throat . . . We had entered the War Office rapids . . . The only course was to fight . . . keeping our bow silent and straight in the heart of an unforgiving and unforgivable incestuous love.' (pp. 72–4)

As we 'see' with musing eye, and 'hear' with the power of poetic language to transform and interfuse different categories of 'reality',[6] we are drawn into the age-old wrinkled face as it turns into the chaos of the rapids. (In a moment the youngest of the crew will die by water, and later in the chapter the boat will hit a submerged rock and its people enter the whirlpool.) The spittle of race-hate on the seamed wrinkles becomes lacy embroidery, and then deadly breakers of foam. Apparent passivity and decay turn first into violence, and then into soul-force of beauty, renewal, and love. The 'memory' of oppression and cruelty boils up again in 'war', and the past claims its toll of youth; but the earlier images of assassinated conquistador and beaten woman, of footfall of love in the forest and threatening 'moonhead' (treacherously 'smooth patch' in the water) are transformed in new meaning. There is disorder in the senses but the dreamer who cannot move[7] and the crew who cannot hear, finally experience a harmony beyond tragedy, as young Carroll dies singing. Communal vision comes when memory reaches into the self to find the 'incestuous' link with the family of others in aboriginal compassion. But History's deformations must be transmuted into a magic 'kerchief' of art woven communally, like the *Kantha* of the Bhils.[8] Love must not 'forgive' but void (in order to renew) the self.

Harris is a Jungian delving through the individual psyche to the collective unconscious. He is also in search of the *anima mundi*, the energy and soul of creation concealed behind appearance. He wishes to turn us and our world inside out. Instead of thinking of ourselves as living behind our eyes, looking out at a world of solid 'reality'; we are to think of an utterly different 'reality', a divine energy, trying to break in, through the scales of our eyes, and transform us. So, now, a more advanced state of Vigilance sees the outer world dematerialize into spider-web through which radiance pours, while Donne finds himself on the windowpanes of worlds of creativity and love. Finally, when all defective kinds of consciousness have peeled away in the 'dying' of the crew, the eye can look straight at the divine energy itself, through the sun; or the energy pour into consciousness through the eye in radiant beauty or the ear in music. What is 'there' is still in one sense the same savannah and a tree with the sun behind it as was looked at 125 pages, or a moment, before. But now it is transfigured into vision and melody. Tree and sun have become the palace of El Dorado the golden one, in which all parts of the self are integrated; a peacock's fan of colour filled with visionary eyes; the golden appletree of the Hesperides; the radiance of the Cross, and of Apollo, God of the Muses; the base matter of the universe transmuted by the alchemy[9] of imagination into gold, through the last peacock stage of the creation of the philosopher's stone. It has always been there for everyone, the sun through a tree, but unrevealed to eyes that merely 'see'. Harris's art takes up the mythic music of *The Tempest*, the sea-change of the drowned ego into something rich and strange; and the magic not of compulsion but transformation; as against Jacobean power politics, or the material prospering of Crusoe. He also chimes with the other Donne, that no man is an island.

For Harris, therefore, the condition of West Indian Man is no mere state of historic deprivation but the ground of new being; and the Caribbean writer can offer a new conception of humanity. For the wretched aftermath of colonialism has finally exposed the destructiveness of the European ideas that gave rise to the Conquistadors, the slave-trade, the exploitations of centuries. If West Indian humanity is a hotch-potch of races and a rag-bag of broken cultures, so much the better. The West Indian is then forced to reconceive himself in a new inclusive and plural form; and in so doing he can offer a necessary decolonization to those who reduced and exploited him, and robbed him of his ancestral heritages. Searching within himself for aboriginal humanity, he must find a 'corrosive sensibility'[10] which will etch through the petrified surfaces of 'reality' as seen by old-world materialist eyes.

Consequently Harris was bound to attack Naipaul as he did in 'Tradition and the West Indian Novel', for seeing conventionally, and producing a commonplace picture of the human being, because he still writes within 'the novel of persuasion', the central tradition of European fiction. This seeks to persuade us that its picture of existence is solidly 'real' – which Harris absolutely denies. To continue in this tradition is to consolidate a reductive view of man as separate individual; to go on thinking of society and culture in fixed forms; to stay in bondage to history. Harris seeks not only to negate Naipaul, but to get rid of the traditional novel altogether; to go behind its invention, and recover ways of seeing and imagining which were available before the fatal advent of renaissance and modern European man.[11]

A House for Mr Biswas,[12] on the other hand, is a fictive 'life-history', from the birth of Mr Biswas in a mud hut on a Trinidad sugar estate to his death 46 years later in a house of his own – jerrybuilt, mortgaged to the hilt, but his. He is unforgettably individual, funny and pathetic, a complex character. His world is indeed built up in massively 'persuasive' detail, and peopled by over three dozen sharply and humorously observed minor characters. Though the book is divided into separate Parts (the first exploring the tensions between the individual and his society and the second registering the effects of change on both) its world is unified by being Mr Biswas-shaped. Yet it is also complex and ambiguous, not merely because it is framed by a Prologue and Epilogue which suggest different ways of looking; and narrated from a shifting point of view; but because of the dense multiplicity of our experience of the man and his world, in change.

Mr Biswas is East Indian, but that way of life is withering in Trinidad. There is no community among the cane-cutters, and his attempt to become a holy man is a farce. Though his caste makes him an acceptable husband, despite poverty, for a daughter of the Tulsis, he constantly rebels against the loss of individuality entailed in membership of that inward-looking mutation of the Indian extended family. For even his smattering of Western education has made him think of himself as an individual, and has given him ideas of self-development, ambition and romance, for which his actual situation offers no outlet. We may laugh at the absurd collection of books which mirror his inner life, and at the comic collisions between his sense of himself and the actualities of his environment. Yet the repeated sequence of aspiration, disillusionment, stoicism, and nausea, is as sad as it is funny. He rebels against being reduced to a 'Tulsi' without individuality and independence; against the disorder and lack of privacy in communal existence at Hanuman House and all the other Tulsi barracks; but his gestures of defiance end in humiliation. He begins to clown, in defence and aggression. But when he is given the chance to 'paddle his own canoe' he discovers the horror of solitude, the deprivation in privacy, the abyss that opens under the rootless man when exposed alone. Unformed, between worlds, he seems unable to manage others or himself – a sardonic contrast with Prospero or Crusoe. In the first shack he builds himself, faced with a tempest without and within, he has the nervous breakdown which ends Part One. Yet Mr Biswas never gives up – for he is hero as well as clown – and Part Two sees him off again, leaving wife and children with the Tulsis, to seek new life in the city. He becomes a roving reporter for a 'yellow' newspaper; making a living out of a rootless man's facetiousness and fantasy; but his life is still precariously balanced over a void. Comic news-stunts lay bare the realities of destitution; and when Mr Biswas becomes a Community Relations Officer all real sense of community is gone. In the ups and downs of his relations with the Tulsis in Part Two, we see the final break-up of the extended family. The big comic set-piece when the Tulsis take over an old Plantation Estate, shows them out of touch with the land and falling apart as a unit; yet there is a 'turn' here, for the devastation of Shorthills comes as much from individualism, in the sons-in-law. Mr Biswas, building another house, with customary inefficiency may set the surrounding land on fire, but Govind and Tuttle systematically plunder the whole estate. Indeed, private enterprise marks a changing Trinidad in several ways. The coming of the Americans and the Yankee dollar during the war provides the new climate, in response to which the economic individualism of the sons-in-law fractures what is left of the communal way of life. In another direction there is intense new emphasis on education as a means of individual advancement. The favoured Tulsi son leaves for Medical School in England, a new generation of Readers and Learners slaves away in Port of Spain, Anand Biswas wins a scholarship abroad – but this kind of private enterprise, too, means the end of the extended family. After a final quarrel with Owad's hypocritical 'communism', Mr Biswas achieves his own house, his nuclear family. This sounds easy, but to him it is an incredible achievement. His wife becomes at last a Biswas. His children will have a home that orders their memories and gives them a sense of belonging. In a strip of garden won from his 'neighbour', Mr Biswas plants a fragrant tree to give protection from the sun. His house is of course a folly, a gimcrack parody of a magazine 'ideal home', hopelessly mortgaged, liable to fall apart. But it is also a sentry box, guarding against the world without and the void within. How terrible (the Prologue had mused) it would have been to have died 'without even attempting to lay claim to one's portion of the earth; to have lived and died as one had been born, unnecessary and unaccommodated'. But the reference to *Lear*, like the novel itself, is both a joke and not a joke. For we must seriously set the 'absurdity' of Mr Biswas and his house against the hostile elements without and the neurosis within that beset the man who belongs nowhere. The 'accommodation' may be a sardonic comment on neocolonial Trinidad, and also on the European ideals of individualism and independence; but its owner is not a houseless wretch, a bare forked animal, a Caliban or Friday. He is Mister Biswas, accommodated man.

One can see what Harris meant by denouncing the 'comedy and pathos' of *Mr Biswas* as a reduction of human potential, a denial of the possibility of 'epic' or 'revolutionary' transformation. Nevertheless, to look more closely at the nervous breakdown at Greenvale, which occupies the same turning-point in Naipaul's novel as the Straits of Memory in Harris's, may reveal more in common than Harris thinks, and suggest a more flexible judgement. After another quarrel, Shama has gone back to the 'Monkey house', leaving Mr Biswas alone with his small son. In isolation he suffers (like Crusoe) from bouts of panic. As 'driver' for the Tulsis in the cane-fields he is hated by those about to lose their allotments, and he has refused employment to two angry men. His ramshackle 'house' has only one room boarded-in, and the secondhand corrugated-iron roof, its holes roughly plugged with pitch, leaks long rubbery 'snakes' which fall on the face in the night. His dog Tarzan is found with its throat cut. A storm breaks, and Mr Biswas thinks he hears menacing voices outside. Black biting ants march in a column across the floor foraging on the 'flying ants' that the rain has brought out. Anand strikes and strikes at them with a walking-stick . . .

> 'A sharp pain ran up his arm. On his hand he saw an ant, its body raised, its pincers buried in his skin. When he looked at the walking-stick he saw that it was alive with biting ants crawling upwards. He was suddenly terrified of them, their anger, their vindictiveness, their number. He threw the stick away from him. It fell into a puddle.
>
> The roof rose and dropped, grinding and flapping. The house shook.
>
> '*Rama Rama Sita Rama*," Anand said.
>
> "O God! They coming!"
>
> "They *gone*!" Anand shouted angrily.
>
> Mr Biswas muttered hymns in Hindi and English, left them unfinished, cursed, rolled on the bed, his face still expressing only exasperation.
>
> The flame of the oil lamp swayed, shrank, throwing the room into darkness for seconds, then shone again.
>
> A shaking on the roof, a groan, a prolonged grinding noise, and Anand knew that a sheet of corrugated iron had been torn off. One sheet was left loose. It flapped and jangled continuously. Anand waited for the fall of the sheet that had been blown off.
>
> He never heard it.
>
> Lightning; thunder; the rain on roof and walls; the loose iron sheet; the wind pushing against the house, pausing, and pushing again.
>
> Then there was a roar that overrode them all. When it struck the house the window burst open, the lamp went instantly out, the rain lashed in, the lightning lit up the room and the world outside, and when the lightning went out the room was part of the black void.
>
> Anand began to scream.
>
> He waited for his father to say something, to close the window, light the lamp.
>
> But Mr Biswas only muttered on the bed, and the rain and wind swept through the room with unnecessary strength and forced open the door to the drawingroom, wall-less, floorless, of the house Mr Biswas had built. (pp. 262–3)

Although Naipaul is intensely 'realistic'; his vision is also as 'mythic', as concerned to reveal the archetypal nature of man and the world, as

Harris. He is even more concerned with history, and with memory; but his scene denies the efficacy of magic, and of epic. It takes protagonist and reader into the void, in a way that must affect the form and meaning of the book. In other words, though Naipaul's 'answers' are so different, he has asked the same questions – and is guilty neither of a crude sense of reality nor an uncritical Western individualism. But he might reply that he finds it necessary to 'realize', rather than dream away, certain actualities. Strip man of the protection of society and family and it is his nature to feel terror. Nature itself is predatory. The idea of harmony between natural man and natural world is a fairy-story like Tarzan, and the dog's death shows a cruel vindictiveness no animal or insect feels. There are snakes in Greenvale and in Adam's bower. Moreover the traumas of history will not heal by wishing. Behind the comic sunhelmet of Mr Biswas on the plantation, are the legacies of slavery, the hatred of the ex-slaves for the indentured 'coolies' who replaced them (and often prospered), and the modern realities of economic exploitation, landlessness, unemployment. Behind Mr Biswas's terror, also, are traumatic personal memories: the voices outside the hut after his father died; the violence of Bandhat, Mungroo, Govind. Above all, what the 'tempest' reveals is the deepest significance of the 'house': no mere gesture of independence or individuality, but a fragile and porous defence against the void. His comic defiance, though apparently directed at the Tulsis, has always sprung from his feeling that he belongs nowhere and stands on the edge of nothingness[13] – like the abyss one falls into in nightmare, or that glimpse of 'a boy leaning against an earth house that had no reason for being there, under the dark falling sky' (p. 171). But the shack on the Trinidad 'heath' inverts the bone-flute metaphor. Blackness comes seeping in through the holes, the doors and windows, overwhelming. Magic and music are powerless. There is no help in hymns, or invoking that great epic the *Ramayana*: no Vishnu the protector in his heroic human avatar, no Miranda/Sita, no Monkey-God/Ariel. There is the tempest, and the horror of man alone. And this must affect not only the view of Hanuman House, but also the form of the book. Part Two must show inversion as well as change; be as funny and terrible an exploration of the individual as of the decaying collective. We must see two-sidedly, clear now that the novel is both satiric comedy and of the abyss; both 'history' and 'myth'; sharing these aspects as related to Conrad and Sartre, as to Dickens. When Mr Biswas achieves his house, the significance of both is ambivalent. It is absurd, and yet it is a defence against the world and the void; he is heroic-and-comic-and-sad; it locates his human dignity and a new affectionate interdependence, but without him it is empty. The fictive 'house' is the creation of Mr Biswas's life, and Anand/Naipaul's art.

Yet that brings us again to the radical difference between Naipaul and Harris. For as Naipaul's subsequent career has shown, he is not merely 'realistic'. His art is also constantly disciplined by relation to a factually experienced world, to what has actually happened.[14] The sentry-box and 'Hanuman House' exist. The career of Mr Biswas (including his illness) follows the stages, though not the order, of the life of Naipaul's father. It is also richly fictive and imagined:[15] but it shows how essentially Naipaul reaches for 'myth' *through* 'history', not against it as Harris does. His imagination seeks the true fictive shape for his sense of the 'real', and this heightens one's sense of his kind of 'truth'.

Indeed it is only when we concede different kinds of creative imagination their own validity that we avoid judging one in the terms of another. Harris's criticism of Naipaul is both true to his kind of vision, and false to Naipaul's. Naipaul might have replied – though he has never done so – that though Harris offers his vision as all-embracing, it is nevertheless enclosed, and far more a 'novel of persuasion' than *Mr Biswas*, in that it only allows one way of looking. In banishing 'character' it reduces the stubborn resistance of the 'other', the differing point of view. This makes the claim to plurality and compassion rather facile, for true compassion has to be for one's neighbour not only as he is but as he wishes to be, and is not achieved by dissolving him into one's own formulae. Harris seeks to undo history, but his first novel does so too easily and notionally, not taking its pressure. It also seems to lack any sense of society, but however ecstatic the vision of the integrated psyche, man cannot live alone.

Yet this could no more invalidate Harris than he invalidates Naipaul. If both imagine 'truly' in their kind, one can only be judged more 'valid' than the other by appealing to theological, philosophical or political, rather than literary premises. What we need is literary discrimination. The usefulness of distinguishing 'myth', 'history' and 'fable' – though I have not used that yet – as different kinds of imagination (which can co-exist in the same work, yet in their mutual proportioning determine its nature), is that they may make us more sensitive to form, and hence more capable of discriminating response. What then becomes highly significant in both writers, is how each has developed new form and vision by pitting these different kinds of imagination against one another in their later work.

Harris's *Tumatumari*[16] ('the sleeping rocks') establishes its mythic nature in a powerful opening which suggests – again – a condition of trauma and an impulse to healing. A woman is beside a pool at the foot of a waterfall, in a world without sun, grey outside and in. It is again a dream; and she is suffering a breakdown after the stillbirth of her child and the horrible death of her husband – whose boat hit a submerged tree above the falls, so that he was swept over and decapitated by the sleeping rocks. Prudence dreams she sees a dark head in the whirlpool, which also suggests the dead body of her baby, and reflects her own features as she feels herself 'equally without root and column'. As she spurns it away it seems to shine 'with the ancient blast of the falls and the flame of the rising sun'. In a contortion of feeling, both self-destructive and self-creative, she lifts the head, cradles it in her arms, and begins to climb the steep bank. She wakes, looking at her husband's Amerindian mistress. In the aftermath of her dream the darkness of Rakka's hair and her face seem to burn: she too is a mask of the sun. So Prudence begins to confront loss, failure, dislocation, dispossession; in marriage, in motherhood, in psyche. But the dream-ritual of carrying the severed head out of the whirlpool and up the slope 'enacts' the birth of day, the return of spring after the death of the sun, the coming to terms with the aboriginal, and the ascent to reintegration after tragic wreck and death.

But this time there is also a deeper engagement with Guyanese history, although, to be true to his kind of vision, Harris had to find a form that would not concede to history too concrete or determining a status. His solution was to recover yet another pre-Renaissance mode of imaging: the Art of Memory which was a branch of Prudentia, and which Frances Yates describes.[17] Since history is a human construct for Harris, and can be transcended in the mind, it was rather appropriate to use 'fable' to stop it becoming a petrifying Gorgon's Head. For the fabulous imagination differs from both 'history' and 'myth' by openly proclaiming that it fabricates, in order to grasp an analytic pattern. It uses emblem, rather than the sense-image of history, or the symbol of myth; and type or 'attitude' rather than character, or archetype; because the function of the fiction is not to portray, or to X-ray; but to analyse.[18] So (though his deepest concern with Prudence is still mythic) when Harris seats her in a 'Chair of History', over the well above the falls, it is now for two different kinds of imagining. Her mythic vision must penetrate again below the surface 'reality', and transmute the past. She must explore the significance of her dream and her husband's fatal destiny; of the prophetic accident when he fell down the well that was to measure the power-potential of the waterfall; of his secret involvement (behind sardonic self-mockery, and apparently ruthless exploitation of his Indians) with their ancient rituals of the hunt of the sun-boar, and the magic death of the midsummer king. She must uncover the mysterious link between the 'lost Indians of the sun', glimpsed for a moment descending the waterfall, and her own ascent with the dead 'one' in her arms; and the connections between herself and Rakka, and her husband and her father. Once again a powerfully sensuous and visionary imagination transforms 'ordinary reality' into revelation. But now Prudence is also allowed to fantasize, and invent diagrams and visual conceits as intellectual tools, to investigate the meaning of history. She composes emblematic canvases and sequences, and scripts for a Theatre of the Absurd; fabling grotesquely, but also seriously, in order to analyse how the traumas of her psyche, marriage, family, and country arise out of history, yet can be overcome in consciousness. Psychic wounds, still affecting sexuality and relationship, spring from the horrors of the slave trade and the shortage of imported women. This also affected the growth of Guyana in that, when it became possible and economically important to develop the interior, the population had not grown enough. In Prudence's mixed-race family, racial prejudice traced patterns of repudiation, hurt and shame. And her father, the historian who saw so much that was wrong, hid his insight and repressed his feelings under a mask of middle-class gentility, until a violent outburst on his deathbed. In order to understand both her family history and what happened in Guyana from 1919 to 1968 – the failure to develop, the racialism, the enclosure and repression – Prudence must grasp how people's conception of themselves dictates private and public life, and how misconception leads to trauma. So, in her Art of Memory, she invents staircases, wheels and chains of emblems, and a Guyanese Nighttown Brothel of Masks, in order to grasp how, at every stage of his life, her father's misconceptions produced psychically deformed children; and how the life of her family reflected, and was reflected in, the deformations of national life. So, also, Roy Solman the engineer became exploiter rather than sun-king; and in his generation, too, bred misconception and death instead of tapping the immense creative energies of the world. Yet in the lives of both, and especially in the 'blows' they strike in death, were intimations of heroism and remorse which Prudence can focus into truer visions.

So she sees an 'Eye' open in the rockface, and the waterfall linking height and depth in a continuous chain of correspondences. It is a vision of destructive power and creative energy; a downrush of compassion and an uprush from humility; a column of fire and mist connecting the dark sewer pool of death and waste with the sunny zenith of aspiration and divine love. But the 'eye' which binds contraries into unity is itself a hairline crack, fissuring the mask of appearance and obsession, and through it floods a newly liberating truth which annihilates inadequate conceptions of the human and the real. So Prudence feels herself psychically plunge over the falls as Roy did, to decapitate her old 'head'; to drown in the flood of new associations; to discover, rising to meet her from the pool, not barren sleeping rock, not severed head or petrifying Medusa, but a smiling reflected face, majestically wreathed and haloed with the sun, reanimated in a Great Game not of politics, but of reconception.

In *Tumatumari* Harris engaged more seriously with history; and also extended the scope of his fiction by giving greater rein to his love of analytic mind-play and diagram, in a form which could combine these with his powerful mythic imagination. Perhaps the gain is not unmixed. *Tumatumari* can be obscure: miss one link in a chain of mental association and wordplay, and a whole passage can become unintelligible. The new form sometimes gives an impression that Harris is writing the novel, and laconic lecture notes on it, at the same time.[19] Fabling increases his tendency to let an original metaphor turn into a cerebral abstraction, and then a term of art, no longer decodable without tracing back to its origin. Yet once again, in essence, we have the overcoming of history by myth; the archetypal 'ceremony' of the bone-flute communing with the dead and the spirits, drawing the world of appearance into a chain of holes or eyes, so that from annihilation and void shall come harmony and vision.

In *The Mimic Men*,[20] Naipaul also sets myth against history, and his title shows that he too is concerned with fable, how men conceive themselves, a theatre of masks. He goes even further than Harris in handing over the whole book to a surrogate writer – an exiled Caribbean politician, trying to make sense of his own failure, and of the outbreak of violent disorder on his island, Isabella. But the novel's three separate books, each using a different kind of imagination, are also seriously questioning *form*: the implications of seeing like this, or like that.

Book One opens and closes with a vision of snow. But it is made up of an initially puzzling mosaic, juxtaposing scenes from different times and places in Singh's life – the young student in London, castaway in a foreign city which has already lost its magic, among equally rootless people from all over the world – the businessman in Isabella, enriched by the bourgeois housing estate he sardonically calls Crippleville, yet weeping as his 'sophisticated' friends vandalize his own Roman villa – the middle-aged exile, writing, in his bare room in a suburban hotel – the dandy young man and his sharp-tongued girl, a marriage drifting to breakdown. Yet what we come to see is that chronology makes no difference because all situations show the same pattern. Rootlessness makes people manufacture identities and rituals, and play at relationships. But these are all two-dimensional, and collapse sooner or later into betrayal, cruelty, and finally empty indifference, the vision of the void. That is the baptism into the blankness of 'snow'. And so we grasp the form of this first book, which could stand alone, perfectly shaped by its own kind of vision. It begins where it must, with the first revelation to Singh of the deeper 'reality' beneath the surface of life. As it goes on, the stage on which 'mimic men' strut and fret is more truly seen as a box-like room, a cell, outside which there is nothing but cold, empty space. It ends with 'a vision of a disorder that was beyond any one man to control, yet which, I felt, if I could pin down, might bring me calm.' (p. 97) Time is not important, nor place nor character, since all periods of Singh's life reveal the same deep-structure. Experience distils symbol, and all the symbols focus on archetypal abyss: a young man with a two-dimensional photograph; a boy outside a hut (again) in the middle of nowhere; or 'heroic' horsemen dwarfed 'below a sky threatening snow to the very end of an empty world'. (p. 98) Mimic men act fables, but fable splits to reveal the deeper 'truth' of myth. (Only this myth sees blankness where Harris saw golden.)

Yet Book One had a moment of doubt, wondering whether 'the personality, for all its byways and wilful deviations, does not hang together'. (p. 31) Singh starts again, searching behind that first vision of snow to discover how he became a mimic man. Book Two is chronological, unlike Book One, because it adopts the method of history to establish cause and effect, development through time, the formation of character. Now he must begin with childhood. The schoolroom contains children of many races, but they all learn to play roles and invent identities because they are ashamed of their backgrounds, and because their island is a collection of displaced people. But their fables keep slipping, revealing what they try to hide. On the beach, Singh has intimations of disorder and shipwreck: the great uprooted tree which has drifted ashore, derelict; the geography of sand crumbled away by rivulets below; a family drowning beyond hope of rescue, and later netted along with fish and a stingray, mutilated. But he saves himself from tragic vision by fabling, that he is different, that an eye up there is on him, like a camera trained on a hero. Soon, however, private playacting turns to public drama. His father, driven by failure and contempt, becomes the leader of one of the half crazy religio-political movements of the Third World, and turns into a holy man. For him and his followers, hurt becomes frenzy becomes role and ritual magic. Mimic men also get caught up in one another's dramas. Singh feels his family 'house' is tottering, and seeks consolation in an incestuous affair with his cousin; but her brother almost shoots him on the beach, while pretending it is all in play. He decides to leave, to seek in England a new life, a truer self, a destiny. But he lands in that attic, with the photograph and the snow. So 'history', though it discovers causation, ends with determinism too; the camera turns into the box again, with the emptiness outside. History explains role-playing; but fable still splits to reveal the mythic vision of the void.

Yet he begins a third time, because the act of writing has changed his vision. To see man as determined is to see him without responsibility; but now, as Singh examines his political career, there is a new language which judges action or inaction, and feels remorse. To say, of the Indian and Black leaders of the independent movement, 'from play-acting to disorder; it is the pattern' (p. 220), is both true and no longer nearly true enough. For if they get imprisoned in the roles that brought them such easy power, if they release forces they cannot control, when the frenzy of the colonized turns inevitably to drama; if they betray hopes that cannot be realized because of the actualities of money and power in a neocolonial situation; nonetheless (he now sees) men *must* 'act', and take responsibility for the roles they choose. Drama can control frenzy, sharpen perception, and raise man's capacity to act well. Singh sees now that his earlier passivity was chosen, not determined. So it was his own self-enclosure and irresponsibility that brought about his downfall, and the race-riots and bloodshed that followed. That cannot be changed, but at the very last we get a re-vision of two ways in which 'acting deliberately' has brought human recovery to Singh himself. The writing of the book, which began as an attempt to fix an image of disorder, has in fact been a process of ordering and humanizing his life, through art. And it has enabled him to choose a new way of acting, extraordinarily limited as yet by the determination to avoid harm, but a scrupulous beginning. He has withdrawn, but in order to start living again with new self-knowledge and responsibility. Man must be mimic. Two moments of horror open up again the abysmal dehumanization of life, when not sustained by role: the experience with the prostitute, of being reduced to a neutral cell of perception; and the paralysis of the displaced man on the railway platform with nowhere to go, while tall trains pass endlessly by. But the terrible vision of myth is not the end, though it must be gone through; nor is history only the record of determinism. The horror and absurdity can be overcome by deliberately 'making' one's life, in full knowledge of the self and the world. Fable comes to the rescue of myth and history; but all three different kinds of imagination need one another, to supply the deficiencies of each alone. The earlier novel built a sentry-box for Mr Biswas; in the later one, the box-like room or cell has turned into the book, the house of fiction, in which the necessary and shaping spirits of imagination are finely distinguished, understood, and harmonized.

Of course the two writers are still radically opposed. Their basic imaginative 'cases' against each other remain, although they have grown closer. Immediately after *The Mimic Men*, Naipaul wrote a history of Trinidad called *The Loss of El Dorado*.[21] Immediately after *Tumatumari*, Harris produced two collections of stories 'reconstructing' myths of the native peoples of Guyana, and a novel, *Ascent to Omai*, containing another attack on 'history' and 'the comedy of manners',[22] and seeking again to create a Golden Man and climb to a lost place of vision. Here another article might begin, exploring a renewed opposition – but still not simply, since Harris begins to archaeologize, and Naipaul to show new compassion for the unhistoried Amerindian and slave. The essential point however was already clear in 1968, though we have yet to do it justice. As metaphors for fiction, relating vision to the void, the 'bone flute' and the 'house' exactly invert each other; yet they contain the same elements; and seek to resolve similar tensions between differing kinds of imagination. Naipaul is a remarkable formal innovator also, though he seeks to break the novel in segments, to promote a multiple view, where Harris seeks new ways of weaving the many into one. Without contraries is no progression. Their opposition is immensely significant, and necessary. They become far more meaningful to us together, held in tension, than either could be alone.

Notes

1 *In* Kirstin Holst Petersen and Anna Rutherford (ed.) *Enigma of Values* (Aarhus, 1975), p. 43; a useful introduction to Harris.

2 *Tradition, the Writer and Society* (London, 1967), pp. 39–40; 'The Unresolved Constitution', *Caribbean Quarterly*, 14 (1968), pp. 44–5; 'History Fable and Myth in the Caribbean and Guianas' (The Mittelholzer Lectures, *Caribbean Quarterly*, 16 (1970), pp. 21. 31.

3 'A Talk on the Subjective Imagination', *New Letters* (University of Missouri), 40 (1973), pp. 144–50. See also 'Yurokon' in *The Sleepers of Roraima* (London, 1970), p. 63 ff.

4 *Palace of the Peacock* (London, 1960). Page references are to the paperback edition of 1968, which has an excellent introduction by Kenneth Ramchand.

5 See Harris on 'the distribution of a frail moment of illuminating adjustments', *Tradition, the Writer and Society, op. cit.*, pp. 35–6.

6 *cf.* Harris on the 'peculiar reality of language', *Tradition, the Writer and Society, op. cit.*, p. 32. Hena Maes-Jelinek, 'The Poetry of Space in *Palace of the Peacock*', *Enigma of Values, op. cit.*, pp. 59–108, is a detailed study of the 'continuous inward revisionary movement' of the language in the novel.

7 *cf.* Harris on Ulysses and the Sirens, *Tradition, the Writer and Society, op. cit.*, pp. 52–3.

8 I owe this to Michael Gilkes, *Wilson Harris and the Caribbean Novel* (London, 1975), pp. 40–41; a perceptive study. In contrast, see Naipaul's account of his dream of unweaving to nothingness, *Area of Darkness* (London, 1964), p. 280.

9 See the account of *nigredo, albedo, cauda pavonis* in the Mittelholzer lectures, *Caribbean Quarterly*, 16 (1970), p. 20. Michael Gilkes points out the pervasive references in the fiction of Harris to alchemy and the *lapis*.

10 *Tradition, the Writer and Society, op. cit.*, pp. 39–40.

11 *Tradition, the Writer and Society, op. cit.*, pp. 21–30.

12 *A House for Mr Biswas* (London, 1961). Page references are to the Deutsch edition.

13 See pp. 83, 118–19, 171, 204.

14 I have in mind here his constant re-immersion of himself in journalism and travel books, and the writing of his history of Trinidad, all of which seem to indicate his need to keep constantly in touch with a 'real world' outside his own imagination, and his distrust of an art removed from life. *In a Free State* (London, 1971), has as one theme the ways in which 'art' can become a mode of unreality, and it is begun and concluded with journal entries. We cannot read *Guerillas* (London, 1975) without in some way 'remembering' Michael X, or *A Bend in the River* (London, 1980) without thinking of Zaire.

15 See Landeg White, *V. S. Naipaul* (London, 1976), p. 124 ff. Naipaul also used, for his opening, his father's autobiographical 'They named him Mohun', see Seepersad Naipaul, '*The Adventures of Gurudeva*' *and other stories* (London, 1976), p. 124 ff. It was this that Seepersad Naipaul read to the Port of Spain literary group.

16 *Tumatumari* (London, 1968). (As it happens, I have discussed the second pair of novels in inverse chronological order. 'The Unresolved Constitution', *op. cit.* shows he had been thinking of Naipaul again. I think it possible that his use of nausea and sardonic humour, as well as of a mimic theatre, may have ironic reference to Naipaul.)

17 Frances A. Yates, *The Art of Memory* (London, 1966). Harris makes particular use of the 'memory theatre' of Camillo (chapter 6 and pull-out) and the Wheel and Staircase of Lull (chapter 7). I am aware that these are 'Renaissance' but their tradition goes back through the Middle Ages to the classical world.

18 For a fuller account of these definitions, see M. Kinkead-Weekes and I. Gregor, *William Golding* (London, 1976), pp. 241–7; and my *Samuel Richardson, Dramatic Novelist* (London, 1973), pp. 419–20 and pp. 466–83. Harris uses the terms in his Mittelholzer Lectures in 1970, *op. cit.*, though as I see it, he fails to distinguish myth from fable.

19 He actually and regrettably does do this in *Ascent to Omai* (London, 1970).

20 *The Mimic Men* (London, 1967). Page references to the Deutsch edition.

20 *The Loss of El Dorado, A History* (London, 1969).

22 *The Sleepers of Roraima* (London, 1970); *The Age of the Rainmakers* (London, 1971); *Ascent to Omai* (London, 1970).

The Uses of Fiction
Edited by
Douglas Jefferson
and Graham Martin

11

The Fourth Novel: Ngugi's *Petals of Blood*

Andrew Gurr

In the twentieth century novels by metropolitan writers have suffered from a fairly substantial kind of shrinkage. The nineteenth-century novel's time scale of years and span of communities or families, the scope of a *Middlemarch* or the great *Bildungsromanen*, has shrunk to the single day of *Mrs. Dalloway* and the solitary psyche of *Herzog*. The reasons for this shrinkage are on the whole clear: a shift of authorial standpoint from objective reporting to the subjective consciousness, the increasing concern with brevity and imagistic economy – even *Ulysses* started out to be a short story – and above all perhaps the pressures of the vast and amorphous society of metropolitan life, which forced writers to give up the attempt to grasp their society whole and to retreat towards the new-found and much more accessible complexities of the individual psyche. For the novel as a form this entailed not only a reduction in scope but also something very like a crisis of identity. Since the novel's form is better suited to large-scale social analysis than to subjective probings, it is not surprising to find the shrinkage of its scope accompanied by so many cries of concern for its declining health.

One can, of course, still argue that the novel is alive and well and living in the colonies. Outside the amorphous metropolitan societies novelists have been better placed to hold on to a sense of social identity. A colony – which I will define very loosely for the present purpose as any community which is dependent politically and culturally on a distant metropolitan centre – has an identity of sorts simply by virtue of its dependence on the distant centre and its consciousness of difference from that centre. It is usually small and distinctive enough to have a conspicuous character of its own, however enervatingly and humiliatingly dependent that character may be. It has an organizing feature or principle which saves it from the amorphous randomness of the metropolis. The colonial identity, with its inescapable social consciousness, counterbalances the writer's tendency to dwell on his subjective consciousness and has given strength to the fiction of Joyce, Patrick White, Doris Lessing, Jean Rhys, V. S. Naipaul, George Lamming, Chinua Achebe, Ngugi wa Thiong'o, and almost all the major writers of realistic prose fiction in the last thirty years.

I think it is fair to say that the novel has always been at its best when it deals with history. The great nineteenth-century novels all tend to hold their subjects at a distance in time, whether at the overtly historical distance of *War and Peace* or the more discreet remove of twenty years or so in *Little Dorrit*, or *Middlemarch*, or *The Mayor of Casterbridge*. That is one of the things the subjective consciousness cannot readily do, and one of the reasons why, with the exception of Lawrence, who from his provincial origins conceived of social and psychological factors as interfused, metropolitan fiction has seemed to be growing weaker. The narrative in egocentric fiction is too concentrated, too immediate for the broad sweep of an essentially social medium. On the other hand historical distance and perspective are perfectly suited to the scope of a novel which is seeking to analyse a colonial society and to find a social identity through its history. Joyce's pattern – leaving his colony to go into exile in the metropolis and from there to create in his fiction the social identity which gave him being – has been repeated many times in this century. Katherine Mansfield in her 'Karori' stories, Naipaul in *A House for Mr Biswas*, Doris Lessing in the Martha Quest novels, Lamming, Achebe, Ngugi, all spent a substantial part of their early careers as writers creating a sense of their own identity by setting out their home colony's history in their fiction. Their concern is with a whole society, not with the individual ego. If an authorial persona appears it is usually on the sidelines as a young observer – Stephen Dedalus, Kezia in Katherine Mansfield's stories, and Anand in *A House for Mr Biswas*. As colonial exiles they utilize the novel form for what it has always done best, social and historical analysis. And their achievements are as substantial as any fiction written in English this century.

There is, then, a peculiar distinction about the works of realistic prose fiction produced this century by writers who are born into a colonial society and who are driven in their youth into a form of exile. It might be either physical exile, as in the followers of Joyce who moved to the metropolis in search of the freedom to write, or the cultural exile of those African and Caribbean writers who are wrenched from their home culture by a metropolitan-orientated education and the adoption of a European language. Either form of exile gives them the distanced perspective which allows them to fulfill the first task of the twentieth-century writer, the search for identity, in the form of a reconstruction of their home society.

The later work of such writers is much more variable. They might settle into the role of permanent exile, like Doris Lessing or Naipaul, and move closer to the kind of fiction generated in the metropolis, focussing on the individual psyche in an amorphous social setting. Or they might face the labour which most Caribbean and African writers have tackled, of returning from exile and grappling with the problems of their home society from inside once more. Again I would assert that the intrinsic qualities of the novel as a form are inclined to favour this second choice, with its continuance of social concerns in preference to the psychological focus of the novel of permanent exile.

The novel of homecoming raises the challenge of form in a distinctive way. It involves a change from the broadly historical analysis of the novels of colonial identity which precede it in each writer's work. It calls for a confrontation not with the past but with the present and the future. So as a social novel it suits the form while as a non-historical work it sets up the challenge of an adjustment to the form used for its predecessors. In the light of that challenge I find it instructive to examine Ngugi wa Thiong'o's fourth novel, *Petals of Blood*.

Achebe and Ngugi, the foremost African novelists writing in English, are true originals. In their own time and place they had no models of any kind to guide them. Naipaul, too, though not quite so much the 'double exile'[1] in language and culture which writers in colonial societies are usually forced to be, had no usable precedents for his writing. Consequently it is intriguing that for all their originality what these three writers have published has followed a markedly similar pattern. The basic impulse of course is the same, the exile's quest for identity, what Ngugi calls in *Secret Lives* 'an attempt to understand myself and my situation in society and in history'.[2] With local variations this impulse started them along remarkably similar paths.

The pattern involves initially the writing of three novels and a book of short stories. That, it seems, is enough for them to complete the exploration of the exile's colonial identity. Achebe started to write a trilogy covering three generations: Okonkwo in *Things Fall Apart*, then Okonkwo's grandson in *No Longer at Ease*; and he only altered his plan because he found the middle generation too perplexing – so his third novel, *Arrow of God*, became a recasting of the first.[3] Ngugi effectively did write a trilogy, covering the colonial history of his people in three stages, from the circumcision crisis of 1927–9 in Kikuyuland, through the guerrilla war of the 1950s, to Kenya's independence in 1963.[4] And Naipaul wrote his short stories, *Miguel Street*, and the two novels about Trinidad, as apprentice work (his own term) for the masterpiece *Mr Biswas*, which ended his quest for identity so completely that he said he felt unemployed after it. Three novels and a collection of stories, the basic route for the novelist who is seeking to establish his sense of identity by recording his society's recent history.

But what follows when that work is done? The uniform pattern then becomes even more apparent, because all three novelists turned – if you except Naipaul's false start with an English identity in *Mr Stone and the Knights Companion* – to write a political novel. By that I mean of course not just a shift in time from history to the contemporary politics of post-colonial society, but a novel about politicians: *A Man of the People*, *The Mimic Men*, and *Petals of Blood*. They are the novels which turn to face the present and the future in the home society, once the past has been created in fiction and the identity – of the situation and therefore of the writer – has been established.

I am of course oversimplifying. There are original writers in the Third World who have followed this pattern more compressedly, George Lamming for instance. There are writers who tackle only the present, and who do not seem to feel the pressures of exile which impel others to recompose their identity, such as Soyinka. They usually employ the directness of poetry and drama rather than novels. Patterns, though, are only devices we employ to help us organize the infinitely variant phenomena we are studying, and that is all I wish to do with this pattern. It focusses attention on the transition these major writers have to make from concern with past identity to present politics. And in the process we can see more clearly the problems of form which confront them as novelists, and how they respond to that challenge. Hence my concern with what I call the challenge of the fourth novel.

Novelists tend to differ from other writers in the spaciousness of their thinking. Their responses are considered, the exposition exhaustive, in a form which calls for a high degree of detached manipulation, for analysis and exposition together. It is obviously the form to use if the writer's aim is, quoting Ngugi again, 'to sensitively register his encounter with history, his people's history.'[5] The form of the novel is best suited to telling a story as a history. Ngugi's achievement in his trilogy, which for me ranks with *Biswas* as among the best fiction written in English in the last forty years, clearly demonstrates this. The question that arises with the fourth novel is whether this essentially historical role can be adapted to the different requirements of the present. In *A Man of the People* Achebe turned from teaching to anger (Ngugi's phrase), a shift which was needful but made it a less weighty achievement than its predecessor. In *The Mimic Men*, also I think a less substantial novel than its predecessor *Biswas*, Naipaul turned away from the society which exiled him to focus on the figure of the exile himself, still a major feat which Naipaul accomplished with his usual deftness, but a retreat from the scale of work he had attempted in the earlier book. Ngugi's *Petals of Blood*, by refusing the easy access to anger and satire and by rigorously keeping his exiles in the heart of their home society, I think accomplishes a good deal more than either of the other two in the pattern.

Ngugi's first three novels are a history of colonialism. They start with the alienation of Gikuyu land and end with the alienation of the social and individual psyche of the colonized. The first begins at a time when the Gikuyu have their land, and the colonial presence is little more than one of missionaries and mission schools, a force which divides the people but does not yet dispossess them. In the second novel they are the dispossessed, tenant farmers, landless labourers or fighters seeking to regain the land which is home. In the third novel the white colonial landlords are going, leaving behind them the traumatized victims of the struggle and the new black landlords who threaten to perpetuate the system of alienation which colonialism set up.

It is a nice semantic irony that alienation, the central concept for both Marx and Freud though used in emphatically different contexts, should also be the term for the Kenyan trauma. The alienation of Gikuyu land is the centre of Ngugi's diagnosis of his people's history under colonialism. The essential point about land alienation had been put by Kenyatta as early as 1938 in *Facing Mount Kenya*. In his novels of the 1960s Ngugi develops the analysis to its utmost, embracing in the process both Marx's concept of the alienation of labour and Freud's concept of the alienated psyche.

Ngugi describes colonialism as a cause of universal exile. It destroys the cohesion of the society it battens on, not only by seizing its land but through the two-edged weapons, education and its foreign language and culture, and the material prizes which go with 'apemanship', imitating the colonialist, in all its forms. Ngugi shows how social pressures create divisions between the members of the colonized society. Loneliness grows up in *The River Between*, is a neurosis in *Weep Not Child* and a condition of life in *A Grain of Wheat*, where Mugo betrays Kihika because Kihika threatens the loneliness which has come to be his refuge. When Gikonyo sees Mumbi with Karanja's child his conclusion is that 'to live and die alone was the ultimate truth'. (p. 135) And with loneliness comes guilt, the consciousness of social failure, the neuroses which grow in the cracks of society once cohesion is gone. That, in very crude summary, is the historical analysis of colonial society Ngugi sets up on his trilogy.

Petals of Blood develops precisely from the trilogy. It covers the twelve years since independence with a broadly historical perspective very like the trilogy, and it does so in three stages. But it has a fourth stage which confronts the future, and it has a cohesive framework which fixes it in the present, with the past as retrospect or flashback and the future as implied consequence of past and present together. Let me give a few details to indicate how the book relates to its predecessors and how it develops from them to face the challenge of the fourth part.

Structurally it is fixed in the present by the murder – a political murder – which is described at the outset and solved, in the sense of the murderer being identified, only at the close of the penultimate chapter. The past, Kenya's history since independence, is thus incorporated as the explanation of the murder, largely in fact the murderer's confession. Post-colonial Kenya is shown as a development of the society described in the last novel of the trilogy, *A Grain of Wheat*. The image of the fertile soil which seems arid dust to the alienated Mugo in *A Grain of Wheat*, for instance, becomes the symbolic drought for the alienated township of Ilmorog in *Petals of Blood*, a drought for which the ambivalent answer is that splendidly evocative symbol the Trans-Africa Highway. In conception an ideal of pan-African co-operation, in practice a grossly exploitative piece of black capitalism, the Highway stands in *Petals of Blood* as an extension of Gikonyo's experience in Chapter 6 of *A Grain of Wheat* over buying the farm. The alienation of man from his land and of man from man remains the central feature of post-colonial society, and stands therefore at the centre of Ngugi's fourth book as it stood in the earlier three.

But what of the fourth section, and the political novel which faces the present, not the past? What is to be done about the central fact that after the colonial presence has lifted alienation continues? In the book of essays which Ngugi published as an accompaniment to his novels, and which he called, inevitably, *Homecoming*, the answer to exile and alienation, he says unequivocally that it is not for the novelist to offer political solutions. Explaining what he saw as Lamming's failure with *A Season of Adventure*, his most politically explicit novel, Ngugi maintained that 'it is not in the province of the novel to give answers.' (*Homecoming*, p. 133) And yet that, on the face of it, is just what Ngugi set himself to do tackling the present and future in *Petals of Blood*. He has analysed the alienating impact of colonialism in his trilogy; in the first three sections of *Petals of Blood* he shows it extended in post-colonial society; if he does no more than that in his fourth novel as a whole then his achievement will be no advance on *A Grain of Wheat*.

One thing he does is to make the implication of Gikonyo's loss of his farm to his M.P. more far-reaching. The first three sections of *Petals of Blood* have titles from Yeats's famous prophetic poem, whose title, *The Second Coming*, has biblical links with the title *A Grain of Wheat*. Ngugi calls his sections, successively, 'Walking', 'Towards Bethlehem' and 'To be Born'. Run together they suggest that their contents are a picture of Yeats's rough beast whose coming will be a foul new apocalypse. The title of *A Grain of Wheat* hints at an apocalypse and at rebirth in society through individual sacrifice.[6] This apocalypse is bleaker. Its apotheosis in the fourth section is not just the beast of New Ilmorog with its concrete tower blocks and its dispossessed peasants turned wage slaves but the explicit suggestion that the second coming is a resurrection of the old colonialism, and will bring the same disasters. The book ends with rumours of 'a return to the forests and the mountains', a new guerrilla war of the peasants against the black colonialists. The title of the fourth section is 'Again . . . La Luta Continua!' Ngugi is turning the primarily historical function of the novel to advantage by deploying Yeats's theory of history as cyclic, so that the future can be prophesied as a renewal of the past.

That is one way in which Ngugi faces the challenge of the fourth novel. To me it is not enough. It says little that is not at least implied in

A Grain of Wheat. It is clever, and as prophecy it might even have a grain of truth, but it does not in itself make *Petals of Blood* a significant advance over the trilogy. To be that it must not only embody the analysis of colonial alienation, but take it further and explore the new implications which arise with independence. And I think that in ways other than the cyclic history device Ngugi does that.

We can get a better perspective on this further exploration in *Petals of Blood* by looking for a moment at what Achebe and Naipaul did with their fourth novels. Achebe resorted to satire, presenting politicians old and new as uniformly subject to human frailty, bringing on themselves by their frailties the crude bludgeon (or the clean sweep if you prefer a less perjorative metaphor) of the military coup. Prophetic it may have been, but Achebe's impulse was more anger than analysis, and *A Man of the People* is a lesser book in consequence. Naipaul's mimic man is really an exile not a politician – the politics are described in cursory fashion; the focus is on the exile and his new identity as a writer, writing to get control of his history and to fill the emptiness of that hideous 'free state' which Naipaul sees as natural to the post-colonial psyche. For the generation which comes after Mr Biswas and his house Naipaul can find no home anywhere. There is a splendidly characteristic irony in his use of that word 'home' in *The Mimic Men*, where he describes Ralph Kripalsingh's 'flight to the greater disorder, the final emptiness: London and the *home* counties'. Both Achebe and Naipaul in their different ways offer negations. Ngugi differs from both in his insistence on the central importance of the concept of home, the return from exile, and on the continuing involvement of the exile with his homeland.

In *Homecoming* Ngugi registers Naipaul's Biswas as 'Caribbean man in search of himself and his place in the world'. The same search is going on in Africa, he says. 'The African masses, together with their West Indian counterparts, are still engaged in a social struggle which may, like Biswas's own struggle, end in a kind of homecoming.' (p. 94) The thing which makes that search necessary is exile, alienation from one's culture and one's home. And after the exile the home will have to be a new one. Ngugi's basic political question is 'how best to build a true communal home for all Africans.' (p. xix) That is the question to which the analysis in *Petals of Blood* is a contribution. Not an answer, I think, but at least an assessment which might clear the way towards an answer. And it is an assessment which has to be seen primarily in terms of exile and alienation.

Consider the names Ngugi gives his characters. They can be divided according to what he calls in *Homecoming* the new tribalism of the Haves and the Have Nots (a division, incidentally, which was first proposed by Sancho Panza's grandmother; it's not exactly a new phenomenon). The Haves enjoy names like Sir Swallow Bloodall or Cambridge Fraudsham if they are white, or Chui, the black headmaster of Siriana, whose name means leopard, and Nderi wa Riera, the Ilmorog M.P., whose name means vulture son of air. All carnivores. The Have Nots are the four central characters, the murder suspects, and their names all signify different forms of alienation. Munira, the teacher turned religious fanatic, has a name which in Gikuyu means a stump, a lifeless, uprooted obstacle. Karega, the younger teacher turned trade unionist and political militant, has a name which translates as rebel, one who refuses. Abdulla, the cripple who used to be a freedom fighter, has a name which also indicates homelessness. Properly called Murira, the mystery man, he gave himself the Islamic name Abdulla thinking it was a 'Christian' name. And the name of the fourth member of the central group of Ilmorog aliens, Wanja the prostitute, means outsider or stranger. The labels are quite explicit, and they explain more clearly than anything else what Ngugi set himself to do in *Petals of Blood*. Where the characters of *A Grain of Wheat* are alienated villagers, the *Petals of Blood* characters are true outsiders. He takes his exiles, his four types of alien, and puts them in a mystery story which poses the question which of them performed the political act of burning down the symbol of New Ilmorog capitalism, Wanja's whorehouse, with its contents, Chui and Nderi wa Riera. While he takes us through the explanation of that mystery he examines the role of the exiles in the society which alienated them.

I think that what Ngugi says of all his exiles is fascinating and illuminating, but there is only space here to look at one of them, the cut-down tree, the stump Munira, the exile who actually did seal up the carnivores in the flames which look like petals of blood. Munira starts out as a teacher with the kind of idealism which created the Trans-Africa Highway. He rides a metal horse in old Ilmorog, and gallops over the landscape, his knight's charger only shrinking to a mere bicycle when he visits the local education offices where he meets the third of the Haves who is to be murdered in the burning whorehouse. Munira has been Christianized – his baptismal name is Godfrey, which, ironically, is also the name of the police inspector before whom he expiates his guilt by writing the confession which is the spinal narrative of the book. Guilt-ridden, like all Ngugi's exiles, he is very conscious of his isolation before his God. He sees himself as 'outside things' (p. 139), a 'spectator' (pp. 269–70), an 'outsider' (p. 274). In the most striking image he calls himself a watcher on the shore of history (p. 212):

> 'His parents had always played it safe and he, Munira, had always stood at the shore and watched streams and brooks flow over pebbles and rocks. He was an outsider, a spectator of life, history.'

The act of arson by which he destroys the Haves is a redemptive, cleansing act which not only cleans out the society of New Ilmorog but redeems his soul and restores him to the society from which he had been alienated. When faced with the corruptions of the Haves he asks what can he do? (pp. 106, 111 and 112), and finds his answer in the petals of fire at the end of the book. This is not the exile coming home, but it is the exile seeing what he can do in the task of building the home.

The watcher on the shore image of Munira's is striking partly because Ngugi uses it in *Homecoming* of himself as novelist. To be precise, he says that the novelist's position is a dual one, simultaneously swimming in the mainstream of his country's history and standing on the bank watching. (p. 39) Through the 1970s, as his imprisonment in Kenya in 1978 shows, Ngugi has increasingly taken what you might call in this context the plunge. He has become more and more the swimmer and less the bystander. He has identified his alienation, his exile, and has chosen not to live with it like Naipaul but to fight it, as each of the four central exiles in *Petals of Blood* choose to do in their distinctive ways.

That, however uncomfortable a shift some of us may find it, is as I see it the key development which takes *Petals of Blood* far past *A Grain of Wheat*. The 'higher consciousness' which he writes of in *Homecoming* as the reward of exile, resulting from 'the state of alienation, strife and uncertainty in the modern world', (p. 110) gives the exile a special role in his society. Munira, Karega, Wanja and Abdulla lead the crusade from drought-stricken Ilmorog which brings them the mixed blessings of the Trans-Africa Highway and New Ilmorog. The new colonialism forces them into different paths, but their responsibility remains with them till near the end. The conclusion is marked by Abdulla, who offers a new metaphor for the rebirth image of *A Grain of Wheat*:

> 'Maybe . . . maybe, he thought, history was a dance in a huge arena of God. You played your part, whatever your chosen part, and then you

> left the arena, swept aside by the waves of a new step, a new movement in the dance. Other dancers, younger, brighter, more inventive came and played with even greater skill, with more complicated footwork, before they too were swept aside by yet a greater tide in the movement they had helped to create, and other dancers were thrown up to carry the dance to even newer heights and possibilities undreamt of by an earlier generation. Let it be . . . Let it be . . . His time was over.[7]

The role of the exile with his higher consciousness is to lead the crusade against the drought, to take part in his society's dance, not to be a bystander. Not for Ngugi the simplicity of Achebe's anger or the essentially defensive ironic detachment of Naipaul.

It might be objected that I am identifying here not an advance in the form of the novel but a development of the novelist's thinking about his material. True enough, up to a point. I don't think the novel as a form is really amenable to drastic redeployment of its essentially descriptive potential. *Petals of Blood* is an advance over what Wilson Harris calls the old novel of persuasion, but it is not the radical new form Harris asks for, and I am inclined to doubt whether we'll ever see such a thing, or not one still marketable as a novel. What I would claim for Ngugi's fourth novel is first the way it consistently builds on its predecessors, unlike the other fourth novels; secondly, the technical ingenuity with which Ngugi structures his narrative to embody past, present and future in the one account, and thus make it a more *contemporary* novel than any other; and thirdly the way it brings the weight of Ngugi's own experience and his own position as double exile into play – facing what Naipaul faces in *The Mimic Men* while refusing to beat the exile's retreat into subjectivity. In its own complex way, it is his homecoming.

Notes

1 The term was coined by Gareth Griffiths (*A Double Exile. African and West Indian Writing Between Two Cultures* (London: Marion Boyars, 1978). Writers who are non-English but use the English language are exiled both culturally and linguistically.
2 *Secret Lives* (London: H.E.B., 1975), preface.
3 See 'Named for Victoria, Queen of England', *New Letters* XL (1973), p. 17.
4 *The River Between* (written 1962, published 1965), *Weep Not Child* (written 1963, published 1964), *A Grain of Wheat* (written 1965–7, published 1968), all London, H.E.B.

5 *Homecoming* (London: H.E.B., 1972, p. 39.
6 See *A Grain of Wheat* (London: H.E.B., 1968), epigraph and p. 15.
7 *Petals of Blood* (London: H.E.B., 1977), p. 340.

The Uses of Fiction
Edited by
Douglas Jefferson
and Graham Martin

12

African Novels of Affirmation

Arthur Ravenscroft

The first volume of Arnold Kettle's *Introduction to the English Novel* appeared in 1951, just a year before *The Palm-Wine Drinkard* by the Nigerian, Amos Tutuola, heralded the vigorous growth of an African literature in English that has become an important means of articulating the experiences and aspirations of the peoples of the 'Third World'. The very nature of African art and of its function in African society has helped to determine the directions taken by anglophone African novelists of repute, and the 1970s saw them using the novel increasingly to analyse contemporary social and political conditions in ostensibly independent African countries, and to examine the relationships between political action and personal ethics.

In *A Guest of Honour*,[1] Nadine Gordimer seems to be using the political situation in a fictional, newly-independent, Central African country as a setting for the sensuous and emotional awakening of a hero past middle age, and his conversion from 'rational' European liberalism to radical political action. Colonel James Bray, the enlightened ex-colonial official, sacked for his active encouragement of the black nationalist political party, is invited to return, a decade later, to join in the Independence celebrations. His one-time protégé, Mweta, is now President of the new nation, but Shinza, Mweta's colleague in the anti-colonialist struggle, has been excluded from government. Bray believes the country can flourish only if they work together, and he attempts the classical liberal task of mediation, while also carrying out an official survey of the country's educational needs.

Bray has been plucked back from an orderly, Proust-reading retirement in Wiltshire, from an apparently firm, civilized marriage that has moved into 'compatibility beyond sex' (p. 145). His re-exposure to Africa (to the very province where he had been District Commissioner in colonial days, where his wife had shared in his hopes for African advancement) releases all his somnolent sensuous faculties and plunges him, almost casually, into vigorous sexuality with a much younger, married woman. A major concern of the novel is undoubtedly this development of Bray's personal character, with its uncomfortable questionings in the reader's mind about such honoured humane values as rationality, as 'the reconciliation of personal passion and impersonal love' (p. 224), as fidelity, as the decencies that had shaped Bray's life of public service. Yet Bray's 'new state of being' (p. 258), which is no mere 'enjoying the last kick of the prostate' (p. 338), is the private concomitant of his seemingly impetuous political involvement with Shinza, when the two leading nationalist figures clash publicly at the first Party Congress after Independence. The chemistry of Bray's private as well as his political change is partly existential, though prompted by a new faith that will 'go ahead into what's coming, trust to luck' (p. 222); he has been fired by an almost jealous admiration of Shinza's bodily vitality and socialist vision for the future of the African masses. Bray's return to Africa reveals to him 'the dark underground lake [in himself] whose eye he had never found' (p. 295) in marriage or career, yet the reader is persuaded that the potential was always there, and Nadine Gordimer evades the trap of exerting an influence of African mystique upon a susceptible European. The realism of her descriptions of landscape and lakeside, of ants dropping on to Bray's papers as he works under a great fig-tree, of dust and zinnias, is too concrete to allow portentous effects, even as one registers a powerful integrating imagination at work throughout the book.

A Guest of Honour appears to have all the lineaments of a psychological novel about an Englishman in Africa, with the political events as background to a study, albeit deep, in character. But that the politics is no simple sightscreen against which to observe Bray explains why *A Guest of Honour* must be judged Nadine Gordimer's first truly mature novel, which has been followed so impressively by *The Conservationist* and *Burger's Daughter*.[2] For the central issue of this book, involving and subsuming Bray's role, is the politics of neo-colonialism, as revealed in the unnamed former colony, the geography, history, capital, countryside, class, tribal and race structures of which Nadine Gordimer creates with confident economy and convincing solidity. The general political conditions are very similar to those in Ngugi wa Thiong'o's *Petals of Blood*,[3] which Andrew Gurr discusses fully elsewhere in this volume. Shortly before Independence, Mweta and Shinza differ seriously about how the Party should implement its socialist aims when it gains power. Mweta chooses gradualism, dependence upon the goodwill of the mining and other industrial interests which have their bases in the West. It is soon clear that the only beneficiaries of black government are expatriate industry and the black élite. Mweta confuses stability with preserving the *status quo*, whereas Shinza wants extensive nationalization and is willing to take the risks of economic upheaval for the sake of an immediate improvement in the lot of the African masses. Ngugi's fictional strategy differs from Nadine Gordimer's in that he presents the ills of neo-colonialism through the consciousness of its peasant and proletarian victims, and in a minutely worked historical context, while she gives it through the perspectives of three sophisticated wielders of power (past power with Bray, present power with Mweta, indirect trades-union power with Shinza), and gains depth of treatment from the interplay of their relationships. Nevertheless, a sense of the burdens of poverty suffered by the workers emerges quite as strongly in *A Guest of Honour* as in *Petals of Blood*, and there is a great deal in common between the two novelists' analysis of the politics of neo-colonialism.

Nadine Gordimer is, of course, a South African novelist, and perhaps it isn't altogether fanciful to see in Bray's awakened adventurousness some authorial speculation about white South African behaviour when the inevitable comes about. This contrasts with one of the most accomplished Afrikaans novels yet published, Karel Schoeman's *Na die Geliefde Land*, translated into English as *The Promised Land*,[4] a novel of the future about Afrikanerdom's self-destroying obduracy after 'the troubles', yet with a hint of enlightened new growth, in the girl, Carla Hattingh's, discontent with her people's sterile nostalgia and despair.

Neither Gordimer nor Ngugi underestimates the power of neo-colonial structures in Africa, nor their corrosive effects upon the lives of the African peasantry and upon the psychology of the African élite. Gordimer treats as axiomatic, Ngugi demonstrates across four novels, the historical origins of the present situation. Both concentrate largely on the interaction of politics and economics by using the realist novel to place characters and narrative, but their marshalling of the minutiae displays, in both, a creative imagination that is visionary rather than documentary. In *Two Thousand Seasons*,[5] the Ghanaian, Ayi Kwei Armah's, fourth novel, realism is abandoned, history turned about, political considerations subjected to establishing the viability of African culture, which itself is claimed to have survived the ages only through the dedication of a tiny minority, the African artists, 'seers' and 'utterers', *griots* chiefly, who have all the sensibility and wisdom of individualist artists but exist with and for the ordinary people and are not élitist. The fable takes the form of a West African clan's history, from their prehistoric migrations across desert and swamp and through forest to a promised land near the Ashanti coast, through the slave-trade and nineteenth-century imperialism to the neo-colonialism of today. The narrating voice represents the collective memory of generations of *griots*, indeed the 'linking of those gone, ourselves here, those coming' (p. xiii). The tone owes much to Afro-American Black Consciousness. It relates a succession of conquests by Arabs and Europeans, of catastrophe upon catastrophe for Africans, with a few breathing spaces whose potential is lost through the apostasy of African 'askaris' and 'zombis'. The book makes a passionate plea for black people to cease to be 'outcasts from ourselves' (p. 3), to turn from the alienating allurements of other cultures that would destroy Africans physically and morally, to find again 'the way, our way', the genuine African way of 'reciprocity' among individuals, of collectiveness and mutual caring in a pristine egalitarianism.

In stylized, image-laden, incantatory prose suggestive of traditional *griot* public utterance, Armah invokes an emotive concept of Black Africanness, asserting that black cultural integrity must come first and all else will be added unto it. The word 'white', associated with Arab as well as European conquerors, becomes an epithet for everything that is evil, loathsome, and destructive in Africa. Many Western reviewers were shocked and in accusing Armah of blatant racialism both misinterpreted his purpose and showed their incomprehension of the violent trauma for Africans of European engagement with Africa over the centuries. The invective that Armah pours upon 'whiteness' in Africa is not so much an absolute judgement upon the European Christian and Arab Muslim cultures, as a means of defining sharply what has proved inimical to Africans, in order to arrive, through inversion, at a clearer understanding of a truly indigenous African way of life not yet fully apprehended by either the masses or the élite; he is trying to incubate a new African reaction to centuries of denegration of African culture by the outside world and by Africans themselves. The device doesn't work faultlessly; Armah does sometimes slip into mere counter-denegration. But, on the whole, he avoids it. The Prologue tells of an ancient prophetess's foretelling 'a thousand seasons wasted wandering amazed along alien roads, another thousand spent finding paths to the living way' (p. xv), and the 'story' is a viable fictional realization of the waste and destruction undergone and the abortive attempts to find in practical living the principles of 'the way, our way' that the succession of *griots* has kept fragilely alive down the centuries. In form a strange kind of modern apocalyptic novel, *Two Thousand Seasons* celebrates and re-enacts the very methods of the 'utterers' who have transmitted the essence of African ways and values. Armah treats time and 'reality' in a free-wheeling, though not arbitrarily fanciful, way. He convincingly dramatizes the centuries of wrong suffered by millions of Africans, but without sentimentalizing the pre-colonial past: the band of escaped slaves, who form a successful guerrilla resistance, train themselves with the utmost mental, emotional, and physical discipline to cope with a demanding present, even if their inspiration comes from the past. With this affirmation of Africanness, Armah turns his back on the nihilism and despair that colour his first three novels;[6] moreover, *Two Thousand Seasons* itself illustrates the functional and didactic role of art in traditional African society. Wole Soyinka has remarked that 'Armah's work is intensively committed to the substitution of another view of *active* history, with re-creating humanistic perspectives as inspirational alternatives to existing society'.[7]

During the Nigerian Civil War (1967–70), Wole Soyinka spent two-and-a-half years in a Nigerian prison, most of it in solitary confinement. After the war he wrote his second novel, *Season of Anomy*,[8] which, although it ingeniously adapts the non-African legend of Orpheus and Eurydice, operates within the cultural assumptions of Soyinka's native Yoruba mythology, especially those relating to the god Ogun. In his essay, 'The Fourth Stage',[9] Soyinka writes: 'Ogun . . . is best understood in Hellenic values as a totality of the Dionysian, Apollonian and Promethan virtues . . . traditional poetry records him as 'protector of orphans', 'roof over the homeless', 'terrible guardian of the sacred oath'; Ogun stands for a transcendental, humane but rigidly restorative justice . . . Ogun [is] the creative urge and instinct, the essence of creativity.' (p. 141) To over-simplify, Ogun's plunging into self-destruction in the Ogun myths in order to re-create himself implies that before there can be wholeness and unblemished beauty, there must be submission, however unwilling, to destruction and disintegration. It is, of course, a profoundly tragic interpretation of experience.

And in 1966 Nigeria endured a profound national tragedy, when there occurred two large-scale massacres of Igbo people living in Northern Nigeria by their Hausa neighbours. *Season of Anomy* is based on those massacres, which Soyinka witnessed. The two central characters are Ofeyi, a commercial libretto-writer working for a monolithic foreign-owned cocoa corporation, and Iriyise, the woman he loves, who sings his songs in cocoa sales-promotion. They belong to the spacious world of Western commercial glitter, but Ofeyi is already disillusioned, for the cocoa industry is part of the Cartel, which systematically plunders the country and is controlled by three corrupt politicians and their instrument, the military commander-in-chief. Ofeyi tries to undermine this power by writing songs that still seem to advance the cocoa sales-drive but indirectly call the power structure in question in such a way that the ordinary people grasp the message without the Cartel's being able to accuse him of actual subversion. In the course of their normal commercial activities, Ofeyi and Iriyise visit a remote communal settlement called Aiyéró, which is self-sufficient, practises common ownership of property and goods, and enjoys an immensely active, rather than complacent, peace of mind. The young people go out into the rest of the country to work, acquire skills, remit part of their income to the community, and always return home eventually. Ahime, an Aiyéró elder, explains: 'All our people know that we founded Aiyéró to seek truth, a better life, all the things which men run after. They also believe that we found it.' (p. 9) As Soyinka presents it, Aiyéró is an idealized African utopia on a modest scale, but it is apparently based on the actual crypto-Christian settlement of Aiyetoro in Nigeria.[10]

In Aiyéró Ofeyi and Iriyise witness the ritual sacrifice of bulls, the opening of 'red sluices for the land's replenishment' (p. 17). In the description of this symbolic ceremony, the language conveys an idea at the heart of the novel's meaning, that out of destruction can flow enrichment and renewal. Iriyise falls under the spell of the Aiyéró ideal; Ofeyi reluctantly finds himself surrendering to it too. Later he enlists the help of the men of Aiyéró who work outside the settlement, to form cells across the country intended to undermine the Cartel and ultimately apply the community's ideals to the nation at large. Before this peaceful evolution can begin to work, the Cartel strikes by organizing an orgy of killing (in the province where it enjoys most support) of all people living there who do not share the tribal and religious affiliations of the majority. Most of the novel covers Ofeyi's clandestine tour of the massacre areas, and it makes for the most bitter and deeply sombre writing yet produced by any African author: a pregnant woman disembowelled in front of a church that has been set on fire with the congregation locked up inside; a man done to death on a country road, his penis cut off and stuck in his mouth. The description of the mass of floating bodies at the irrigation dam site where the Aiyéró workers had been well organized (pp. 172–4) makes Soyinka's insistence in reporting such horrors very clear: it is a facing of the obscene reality of what Nigerian could do – has done – to Nigerian, African to African, man to man. In Soyinka's own words, 'a testament of damnation on earth'.

In terms of the narrative, Ofeyi observes all these horrors while on his quest for Iriyise, after her abduction by Cartel agents. It is during this descent into hell that Ofeyi is converted from his former rather facile humanism to the doctrine of the superbly created character, the Dentist, a professional assassin, and, surprisingly, also a man of Aiyéró. But the euphemistic name conveys exactly what seems to be Soyinka's new post-war concept of the legitimate use of violence as social surgery to prevent putrefaction from spreading. It is an important change in his thinking, when one recalls that in his early play, *A Dance of the Forests* (1963) he satirically made the deity Forest Head complain that what frightened him most about human beings was 'their latent violence'. Near the end of the novel Ofeyi finds Iriyise secreted in the very centre of a hell-like prison and in a coma. With the Dentist's help she is rescued. Here the correspondence with the Greek legend ends, for there is medical hope of Iriyise's recovery as the little procession takes to secret forest paths back to Aiyéró. While the Orpheus-Eurydice schema in the novel does lend intensity to the horrors that Ofeyi witnesses, what is crucial is the departure from the details of the legend. One has only to list the five sections into which the novel is divided: Seminal – Buds – Tentacles – Harvest – Spores; words associated with birth, life, growth, death, *new* life, not with death and damnation. The powerfully described ceremony early in the novel, of the blood of the bulls showering new life into the earth, recurs later and as a firmly established image suggests, together with the cyclic section-headings, that in trying to 'stay the season of [his] mind', to extract meaning from the massacres and the Civil War that followed them, Soyinka is affirming that the terrible Nigerian blood-letting is capable of providing replenishment for Nigeria's future. *Season of Anomy* announced a new radical political development in Soyinka's thinking since he wrote his first novel, *The Interpreters*.[11] The mythic mode is put to use in a devastating analysis of a further stage in neo-colonialism, its alliance with the local military. Against this destructive power Soyinka sets, in Aiyéró, the promise, however faint, of an African version of renewal through communalism.

Bessie Head's third novel, *A Question of Power*,[12] is set in rural Botswana, far removed from cartels and western-type commerce, but it is no idyll. The local, poverty-stricken people are being taught by foreign volunteers to wrest an austere living from a harsh environment, which seems an unlikely place for the moral luxury of the heroine's deep psychiatric disturbance. But, as the title indicates, *A Question of Power* deals with much more than the nervous breakdown of Elizabeth, a 'Coloured' South African trying to overcome the racial ignominy of her upbringing and to make a new life in Botswana. With no command over a single African language, with a religious and cultural background that is essentially 'European', she feels so alienated racially that over a period of three years her nights are plagued by nightmares of mental torture, and hallucinations later intrude into her waking hours also. There are two protagonists in the terrifying drama of her dreams, simultaneously partners in the attempted destruction of her personality, and adversaries for her allegiance. They bear the names, Sello and Dan, and the physical appearances, of two real people in the village whom Elizabeth knows only by sight. At first a god-like, becassocked figure, Sello enacts the lust for moral and spiritual powers in Elizabeth's personality; Dan enacts the carnal. Yet this level of meaning merges always with the macrocosmic, with the human use and abuse of spirituality and carnality in general, through the invocation of ancient Egyptian (Osiris and Isis), Hebrew (David and Uriah), Greek (Medusa) and Hindu (Mahamaya) myths, and frequent references to the wretched and oppressed throughout history, including 'the poor of Africa' (p. 31). Sello's association with Medusa suggests that even the most spiritually admirable human impulses are ultimately tinged by the hypocritical in private conduct and in the wielding of political power, so that Elizabeth is forced to the conclusion that God as an abstraction is the hideous confluence of Good and Evil.

In Part I, 'Sello', Elizabeth is deprived of any reliance upon the beneficent power of idealism: 'people . . . had been killed and killed and killed again in one cause after another for the liberation of mankind' (p. 31). In Part II, 'Dan', the Dan figure, all masculinity and practicality, with 'a huge, towering black penis', subjects her to a lurid cascade of obscenities, taunting her with being un-African, humiliating her, ultimately reaching his hands into her skull to destroy her mind. In Part I Elizabeth's torturing by Medusa becomes a symbol of humanity's sufferings, and in Part II the sexual obscenities symbolize the depravities in the human unconscious that surface from time to time to be practised under vicious political regimes. The whole vivid, whirling, at times bewildering, exhibition of Elizabeth's phantasmagorical inner life also constitutes a debate about the present and future of Africa, about its political experiments and the sort of power that is being exercised in African states. These brilliantly created scenes of nightmare are ironically interspersed with accounts of Elizabeth's calm daylight experiences in successfully establishing a co-operative vegetable garden as part of the local industries project in the village. Here, unconsciously, with simple, peasant people, Elizabeth is forging personal links of respect and love with the very Batswana who treat her with racial contempt in her nightmares. The almost lyrical descriptions of sunrise and sunset, of landscape, foliage, and birdsong, the simple ordinariness of human relationships in her waking life appear dreamlike beside the agonies of Elizabeth's nights, but it is this healthful normality that prevails. Elizabeth's acceptance of her full part in the austere but rewarding co-operative enterprise of making a garden out of barren sand heals the ravages of her own intellectuality, and makes her fully accepted in an Africa to which she comes to feel she belongs. I have discussed *A Question of Power* more fully elsewhere[13] and observed that Bessie Head's resilience as a novelist lies in the single-mindedness with which she confronts the tendency of political leaders, however laudable their aims, to lust in the injuring of ordinary people as they carry out those aims. *A Question of Power* recognizes this tendency as a horror that mankind can deal with, especially in Africa, not through cynicism or liberal abstention from action but through modest, practical action that undermines the absolutes and is energized by collective purpose.

These five utterly dissimilar novels by Nadine Gordimer, Ngugi, Armah, Soyinka, and Bessie Head that I have singled out do share some common thematic preoccupations: the predicament of the African peasantry and proletariat since Independence; the part played by Western-based industry in the economic exploitation of Africa; the implication that the highest demands of personal integrity must transfigure political action; the assurance that Africa can find itself again, that it has inherent resources of political power and energy of spirit yet to be tapped through communal enterprise. Whether by means of psychological and realist modes, or prophetic declamation, or by working through the mythic, the five novels handle very real twentieth-century political problems in Africa and do so on a substantial, comprehensive, and compelling scale. Because of the inventiveness with which the novelists apply their creative imagination to the relationship between individual and community in the context of the major political problems of Independent Africa, each of these five novels of the 1970s is, whatever its particular shortcomings, a disturbing, uncomfortable, but ultimately affirmative work that testifies impressively to the vitality of the African novel in English.

Notes

1 Nadine Gordimer, *A Guest of Honour* (New York, 1970; London, 1971), pages references are to the Penguin edition, 1973.
2 Nadine Gordimer, *The Conservationist* (London, 1974) and *Burger's Daughter* (London, 1979).
3 Ngugi wa Thiong'o, *Petals of Blood* (London, 1977).
4 Karel Schoeman, *Na die Geliefde Land* (literally, To the Beloved Country) (Cape Town, 1972); translated as *The Promised Land* (London, 1978).
5 Ayi Kwei Armah, *Two Thousand Seasons* (Nairobi, 1973; London, 1979), page references are to the Nairobi edition.
6 Ayi Kwei Armah, *The Beautyful Ones Are Not Yet Born* (London, 1968); *Fragments* (New York, 1970); *Why Are We So Blest?* (New York, 1972).
7 Wole Soyinka, *Myth, Literature and the African World* (London, 1976), p. 110.
8 Wole Soyinka, *Season of Anomy* (London, 1973).
9 Wole Soyinka, 'The Fourth Stage', in *Myth, Literature and the African World*.
10 See E. M. McClelland, 'The Experiment in Communal Living at Aiyetoro', *Comparative Studies in Sociology and History* (The Hague), vol. IX, no. 1 (1966), pp. 14–27; I am indebted to the Rev. M. Jarrett-Kerr, C. R., for drawing this article to my attention.
11 Wole Soyinka, *The Interpreters* (London, 1965).
12 Bessie Head, *A Question of Power* (London, 1974), page references are to the Heinemann paperback edition.
13 Arthur Ravenscroft, 'The Novels of Bessie Head', in Christopher Heywood (ed.), *Aspects of South African Literature* (London, 1976).

The Uses of Fiction
Edited by
Douglas Jefferson
and Graham Martin

13

Burger's Daughter: The Synthesis of Revelation

Margot Heinemann

Speaking some years ago about African writing (including in that term writing about Africa *not* by black Africans), Nadine Gordimer noted that its themes are very different from those that have preoccupied modern European and American writers.

> 'European writers from Beckett to Marguerite Duras are obsessed with human alienation and its consequent problem of communication . . . In Africa, it seems, the lines are still clear. The possibility of communication between man and man is taken for granted, it is what is conveyed that matters. Human beings still clash, rather than near-miss, in African writing.'[1]

Although her subject-matter and her perception of it as a white radical intellectual is inevitably different from that of black African writers, Nadine Gordimer is at one with them in rejecting 'hyper-introspection' and the impossibility of communication as major themes. One can't, however, consider her simply in specialist terms as a South African writer: still less as one whose best work timelessly transcends the setting from which it comes. It's because she has remained obstinately rooted in the tragic situation of her own country that hers has become a major voice in world literature.

Her novel *Burger's Daughter* (1979) is the outcome of a long process of development in her art, in her way of seeing, and in the world she writes about. This development becomes very striking if one reads her own selection of her short stories, *No Place Like* (Penguin, 1978) in the order in which they were written. As she says in her preface to that collection:

> 'I had wanted to arrange the selection in sequence from the earliest story collection to the latest simply because when reading story collections I myself enjoy following the development of a writer. Then I found that this order had another logic to which my first was complementary. The chronological order turns out to be an historical one. The change in social attitudes unconsciously reflected in the stories represents both that of the people in my society – that is to say, history – and my apprehension of it; in the writing, I am acting upon my society, and in the manner of my apprehension, all the time history is acting upon me.' (p. 13)

'Politics is about people' – it's a truism. But the political situation in South Africa, and hence its effect on people, is very different now from what it was thirty years ago. The white girl in an early Gordimer story like 'The Smell of Earth and Flowers', experiencing 'her generation's equivalent of religious ecstasy' through the unity of black and white in the passive civil disobedience campaign, belongs to the early 1950s. In later stories like 'Africa Emergent' or 'Open House' of the 1970s, white liberalism itself is collapsing. White sympathizers with the African cause now may often be regarded with suspicion (not without reason) as possible BOSS agents, rather than welcomed by black radicals with open arms.

With a great part of the African continent now independent of white rule, directly as a result of military action by black guerrillas and independence armies, civil rights in South Africa have been yet more drastically curtailed. Political campaigning has been driven underground, towards armed resistance. Segregation is stricter, black consciousness more intense. In Gordimer's early stories we have humble black servants fatalistically bemoaning their lot (as the Burgers' servant Lily or old people in Soweto still do in *Burger's Daughter*). In the later ones young black political refugees awaiting military training, or children demonstrating against Bantu education in defiance of the guns, become central to the fiction because they have become central to the consciousness of the time.

> 'In a certain sense the writer is "selected" by his subject – his subject being the consciousness of his era. How he deals with this is, to me, the

> fundament of commitment, although commitment is usually understood as the reverse process: a writer's selection of a subject in conformity with the rationalisation of his own ideological and/or political beliefs.' (*No Place Like*, p. 14)

The growth and complexity of *political* consciousness and involvement imposes changes in style and tone which are frankly disapproved and resented by some critics who greatly admired the earlier work. Thus the American critic Robert F. Haugh in his book-length treatment[2] places Nadine Gordimer 'among the masters' on the strength of a few 'timeless' short stories like the very early 'Is There Nowhere Else Where We Can Meet?' But when it comes to the novels, and especially later ones like *A Guest of Honour* (1970), that deeply felt study of tension and conflict in an African state after independence, Haugh compares her blacks regretfully with Shakespeare's Othello and Conrad's James Wait, for him 'the supreme creations of black men in literature' because they are 'superb human beings', 'authors of their woe'. Gordimer's novels, he thinks, over-emphasize race and sociology. 'Frequently the trouble is that in seeking a more sustained story structure Miss Gordimer is drawn into the sort of direct racial confrontation that she avoided in her most successful short stories.' (p. 161) Essentially it's the human and political implications of that 'direct racial confrontation' that the critic can't take.

And in one sense Haugh is right. In a short story the social origins of action and pain can still be mysterious, inexplicit; as a reader one can fill in the blanks or not, as one wishes, and yet feel one's taking the central point. In the later novels this is no longer possible: they're not just accumulations of impressions, but contain within themselves the movements and connections of history.[3]

Most modern political novels, at least in English, have dealt with people concerned with politics only to the extent that seems 'average'. From E. M. Forster's *Passage to India* to Paul Scott's *Raj Quartet*; from Graham Greene's *The Third Man* to *Our Man in Havana* or *The Human Factor*; from Alan Sillitoe's *Saturday Night and Sunday Morning* to Raymond Williams's *Border Country* – the people don't *want* to be involved in politics, it happens to them. This has been the form in many of Nadine Gordimer's novels and stories too, from *Is There Nowhere Else* and *A World of Strangers* (1958) to *Livingstone's Companions* (1972) and *The Conservationist* (1974). But because in the increasingly polarized situation in South Africa 'society is the political situation' and 'politics is character'[4], she now bases much of her fiction on people for whom political action to change society is at the centre of their lives – like the Indian working mother duplicating leaflets and going to prison in the story *A Chip of Glass Ruby* (1965), or the heroes of novels like *The Late Bourgeois World* (1966) and *A Guest of Honour* (1970), or now *Burger's Daughter* (1979) where she explores what it's like to be a Communist in a fiercely repressive capitalist society. And this is in some ways a rarer and more difficult achievement.

Nadine Gordimer is not a Communist. 'Non-political' is how she describes herself, in the sense that she has never joined a political party. But she's close enough to the subject to render her Communists, like her other characters, with that combination of 'close identification and monstrous detachment' which she sees as crucial to the novelist's art. 'The tension between standing apart and being fully involved; that is what makes the writer . . . The validity of this dialectic is the synthesis of revelation; our achievement of, or even attempt at this is the moral, the human justification for what we do'[5] – the justification, that is, for using other people's lives and sufferings as raw material. She avoids presenting any kind of 'typical Communist', whether romantic or steely-eyed. 'The faithful' are identifiable by what they do – a practical stubbornness and courage – but are otherwise very different people. It's not a question of a particular psychological or personality type – fanatical, insecure, father-fixated or whatever – being drawn to this kind of activity, though the activity itself, persisted in through the illegality and danger, may well bring out certain qualities in the activist.

The framework of *Burger's Daughter* is extremely simple. Plot in the ordinary sense is minimal; the underlying movement is in the mind of Rosa Burger. Child of two leading Communists – Lionel a doctor, Cathy former organizer of a mixed-race trade union – brought up in an atmosphere of political struggle and through years of increasing defeat and repression of the Left, so long as her much-loved father is on trial or serving a life-sentence Rosa feels she must unquestioningly bear her responsibility as last survivor of his family and his sole link with the outside world. When he dies in prison, she is free for the first time to choose what do with her life. She contrives to get herself a passport and leaves South Africa for Europe. There, staying in the South of France with her father's first wife Katya – who, unlike her own parents, has chosen to live for the sensuous present – she meets a French academic with whom she falls in love and has an idyllic affair. She plans to take a flat and make a life near him in Paris: he has a wife and family whom he can't leave, but they might have a child. But visiting London, she comes into contact with South African political exiles who reject much of what her father stood for. Renouncing the happiness of the Paris plan, she returns to South Africa and at the end – inevitably – to prison. And that's about all.

It's the meaning of this movement that the novel explores, mainly through Rosa's own consciousness (distinctly a 'fine consciousness' in Henry James's sense, observed as well as delicately observing). Her memory recreates her own childhood, in slightly easier times; the open hospitality of 'that house', the Burger house, where colour wasn't divisive (the children sharing baths and games with the little black boy, Baasie, son of an absent comrade), and it was taken for granted that you 'didn't belong to yourself' but to others, to the socialist and liberation movements, something you learned 'as other children learn to wash their hands'. The personal memories and flashbacks span also the historical and political changes of those years. As Rosa's driven to question and test old loyalties and principles, we're made to feel, as well as rationally to assess, the weight of the overpowering decision: can she, should she, how can she defect from the commitment and philosophy into which, without willing it, she was born?

Very little overtly happens or can happen in the novel, except the inner history of the heroine. Always in South Africa she's under surveillance, a 'named person'. Close friends are watched, in prison or under house-arrest. When she escapes, it's to a world where, by the terms of the understanding on which she's granted a passport, she can meet no-one significant to the South African struggle. A similar focussing on the inner action is at the centre of *Samson Agonistes*, another work about a revolutionary enduring the aftermath of disaster and the failure of the good old cause.

The narrative method is flexible, centred in Rosa's own observation, but shifting easily to other minds, to the impersonal reports of 'surveillance', the hostile record of the political police – in the main quite unobtrusively. One notices these changes only when a particular contrast in angle of vision is important to the story. Crucial moments are often represented not in narrative form but as scenes, in highly articulate conversation and discussion among the characters – the kind of thing which R. F. Haugh dismisses as 'sociological', but which the intensity of the underlying conflict sustains and makes exciting.

Strict adherence to a single point of view, whatever its formal and dramatic advantages, could have given only a linear version of what needs to be shown as a highly complex process. Nadine Gordimer deliberately uses a montage of different views and voices, integrated to represent a single action. She doesn't, in fact, allow 'point of view' to get in the way of the human story she has to tell, but she does exploit it for dramatic and ironic effect. The cutting between different views places the central consciousness of Rosa (as of Bray in *A Guest of Honour*) within a society, while allowing the reader freedom to move and evaluate. Like the novelist, we're obliged to be both objective and involved.

Moreover, Rosa's first-person monologue – partly because of her isolation, there is unfashionably much of it – is itself subtly varied in presentation. As she explains at the beginning:

> 'One is never talking to oneself, always one is addressed to someone. Suddenly, without knowing the reason, at different stages of one's life, one is addressing this person or that all the time, even dreams are performed before an audience.' (*Burger's Daughter*, p. 16)[6]

What we call the self is, in fact, socially created. In the first part of the book, in South Africa, Rosa's inner speech is usually addressed to her drop-out friend Conrad. Later, in the French section, there's a good deal of 'straight' talking to herself, but sometimes briefly she'll converse in her mind with Katya or with her lover Bernard. Only in the final South African episodes are her thoughts addressed to her father: a connection is resumed.

The dominating consciousness remains Rosa's, and our sympathy with that sensitive, tough, self-mocking, occasionally bitchy voice organizes the novel. The other views distance the events, carry us quickly through historical time (in conversations with Burger's biographer), or allow us to see Rosa as well as see through her eyes. But the commentary on her thoughts and actions, the discovery of what she's really doing, has to be her own; and it's the absence of omniscient narrator here that makes the moments of inner climax dramatic and astounding.

Thus at the opening of the novel, when Rosa as a schoolgirl stands outside the prison gates with comforts for her mother, the description we're offered is at first strictly external, the impersonal view of 'surveillance', or of her headmistress. Fourteen years old, a 'promising senior' in her brown and yellow school uniform, she's small for her age, 'slightly bottle-legged (first hockey team)', with a strand of her hair 'bleached lighter due to contact with chemicals in the school pool (second swimming team) and exposure to the sun.' Such details imply the contrast between what might reasonably be her preoccupations at that age and what, for Burger's daughter, they have to be. At school, we're told,

> 'Her matter-of-fact and reserved manner made it unnecessary for anyone to have to say anything – anything sympathetic – indeed, positively forbade it, and so saved awkwardness. She displayed 'remarkable maturity'; that, at least, without being specific, one could say in the report.' (p. 9)

Contrasted with this, in the next brief shot, an emotional sympathizer describes 'little Rosa Burger . . . dry-eyed and composed . . . an example to us all of the way a detainee's family ought to behave.' (p. 12) But the ironic inner voice of Rosa herself immediately places this as the view of a sentimental amateur, 'a grown-up who made me feel older than she was'. (p. 15) For Rosa is by birth and training a professional revolutionary. On her own initiative she brings a hot-water bottle, something her mother never uses, so as to smuggle in a note twisted round the stopper. In secret – neither surveillance nor sympathizers will know this – she's coping with a bad adolescent period-pain: that's the extra suffering that sticks in her memory. Here, as throughout the novel, we're reminded that these highly articulate, intelligent activists live not only through the brain, but like anyone else, physically and sexually from the waist downwards.

Through Conrad, the hippy student she partly lives with in a casual, intermittently sexual relationship during her father's trial and life-sentence, Rosa's inherited values are forced onto the defensive. Freedom, to him, is wholly individual and asocial, the right to do your own thing. Parents and their values are part of what you reject or escape from. (His own mother had a lover: he hated and desired her.) As for Rosa, she's grown up entirely through other people, he tells her, doing what they told her was appropriate: rationality, extraversion. 'Life isn't there'.

> 'Among you, the cause is what can't die . . . It's immortality. If you can accept it. Christian resignation's only one example. A cause more important than an individual is another. The same con, the future in place of the present. Lives you can't live, instead of your own. You didn't cry when your father was sentenced. I saw. People said how brave. Some people say, a cold fish. But it's conditioning, brain-washing: more like a trained seal, maybe.' (p. 52)

Conrad, of course, speaks for many young radicals of his and Rosa's generation. And while she effectively answers him back, at deeper levels the conflict goes on in her mind, fuelled by the feeling of guilt that so often goes with bereavement:

> 'When I was passive, in that cottage, if you had known – I was struggling with a monstrous resentment against the claim – not of the Communist Party! – of blood, shared genes, the semen from which I had issued and the body in which I had grown . . . My mother is dead and there is only me, there, for him . . . Only me. My studies, my work, my love affairs must fit in with the twice-monthly visits to the prison, for life, as long as he lives – if he had lived . . . And now he is dead! . . . I knew I must have wished him to die . . ' (p. 62)

All her life has been geared, as she now sees it, to her parents' commitment. Before she'd ever had a real love-affair she had to pretend to be engaged to a prisoner, a boy with Frelimo links, so that she could use the fiancée's privilege of letters and visits to keep him in touch with the movement. The pretended feelings became, on her side, desperately real: but if her mother realized Rosa's passionate involvement 'she didn't choose to see'. Released, the boy left South Africa at once; she didn't meet him again. Recalling that time, Rosa accuses both mother and father.

At the initial crisis of the book she refuses – for the first time in her life – to do what 'the faithful' expect of her. She has recently renewed contact, illicitly, with her father's old friends and comrades, the house-arrested Terblanches. Just afterwards their daughter seeks Rosa out to ask her to borrow her firm's key to the photocopying room, so that they can get a duplicate made and print leaflets there. Rosa won't do it. Even more of a break with the tradition – she explains to Clare Terblanche *why* she won't. She's no longer prepared to conform, to sacrifice everything to *The Future* that never comes, and that might be unfree and repressive if it did. Dismissing Clare's arguments (which she knows already), Rosa notes her snuffling ungracefulness, her lack of sexual charm – irrelevant logically, but a kind of retaliation for her own sense of guilt.

The relationship with the older Terblanches is wonderfully done, and crucial for the novel. They are incontrovertibly good and heroic, in terms of action and selfless service to their cause (both have been in prison). They are also, as Rosa at this point sees them, ungraceful, uncharismatic, physically ageing, mentally inflexible, as parents demanding, as friends tactless. The mixture of feelings – love and admiration, fear and recoil, as from something threatening – permeates the precise physical observation which allows Rosa to see *the cause* separate from the deep emotional commitment to her own parents.

> 'Like many people who have high blood-pressure, Ivy Terblanche's emotions surfaced impressively: her voice was off-hand but her eyes glittered liquid glances and her big breast rose against abstract-patterned nylon. Lionel Burger once described how, when she was still permitted to speak at public meetings, she "circled beneath the discussion and then spouted like some magnificent female whale".' (p. 107)

The passage implies more than it states. Ivy is ageing and unattractive, her clothes cheap and ugly, her rhetoric out of date. Yet her courage and persistence are beyond praise. And the charming, civilized voice of Rosa's father – accepting and valuing her, yet able to 'place' her with saving humour – is no longer there to distance her demands.

> 'In the enveloping acceptance of Ivy's motherly arms – she feels as if I were her own child – there is expectance, even authority. To her warm breast one can come home again and do as you said I would, go to prison.' (p. 114)

Dick is even more touchingly heroic. An old sheet-metal worker, in 'solitary' he couldn't remember poems as some prisoners could, to keep his mind occupied, so instead he carved in his imagination a whole dining-room suite, 'barley-sugar uprights, with round knobs on top . . . man, it was craftsmanship'. (p. 107) And it's he who hints of hope:

> 'Not long now, Rosa. Angola will go, Mozambique; they won't last another year . . . Too late for Lionel, but you're here, Rosa. (p. 108)

But Rosa isn't with him (ironically, since the reader must know that Angola and Mozambique *did* 'go'):

> 'Dick, with those ugly patches on his poor hands, said to me like a senile declaration of passion: we are still here to see it. He thought I was overcome at the thought of my father. But I was filled with the need to get away as from something obscene – and afraid to wound him – them – by showing it . . .'

His still-passionate optimism seems grotesque to her because the world in which the unquestioning belief of these old Communists was formed – the confidence that shines from their faces in Moscow peace conference photographs of the 40s and 50s – no longer exists. It's not only the bitterness of one defeat after another that makes it all seem 'obscene'. Even more, it's the question from a girl brought up to feel public tragedies as acutely as personal ones – after Hungary and Prague, what can one still believe?

> '. . . When the Russians moved into Prague my father and mother and Dick and Ivy and all the faithful were still promising the blacks liberation through Communism, as they had always done. Bambata, Bulhoek, Bondelswart, Sharpeville; the set of horrors the faithful use in their secretly printed and circulated pamphlets. Stalin trials, Hungarian uprising, Czechoslovakian uprising – the other set that the Liberals and right-wing use to show it isn't possible for humane people to be Communists. Both will appear in any biography of my father.
>
> 'In 1956 when the Soviet tanks came into Budapest I was his little girl, dog-paddling to him with my black brother Baasie, the two of us reaching for him as a place where no fear, hurt or pain existed. And later, when he was in jail and I began to think back, even I, with my precocious talents for evading warders' comprehension now in full maturity, could not have found the way to ask him – in spite of all these things: do you still believe in the Future? The same Future? just as you always did?' (p. 115)

The contradiction is unresolvable. Yet she does not find it easy to break her commitment to the Terblanches and her childhood, harder still to give up the sense of unity and solidarity directly with black militants. How hard, we feel when she embraces Marisa Kgosana, friend of her father and A. N. C. leader, met by chance in a department store. Just back from visiting her jailed husband on Robben Island, Marisa is trying out the face-cream 'being rubbed on to her plum-dark skin with one white finger' by an admiring saleslady (who assumes the beautiful black woman must be a visitor from the *French* islands). Her dignity is complete and relaxed. She doesn't even need to be physically faithful like Penelope: one lives as one can. Restriction and surveillance are a different matter if one comes from Soweto:

> 'The comfort of black. The persistence, resurgence, daily continuity that is the mass of them. If one is not afraid, how can one not be attracted? . . . Marisa and Joe Kgosana have all this to draw on . . . Behind *our* kind, who are confined to the magisterial areas of the white suburbs, are people who sent obscene letters calling my father a monster.' (p. 143)

It wouldn't take much to draw Rosa into that orbit, as she realizes when she goes, illicitly, to a party in Soweto. 'I felt a dangerous surge of feeling, a precipitation towards Marisa . . . a longing to let someone else use me, lend me passionate purpose, propelled by meaning other than my own.' She's saved from that by the young 'black consciousness' activists she meets at the same gathering, hostile to all whites including herself. The sincerity and sacrifice of people like her father, so admired by the older generation of blacks there, is rudely ignored or rejected by the younger, who have no experience of any joint struggle with whites (the stricter Apartheid laws have seen to that!). Although theoretically Rosa understands their bitterness, emotionally their reaction makes it easier for her to apply secretly for a passport (something none of 'the faithful' would ever do, except on orders) and to leave South Africa, perhaps only for a holiday, perhaps for good.

Everything experienced up to now contributes to this step. The kindness of well-off liberals like Flora Donaldson, who 'fellow-travels beside suffering as a sports enthusiast in a car keeps pace alongside a marathon runner'; the complacency of the new African small-business people; the old man found insanely beating a donkey to death, whom Rosa dare not hand over to the police because he's black – after all this 'I don't know how to live in Lionel's country.' In the end, she goes to Europe to defect from him.

The South of France scenes are perhaps less convincing. Katya and her friends – ageing beauties, warm-hearted courtesans a little past it, homosexuals running gay bars, handsome young lovers bought by rich Americans – have charm enough, but scarcely the substance to sustain their part in the novel. They can't provide a strong enough image of what's attractive in European civilization, even a decaying civilization, to suggest that 'whole world outside what Lionel lived for'. And Katya herself, still in middle age living sensuously for sunshine and nightingales, is perhaps too directly the mirror-opposite of Cathy Burger, a dream-alternative mother who makes no demands and only wants the child to be happy in the enjoyment of sex and French cuisine.

But the weakness, if it is one, is peripheral. For the love-affair, for which this is only the setting, is admirably rendered in all its sexual delight and ambiguity. Bernard Chabalier, young, sympathetic and sensitive, is distanced not only from Rosa's particular South African experience, but from the need to act on one's convictions which is more hereditary and enduring than the unquestioning conviction itself. The curious recent relation of many near-Marxist European intellectuals to the untidy and tragic political struggle has never been better shown. It's delicately suggested by Bernard's flippant description of the thesis on French colonialism he's writing (p. 272):

> 'You choose something you hope someone else isn't writing about already. That's the extent of the originality . . . If you are too topical, the interest will have passed on to something else before you've finished . . . But the influence of former French colonists who've come back to France since the colonial empire ended – I haven't got a working title yet – that's something that will go on for years. I don't have to worry.' (p. 272)

And when Rosa, fascinated by the theme, asks why he can't write a book rather than a thesis, he answers frankly that he needs the Ph.D., or he won't get out of school-teaching into a University job.

> 'You don't know how careful we are, we French Leftist bourgeoisie.'

The space between thought and action seems to Bernard normal and natural for his kind. He lives within it, signing Amnesty petitions protesting against the abuse of psychiatry in the Soviet Union and censorship in Argentina, giving talks on *France Culture* – 'usually the sociological consequences of political questions – that sort of programme'. For him, disillusion with the Future assumed as inevitable by 'the faithful' produces not an agonizing conflict – as it must for Rosa Burger – but a freedom from responsibility for any future at all.

The contrast defines itself during a cosmopolitan intellectual discussion where Bernard attacks 'the new anti-Sovietism of the Left' as still not sharp enough in condemning Socialist illusions. 'Socialism is the horizon of the world, but it's a blackout.' Following up, an English Parliamentarian rejects the entire Socialist vision as 'evil utopia'.

> 'When rationalism destroyed heaven and decided to set it up here on earth, that most terrible of all goals entered human ambition. It was clear there'd be no end to what people would be made to suffer for it . . .' (p. 295)

Suddenly Rosa sees the whole group with amazement, and Bernard as one of them. 'For a moment her presence went among them like an arm backing them away from something lost and trampled underfoot' (a poetic image that precisely conveys the *emotional* intensity of the political moment). She mocks their proposition – to her absurd – that 'you can't institutionalise happiness'.

> 'There isn't the possibility of happiness without institutions to protect it . . . I'm talking about people who need to have rights – *there* in a statute book, so that they can move about in their own country.' (p. 295)

'Oh well, ordinary civil rights. That's hardly utopia.' In conceding her point they dismiss it. But Rosa carries it further, as if seeing for a moment the relations of things.

> ' "But the struggle for change is based on the idea that freedom exists, isn't it? That wild idea. People must be able to create institutions – institutions *must evolve* that will make it possible in practice. That utopia, it's inside . . . without it, how can you . . . act?" – The last word echoed among them as "live", the one she had unconsciously substituted it for.' (p. 296)

But although the distance between the lovers, instinctive as well as rational, has been tellingly established, it's not at this point that the love-affair gives out. (Gordimer is too subtle an observer for that.) Indeed Rosa is so much physically in love (as she never was with Conrad) that Bernard's honesty doesn't seem to break what's between them, even when he tells her:

> 'I want to say to you – you can't enter someone else's cause or salvation. Look at those idiots singing in the streets with shaved heads a few years ago . . . They won't attain the Indian nirvana . . . – The same with your father and the blacks – their freedom. You'll excuse me for saying . . . the same with you and the blacks.' (p. 297)

The way out opens into the personal life. For the time being the flow of feeling carries her on towards it with a sense of release – the more that it does not even require the public status and obligation of marriage. Yet this conversation prepares the way for the decisive confrontation of the book – one which, in its violent and overwhelming discharge of accumulated tensions, is even more deeply related to Henry James than are the delicate elaborations of style.

Rosa has not reacted, at any conscious level at least, against Bernard's dismissal of her heritage. Awaiting him in London, she feels free to make contact with the anti-Apartheid circles she has avoided so long as she intended to go back to South Africa. At a social gathering of political exiles, black and white, she is the centre of sympathy and moving speeches, as Burger's daughter. Ironically, at the moment when she's being publicly acclaimed she has already opted out. And it's exactly at that point that she recognizes the little black boy Baasie ('little master'), with whom she shared a bed and a bath and a father, till her parents were taken to prison and the children were split up. The meeting after twenty years is awkward, strained: but she presses her phone number on him. Later at night he rings her – angry and insulting – and the whole thing explodes in her face as he attacks not only Rosa but the memory of her father:

> 'Everyone in the world must be told what a great hero he was and how much he suffered for the blacks. Everyone must cry over him and show his life on television and write in the papers. Listen, there are dozens of our fathers sick and dying like dogs, kicked out of the locations when they can't work any more. Getting old and dying in prison. Killed in prison. It's nothing, it's us, we must be used to it, it's not going to show on English television . . .' (p. 319)
>
> 'Whatever you whites touch, it's a takeover . . . Even when we get free they'll want us to remember to thank Lionel Burger.' (p. 320)

For Baasie has moved on. He's no longer the 'little black kid' she remembers. His father too has died in prison, reported hanged with his own prison pants. Why should he want to know her? In his need to make his future he, even more than she, has remade and devalued the past. Her reaction is an intense contradiction of feelings – rage, nausea, desire to defend her father, revulsion and hatred of Baasie. 'Impulses of cruelty' come 'exhilarating along her bloodvessels' as she snaps out one insult after another, accusing him of wanting money, implying that he ought to be in the bush with the Freedom Fighters, denying that either of them has the right to judge her father, 'unless you want to think being black is your right'. When it's finished, she's left with the overwhelming awareness of a commitment from which she will *never* be able to escape.

It's in the shock after this experience that her thoughts, for the first time in the book, become conversation with Lionel Burger himself. The effect is startling and strangely moving. What she strives for above all is his cool rationality. Her father would have understood Baasie's anger as a phase in the growing movement, never retaliated in a way she herself now feels to be 'filthy and ugly'. And now, inevitably, she has to go back. The idyll with Bernard, perfection of a kind, is never mocked. Simply, she realizes that 'no-one can defect'.

The change we feel when she returns to South Africa, however, isn't only in Rosa but in the political situation itself. For the black people's movement, quiescent for years, suddenly bursts into action on a vast and unexpected scale. No longer fighting the bond of feeling she inherits from her father, Rosa passionately observes and interprets as if for him the Soweto school riots of 1976, where tens of thousands of black children protest against the inferior education (compulsorily in Afrikaans) that sums up their oppression by whites in their own country. In a way Lionel couldn't have foreseen, the children are radicalizing the parents; yet such unforeseeable transformations are the essence of his vision. As Rosa herself puts it, 'the real Rosa [she means Rosa Luxemburg] believed the real revolutionary initiative was to come from the people: you named me for that'.

The children's protest, even if it's still blindly anti-white, in its courage recalls Lionel Burger. It liberates Rosa from the sense of futility and mere habit in continuing her parents' work. Whatever was mechanically copied from older generations has to be relearned; the role of whites in the movement can't be the same as in the past. Yet they have to be there: 'Like everyone else, I do what I can.'

As a physiotherapist Rosa helps to rehabilitate black children smashed up by the police. And secretly she renews contact with Marisa Kgosana and the black activitists in Soweto. Before long continuity asserts itself in another way; she's arrested without charges, perhaps to be used in a big political trial of Marisa herself. Rosa, Clare Terblanche, Marisa are all held in the same prison. The sympathizers standing outside the gates provide visits and parcels on her behalf, as she did for her mother at the beginning.

The ending is still in some degree 'open'; for Nadine Gordimer deliberately presents the reader with a fine balance between despair and difficult hope. It would be possible to see what happens to Rosa as simply the working-out of an Oedipal fixation, a tragic inability to free herself from her father's deluded shadow and to live. Yet we learn through indirect report that even in solitary confinement she's in touch with the others. Marisa sings hymns and pop-songs that can be heard outside her cell: she develops a mysterious spinal ailment for which Rosa is allowed to give her physiotherapy. 'Laughter escaped through the black diamond mesh and bars of Rosa's cell during these sessions.' The symbolic sensual contact of black and white is re-established. As for Rosa herself, her only permitted visitor, the maligned but loyal Flora Donaldson, testifies, 'She's all right. In good shape. She looked like a little girl . . . About fourteen . . . except she's somehow livelier than she used to be. In a way. Less reserved.' One would have to bring an irremovable set of responses (Conrad's, perhaps?) not to feel some renewal of hope.

To represent a revolutionary hero is in some ways a particularly difficult thing for the novelist, and just painting in a few warts is no solution. For here the simple one-to-one equation of radical politics and immediate everyday human motive no longer operates. 'I am not a politically-minded person by nature,' says Nadine Gordimer. 'I have come to the abstractions of politics through the flesh and blood of individual behaviour. I didn't know what politics was about till I saw it happening to people.'[7] But if the novel is to be a novel and not a tract, how does the writer depict a character who, as well as a humanitarian activist, is a leader who has to deal with 'the abstractions of politics'? For the fully-committed revolutionary leader doesn't simply *experience* racial oppression and class conflict spontaneously, as personal material fact, on the time-scale of his single human life. He must also perceive what's outside himself and analyse it rationally, conceptually, in the lives of others as in his own, in order to intervene in history, knowing that the time-scale of change he must consider spans many generations. And it's this quality in her father to which Rosa finally and unsentimentally returns – the 'sane habit of analysis of our kind', the 'sweet lucidity' which gives him, in the face of all that can be done to him in the moment, a sublime calm.[8]

That people can rule their lives like this gives them, to outsiders like Conrad or Katya or in the end Bernard, a chilling quality that's slightly unreal. For the reader living in a less extreme situation, the stance could easily seem priggish. Yet in a novel about this particular (and far from unique) history, it is, I think, convincing – and not only because of the known analogies between the heroism of Lionel Burger and that of real-life leaders like Bram Fischer or Nelson Mandela, on which it's partly based. What impresses in Burger's life, as in his speech from the dock (the only time we hear his voice), is not a blind faith, but a reasoned though fallible one based on the best available evidence; not a heroic adventurist gesture but a calculated risk; not the courage of one man alone but that of thousands. His daughter sums it up:

> 'Who among those who didn't like your vocabulary, your methods, has put it as honestly? Who are they to make you responsible for Stalin and deny you Christ?' (p. 349)

Even on the left different readings are possible. The oddest critical view of *Burger's Daughter* I have read is that it 'has nothing to say', is not revolutionary, and hardly deserved the honour of being banned in South Africa. (The chairman of the censors, rescinding the ban, said almost the same thing.)[9] But of course a political novel, if it's any good, is not as a rule political in the same way as a pamphlet or a treatise. Its effect is diffused and tends to operate more slowly, at different levels and over a longer period. Nadine Gordimer herself said of this book 'I don't have any intention in the way [the censors] say I do. I'm not preaching, I'm exploring.' To do that, in the fearless sense she understands it, is commitment enough.

Notes

1 *African writing*, Lectures given at University of Cape Town's Public Summer School, Feb. 1972 (Cape Town, 1972).
2 R. F. Haugh, *Nadine Gordimer* (New York, 1974).
3 Indeed it could be argued that as novels they have almost *too* much unity: that *every* detail is relevant to the central meaning, as in the short story it must be, and we miss something of the randomness and oddness of the world we know, where some details matter and others are merely there, uninterpreted, relevant perhaps to some other story about different people – an effect on which partly depends the sense of space and openness one gets from *War and Peace* or *Anna Karenina*.
4 Nadine Gordimer, 'A Writer in South Africa', *London Magazine*, Vol. 5, No. 2, May 1965.
5 Author's introduction to *No Place Like* (Hardmondsworth: Penguin, 1975), p. 12.
6 This and subsequent quotations are taken from *Burger's Daughter*, London 1979.
7 'A Writer in South Africa', *loc. cit.*
8 Bray, the hero in *A Guest of Honour*, achieves this kind of rationality, though it doesn't save his life. Max, the young saboteur-betrayer in *The Late Bourgeois World*, who lacks it, is consumed by a personal need for recognition which makes him a traitor and destroys him in the end.
9 The novel was banned by the South African censorship in June 1979 on the grounds that 'the authoress exploits the black–white dichotomy in South Africa for political ends. The negative is stressed; the positive ignored.' In October 1979 the Publications Appeals Board lifted the ban, the chairman, a former judge, commenting afterwards that the book was 'very badly written . . . this is why we eventually passed it. We knew our people wouldn't read it anyway.' (From feature article in *Observer*, 23.3.80.)

The Uses of Fiction
Edited by
Douglas Jefferson
and Graham Martin

14

Love and Sympathy in Virginia Woolf

Barbara Hardy

The novel is an affective medium. Not wholly so, because it argues and discusses as well as expressing feeling. Indeed, its mode of inquiry cannot be separated from its expression and manipulation of feeling, since its medium is mixed, conducting experiments and inquiries in ways which are impassioned, personal, and particular. Its expression of feeling, conscious and unconscious, personal and social, is controlled and checked by its habits of investigation. It expresses and meets affective needs in author and reader, but also questions the nature and function of the affections. As it creates character, in the forms of symbol or realistic image, it erodes and modifies myths, fictions, and conventions about feeling and passions. In the novels of Virginia Woolf, fictitious characters are equipped with a reflective intelligence which analyses their affective experience; she creates dynamic models of feeling which are experimental and questioning. Like our first novelists of sensibility, Richardson and Sterne, she also uses explicit comment, generalization, and interrogation. In *Jacob's Room* (1922) for instance, she observes that though we have maps of London, the passions remain uncharted.[1] Like her contemporaries, D. H. Lawrence and E. M. Forster, she is aware of our ignorance of feeling and passion, and this awareness brings her art close to Lawrence's own declared effort to use fiction to educate the feelings.

Like all novelists, she uses the traditional form of the love-story, and like many novelists, rebels against its constrictions and conventions. In her first novels, *The Voyage Out* (1915), *Night and Day* (1919), and *Jacob's Room*, analysis of feeling is expressed in the double medium of authorial guide and dramatized characters. The guide comes to be replaced by the analytic drama of characters, which itself becomes more fragmented until it is undermined by the lyricism and self-questioning of *The Waves* (1931), where Bernard's doubts as to whether there can really be 'a story' reinforce the breakdown of narrative patterns of feeling. The seeds of doubt appear from the start. Even her early characters feel, then doubt what they feel, always alert to puzzles of love and sympathy. They feel, act, meditate, act again, undo action, and make provisional decisions and ties. They reveal, hide, express, suppress, darken, clarify, misunderstand, and understand what they are, as feeling creatures. Sometimes they sound the ancient theme – older than the novel – of reason's conflict with passion. They are up against the difficulty of using our inadequate language for feeling – what are these things called love, hate, anger, jealousy, and fear? The passions often appear in their traditional guise, calling attention to their nature and function, so as to question received opinions. Like all novelists, Virginia Woolf has special interests within the common stock of human passions. She tells and changes the story of desire, union, and separation, but enlarges this story, seeing romantic and sexual love as aspects of creativity, sympathy, and empathy. She is also especially alert to the influence of social roles in the life of feeling, analysing the emotions of parent and child, mother and father, man and woman.

One of the central themes in her novels is the collision between what we are expected to feel with what we do feel. She conceives characters whose social and sexual self-awareness creates new stereotypes, like Lily Briscoe and Miss La Trobe, artists whose modes of love and sympathy bring new questions and discomforts. She is good at blurring the lines between defined roles, showing unexpected or incongruous motions of feeling, like Lily's blend of aesthetic imagination with reluctant 'womanly' sympathy, or Mrs Ramsay's private rebellions against the demands of maternal and wifely love. Her sense of socially determined patterns of feeling seems to lead Virginia Woolf to an awareness of a conscious tension between freedom and determinism. She can catch her characters in the very act of fighting or succumbing to their roles. Indeed, she can show them catching themselves in the act of feeling more or less than the social role requires. Mrs

Ramsay's inner life is seen as larger and vaguer than the social selection and reduction which is on public view. Virginia Woolf is sensitive to the strange stop–go of passion, the instability of the emotional pulse, the irregularity and complexity of loving compared with the regularity and singleness of loving in love-stories. She is alive to the nuances of public appearances and private experiences. She shows how affective roles display themselves, in language and act, as distortedly hard-edged and definite. She is too intelligent not also to know and show that patterns of feeling may seem clear and secure and defined at one moment, blurred or dark in the next. The inner life is inspected, dramatized, and scrupulously placed in the environment of external constraints.

Manner and matter are welded together: the artist's mode of presentation is her mode of analysis. She creates characters who question sympathy, and who awaken the reader's sympathy. She promotes various types of aesthetic continuity in her narrative and drama, yet questions the nature of continuity. She uses the traditional tropes of metaphor, metonymy, and allegory, to define, fix, and excite, in a rhetoric which works on the reader, but which is internalized and made visibly characteristic of the generation of feeling in her characters. As the characters act out and act in love-stories, they examine the nature of love. As her artists respond, invent, and imagine, they examine the process of perception and making. The methods and materials shift as her art moves through a noviciate into maturity. Her novels examine the nature of feeling in a constantly re-created variety of affective forms.

In her first two novels, *The Voyage Out* and *Night and Day*, Virginia Woolf follows a long tradition of the analysis of love. She inspects conventions and assumptions of feeling, in carefully defined environments of society and nature. In *The Voyage Out* Terence reads a passage from a silly novel, making Rachel ask 'Why don't people write about the things they do feel?' and 'What are the things people do feel?' (p. 304). One of the things people feel in good novels is that they aren't sure what they feel. Stendhal, Thackeray, and Hardy raised the question of uncertain, ambiguous, amorphous, and malleable feeling, in a social and psychological analysis of individual lives and specified environments. Julien Sorel, Pendennis, Blanche Amory, and Eustacia Vye feel that they can change and influence their affective life by taking ambitious thought. Through the characters' efforts, successes and conflicts, their authors unravel a tangled process of moving from feelings which seem real, sincere, or genuine, to feelings which seem illusory, imagined, provisional and assumed. What they recognize and show in these characters, their social contexts, and their social movements, is not simply the distortion of the life of feeling. *Le Rouge et le Noir*, *Pendennis*, and *The Return of the Native* show that performance and assumption can move an act into reality. These novels brilliantly undermine what may seem like the hard-and-fast distinction between sincerity and insincerity. They also contemplate social determinism. Virginia Woolf's analysis of feeling is not always as radical or as subtle as that of these great predecessors. It is, however, freshly enterprising. She is not a socially innocent novelist, but her social analysis tends to take place in a narrow space, and that narrow space does not expand, microcosmically, like Jane Austen's narrow spaces. When Virginia Woolf looks at conventions and restrictions, they tend to belong to a class, rather than a cross-section of society. This is no reason to be ungrateful for what she does, but she is narrower than Stendhal and Thackeray because their great subjects of social movement, class conflict and class aspiration, lie beyond her scope.

She is, however, aware of society's power to restrict and falsify the emotional and erotic relationships of men and women. In *Night and Day* Katherine Hilbery is cleverly placed in a bookish environment, but deprived of conventional literary misdirection. Neither a Catherine Morland nor a Maggie Tulliver, she helps her mother write a biography and takes refuge (not wholly convincingly) in the secret pursuit of mathematics. She is sickened by the great theme of literature, 'that perpetual effort to understand one's own feeling, and express it beautifully, fitly, or energetically in language' (pp. 38–9). This literary antipathy may act as authorial disguise in a fairly autobiographical novel, but it is not merely a mask. Disliking literature makes Katharine ignorant of what literature might have shown her – a girl who had read more mightn't have been so amazed by the irregular pulse of love. The antipathy makes her so impatient of self-examination that she adopts the most conventional course open to a young woman of her class and time, and gets engaged with a perversity almost worthy of Edith Dombey. (But Katharine is milk and water compared with Edith's fire and ice.) She is so doubtful about love that she decides to do without, until her author puts her in the way of the real thing.

The second stage in her sentimental education is the process of confusion, identification and anxiety. The novel analyses a complex consciousness, for instance, as Katharine only half-listens to the story her lover relates, and infers love from a state of happiness. The narrative rhythm reveals any lapses of feeling, when desire and affection switch off. The characters are taken rather too seriously as they dash around and analyse their erratic rhythms, and as usual in Virginia Woolf, the course of love gets rather oddly, because sexlessly, done. But the novel faces the disconcerting experience of real feeling, as opposed to expected feeling. It puts out tentative antennae into possibilities of new forms of relationship.

The third novel, *Jacob's Room*, is not an analysis of affection and sentiment but takes its place in the history of feeling in fiction because of its delicate and sympathetic understatement. The narrator adopts a tentative, exterior view of her characters, sometimes vouching for their inner lives but usually presenting them as persons to be read, like most people outside novels, from distant or objective views. They are inferred through objects, rooms and houses. The narrator is not 'a character' like Conrad's Marlow, but fully fleshed in feeling, like the narrator in George Eliot's late novels. The commentary is written in a personal voice which speaks only in general terms, like the tones of an autobiographer who can only express feeling without narrative causality. The feeling often emerges from a character's feeling, as in this passage, which is provoked by Clara Durrant's entry in her diary, 'I like Jacob Flanders,' (p. 68), and by several other opinions, indifferent or warm:

> 'It seems then that men and women are equally at fault. It seems that a profound, impartial, and absolutely just opinion of our fellow-creatures is utterly unknown. Either we are men, or we are women. Either we are cold, or we are sentimental. Either we are young, or growing old. In any case life is but a procession of shadows, and God knows why it is that we embrace them so eagerly, and see them depart with such anguish, being shadows. And why, if this and much more than this is true, why are we yet surprised in the window corner by a sudden vision that the young man in the chair is of all things in the world the most real, the most solid, the best known to us – why indeed? For the moment after we know nothing about him.
>
> Such is the manner of our seeing. Such the conditions of our love.' (p. 69)

Granting the substantial differences between a novel written in 1859 and one written in 1922, this sympathetic narration can be put beside George Eliot's narrative commentaries. Like them, it speaks with anonymity, impersonality and authority, on behalf of a common attitude, in tones of love. Virginia Woolf's commentary is more melancholy and sceptical than George Eliot's, but at times there's only a hairsbreadth between their feeling utterances. That hairsbreadth lies, I think, in Virginia Woolf's disclaimer of full knowledge: here the narrator gives a conventional bit of dialogue and inner monologue, and comments that 'though all this may very well be true – so Jacob thought and spoke – so he crossed his legs . . . there remains over something which can never be conveyed to a second person save by Jacob himself.' (p. 70) This is the modern novelist speaking, admitting not only the fictional nature of the fiction, but the difficulty of her enterprise. She admits, too, all the things that go to make up a character, which we can't assess, or don't want to put in, or must distort:

> 'Moreover, part of this is not Jacob but Richard Bonamy – the room; the market carts; the hour; the very moment of history. Then consider the effect of sex – how between man and woman it hangs wavy, tremulous, so that here's a valley, there's a peak, when in truth, perhaps, all's as flat as my hand. Even the exact words get the wrong accent on them. But something is always impelling one to hum vibrating, like the hawk moth, at the mouth of the cavern of mystery, endowing Jacob Flanders with all sorts of qualities he had not at all – for though, certainly, he sat talking to Bonamy, half of what he said was too dull to repeat; much unintelligible (about unknown people and Parliament); what remains is mostly a matter of guess work. Yet over him we hang vibrating.' (p. 70)

This passage is typical of the affective medium of narration. Its cool tones are part of a complex and varied notation, coloured by appropriate feeling according to the occasion, as in some Victorian narrative commentaries. Yet the registration of the characters' feeling is entirely modern. It presses lightly where Dickens and George Eliot pressed weightily, using understatement, suggestion, and implication. The pity and love of bereavement are whispered. The novel ends with the mother holding out a pair of Jacob's old shoes and asking Bonamy, the friend who loved him, 'What am I to do with these, Mr Bonamy?' (p. 173) The moment vibrates. Its resonance is created by understatements and undiscerned anticipations, which have brought the war so suddenly upon the characters and the reader, at its end. Jacob goes to war on the penultimate page, and we do not see him go. We only hear the thought of his mother, reported in free indirect style, that her sons are fighting. There is muted report, a fragile object's appeal, a quiet question. The feeling behind the novel is one of compassion and anger, and the novelist has carefully prepared the shock of its ending.

The last page is unlike any Victorian death-scene, but it uses some ancient effects. There is incantatory language and repetition, making the scene lyrical. The motif of the empty room, 'Listless is the air . . .' (p. 172) is repeated and consummated. Feeling is bounced off objects: letters, bills, arm-chair are resonant. There is a little sympathetic nature: 'leaves seemed to raise themselves'. A casual street-cry is made fully appropriate, 'A harsh and unhappy voice cried something unintelligible.'

Mrs Dalloway (1925) deals in emotional extremities. They are emphasized in the contrast of Clarissa Dalloway with Septimus Warren, where similarities of vitality and goodwill are balanced by dissimilarities of disintegration and harmony. The oscillation of extremes is also present in the narrated track of feeling. Clarissa herself veers from loving to hating, in her feelings about life in general, and in some particular sentiments. For instance, she sees Miss Kilman as a monster when she is absent, because then – as she knows – she is possessed by the power of the idea. In Miss Kilman's presence, the sense of monstrosity dwindles. Virginia Woolf uses the allegory of feeling in order to represent the disconcerting experience of being overpowered by feeling, amazed by the perceived action of the affections. The characters perform their own analysis of feeling, because it is the very experience of division and abstraction which they feel. The allegory is appropriate machinery. Rhetoric and psychological analysis are perfectly matched, for instance, when Clarissa's hatred of Miss Kilman is imaged as a spectre:

> 'For it was not her one hated but the idea of her, which undoubtedly had gathered in to itself a great deal that was not Miss Kilman; had become one of those spectres with which one battles in the night; one of those spectres who stand astride us and suck up half our life-blood, dominators and tyrants . . . (pp. 12–13)

The act of hyperbole is seen in the making. The exaggeration itself creates a powerful image, lucidly and consistently inflated; the character feels both a monstrous enlargement of dislike and a rational awareness of the enlargement. The figure is an objective correlative of violent passion and a measure of internal reflection and diagnosis. The defiance and recovery in the 'Nonsense, nonsense' (p. 13) which follows is characteristic of the character's resolute self-rejection and resilient grasp of the solid world. It is within Clarissa's mind that the monsters are made, but as she is aware of the occasion and process of making, she can throw off the passion. She can clearly distinguish between the outer and inner world, and command her passions. On a later occasion, the process and pattern are repeated, as Clarissa feels the presence of the monster, less as a personification of her own feeling than an image of Miss Kilman, 'stand she did, with the power and taciturnity of some prehistoric monster armoured for primeval warfare,' (p. 112). She loses malignity, 'became second by second merely Miss Kilman, in a mackintosh, whom Heaven knows Clarissa would have liked to help.' Clarissa laughs at the dwindling of image and passion. But they can and do return in full force:

> 'Love and religion! thought Clarissa, going back into the drawing-room, tingling all over. How detestable, how detestable they are! For now that the body of Miss Kilman was not before her, it overwhelmed her – the idea. The cruellest things in the world, she thought, seeing them clumsy, hot, domineering, hypocritical, eavesdropping, jealous, infinitely cruel and unscrupulous, dressed in a mackintosh coat, on the landing; love and religion.' (p. 112)

Definition and analysis go together. Here again, the course of feeling is disconcertingly dramatized, in a quickly-moving trajectory. Within one paragraph, Clarissa's mood shifts from hating to caring for the old woman opposite: 'Let her climb', then back again to hating, 'love and religion would destroy that, whatever it was, the privacy of the soul. The odious Kilman would destroy it' (pp. 112–13). Then follows the excellently observed magnetism of strong feeling, as even Peter Walsh is seen as a part of the distasteful passion of love, and rejected too. Virginia Woolf uses the free indirect style to register the pressure and growth of feeling. She tears her characters out of their affective privacy, showing how passion is checked and qualified, as it gathers momentum and material from external sensations and events.

A piercing insight shows the difference between the double motion of Mrs Dalloway's strong feelings, constantly moderated by the outside world, and the disastrously single affective action of Septimus Warren, which transforms that outer world into metaphors for his inner vision:

> 'But they beckoned; leaves were alive; trees were alive. And the leaves being connected by millions of fibres with his own body, there on the seat, fanned it up and down; when the branch stretched he, too, made that statement. The sparrows fluttering, rising, and falling in jagged fountains were part of the pattern; the white and blue, barred with black branches. (p. 22)

Once more, rhetoric and analysis blend. The heightened and bizarre sensibility of Septimus has the advantage of brilliant vitality and originality, and the danger of distortion and solipsism. The counterpoint of Clarissa and Septimus creates an implicit commentary on the affective life. Two strong sensibilities are contrasted, the one placed and controlled by a sense of the world outside, the other split off from external constraints. And the obsession of Septimus Warren has social implications, in its doctrine of love and peace, its anti-militarism. Its terrible honesty makes a moral plea, especially conspicuous in a novel about the aftermath of the First World War. It also kills him.

If *Night and Day* showed signs of moving the enquiry about feeling into an enquiry about marriage, the later novels do not. They introduce an important new love-theme, the need to rest from negative capability. Love is not shown as tireless, and Virginia Woolf provides images and definitions of love which depend on images and definitions of what love is not. Mrs Dalloway's excess of empathy is the other side of Septimus Warren's schizophrenic isolation, and in *To the Lighthouse* (1927) Mrs Ramsay's radical loving of husband, children, friends, must be arrested and allowed to fall back into the darkness of self-repose:

> 'one shrunk, with a sense of solemnity, to being oneself, a wedge-shaped core of darkness . . . this self having shed its attachments was free for the strangest adventures.' (p. 60)

There is another darkness, too. The vitality and radiance in Virginia Woolf is presented in a melancholy, sometimes hysterical, medium. It makes its presence felt in different ways. In *The Voyage Out* the enquiries of Terence and Rachel are checked; Rachel's eager question, 'tell me about the world' (p. 305) is soon answered. Barbara Bodichon wrote to George Eliot that she found the first part of *Middlemarch* unbearable, because of the sense of what was to come for Dorothea, 'like a child dancing into a quick sand on a sunny morning'.[2] Virginia Woolf's novels have a similar effect, shadowed as they are by death. Even the ones who don't die in the novels, are shown as decidedly mortal. (Not all characters in fiction are.) Their love of life, people, and self, all have a special urgency. It is sometimes said that the Victorian preoccupation with death has been replaced by the modern preoccupation with sex, but this is not true of the Georgian novelists.

Abrupt deaths in Virginia Woolf and E. M. Forster give an edge to sentimental history, and both novelists are good at conflating the shock within the novel and the shock without. In the telling of Mrs Ramsay's death, for instance, there is suddenness and foreshortening. The presentation of feeling is not naïve; the novelist knows that the reader was brought up to expect deaths in fiction to be signalled by early warnings. Sudden death – in literature alone – is novel, leaving us, like Mr Ramsay, unexpectedly empty-handed.

> [Mr. Ramsay stumbling along a passage stretched his arms out one dark morning, but, Mrs. Ramsay having died rather suddenly the night before, he stretched his arms out. They remained empty.] (p. 120)

Death in *To the Lighthouse* is introduced in the prevailing medium of melancholy, a melancholy present in the quality of the characters' beliefs and feelings, in the incantatory rhythms and images, in the central symbols, and in the very act of understatement. Virginia Woolf does not use simple understatement, and the bereavement is narrated after three pages of intensely imagistic and rhythmical language, introduced by the bridge passage 'Well, we must wait for the future to show', at the beginning of *Time Passes*.

Five people put out their lights, and disintegration continues in the landscape of night, rain, confounding darkness, winter, storm, and destruction. One night's darkness and breakdown is extended into many. The understatement occurs in a heightened and portentous context. Its narrative brevity, its brackets, and its abruptness, link the widower in the book with the reader of the book.

Mr Ramsay is conceived as a very Victorian character, responding conventionally and expecting conventional response. He performs the part of a grief-stricken husband (which he really is) and expects sympathy from Lily Briscoe. The only moment when the novelist leaves his response to his wife's death uncriticized, and accepted as spontaneous and true, is within the square brackets. They make a brief space for the pang, acted out in the stretching-out of his arms. (A similar gesture from a widowed husband in *The Years*, is not accepted as sincere: Colonel Pargiter's daughter comments grimly on his self-dramatized exit from the deathbed with arms outstretched and fists clenched.) What is especially interesting in Virginia Woolf's analysis and drama is her recognition of the transcendence of social roles. The sympathy Lily Briscoe feels she should feel for Mr Ramsay is the feeling she knows is demanded by men of women, and provided for men by womanly women like his dead wife. Even as a guest at the Ramsay table, Lily had felt the impulse to do the proper womanly thing by feeding men with interest and sympathy, and the counter-feeling to resist Mrs Ramsay's direction of the love-feast. Lily is Mrs Ramsay's opposite, epicene, independent, professional. She is equipped to question, criticize, appreciate and re-define a woman's protective role, and comments clearly on its attraction and repulsion. Unlike the reader, she has not had access to Mrs Ramsay's inner darkness or to the interruptions and constraints of her love. Lily's commentary, sensitive as it is in its effort to imagine Mrs Ramsay's imagination, simplifies Mrs Ramsay's affective life. Lily sees it only in its public appearances and projections but the reader has larger access, and can see the ironical appropriateness of Mrs Ramsay's apparition, which provides Lily's picture with a wedge-shaped darkness. It was precisely that inner dark which gave Mrs Ramsay strength to give and imagine. It is the necessary darkness of the imagination which these two women share.

Lily's attempt to do the womanly thing and sympathize with Mr Ramsay is also a parallel to Mrs Ramsay's inability to say 'I love you'. Lily is less unlike Mrs Ramsay than she thinks, both in this inhibition, and in the discovered symbolic language. Mrs Ramsay had thought 'Anything will do,' when looking for an image or anecdote to replace 'I love you' (p. 112). Lily finds that praising Mr Ramsay's beautiful boots can replace condolences. Mr Ramsay himself accepts the substitute with pleasure, his self-dramatized and indulgent demand falling away into a simple human gratitude for simple human communion. The indirect and understated language of the affections is delicately exhibited and explained.

In her last three novels, *The Waves* (1931), *The Years* (1937) and *Between the Acts* (1940), the analysis of emotion continues, but the subject of love and sympathy becomes displaced by concerns with time, history, mortality, and the breakdown of art and relationship. The novels are pierced with insights into the irregularity and discontinuity of human feeling and the need for regularity and continuity, especially in *Between the Acts*. The awkwardness and fragmentariness of the village pageant create a new version of Lily Briscoe's insight into the collaborations of art and nature. The comic mooing of the cows fills the gap in art, and provides for the audience within the novel a bizarre continuity which parallels the novel's own emotional continuity. The last important contribution to the analysis of emotion comes in *The Waves*, which like its successors, fights against narrative fullness, development, and continuity. Like the novelist, Bernard is always looking for a story but comes to give up the search as artificial, false, and arbitrary. More clearly than the other characters, he mirrors and contemplates the affective life. Two of his insights into feeling express and perhaps explain the novelist's discontent with her analysis. As Bernard mourns the death of Percival, whom he has loved, he explicitly rejects language as an affective register:

> 'But for pain words are lacking. There should be cries, cracks, fissures, whiteness passing over chintz covers, interference with the sense of time, of space; the sense also of extreme fixity in passing objects; and sounds very remote and then very close; flesh being gashed and blood spurting, a joint suddenly twisted – beneath all of which appears something very important, yet remote, to be just held in solitude.' (p. 178)

He confronts the problem which exists for the man and the artist. As a man he has to experience sympathy, and even plans carefully the time and place, 'Now in this drawing-room he is going to suffer.' (p. 178) Death had 'crashed' into a time of happiness, so there is a conflict of feeling. Bernard has to carry forward his grief and love, into 'the first morning he would never see', stating the need for continuity and change in images which wring sympathy out of the reader, 'the sparrows were like toys dangled from a string by a child' and 'Madonnas and pillars, arches and orange trees, still as on the first day of creation, but acquainted with grief.' (p. 178) The Biblical echo 'acquainted with grief', makes its point: rhetoric's traditional generalizations are examined as they are expressed. 'For pain words are lacking,' is an insight stated in words.

The other powerful example comes earlier where Bernard is commenting 'in the midst of . . . anguish' (p. 168) on Susan, who makes her own emotional judgement of emotion in her repeated 'I love; I hate' and her comment that love and hate are identical. Bernard sees himself observing and narrating even in agony, dramatizing and inventing a story for Susan in which 'some witless servant could be heard laughing at the top of the house as she whirred the wheel of the sewing-machine round and round.'. He quotes the snippet of story, deducing that we are incompletely 'merged in our own experiences':

> 'On the outskirts of every agony sits some observant fellow who points; who whispers as he whispered to me that summer morning in the house where the corn comes up to the window, "The willow grows on the turf by the river. The gardeners sweep with great brooms and the lady sits writing." Thus he directed me to that which is beyond and outside our

> own predicament; to that which is symbolic, and thus perhaps permanent, if there is any permanence in our sleeping, eating, breathing, so animal, so spiritual and tumultuous lives.' (p. 168)

The analysis blends image and commentary, marking flux, the attempt to wrest moments from flux, and the awareness of the attempt. Like the novelist, Bernard sees that there is always the 'fringe of intelligence' which catches those undifferentiated materials on which art works. The unwinnable race between form and material, order and disorder, past and present, emerges as a major theme in the last novels. Bernard's statement of his grief and sympathy, undercut by the very act of analysis, at once expresses and analyses a truth about love and imagination.

Notes

1 *Jacob's Room*, p. 93. The text of all quotations from the novels of Virginia Woolf is from the Uniform Edition published by The Hogarth Press. But for ease of reference, page numbers following quotations refer to the Panther paperback editions.
2 *The George Eliot Letters*, ed. Gordon S. Haight (Yale University Press, 1978), Volume IX, p. 34.

The Uses of Fiction
Edited by
Douglas Jefferson
and Graham Martin

15

The Name's Familiar: An Aspect of The Fiction of Henry Green

Alistair Stead

I

> 'Prose is not to be read aloud but to oneself alone at night, and it is not quick as poetry but rather a gathering web of insinuations which go further than names however shared can ever go. Prose should be a long intimacy between strangers with no direct appeal to what both may have known. It should slowly appeal to the feelings unexpressed, it should in the end draw tears out of the stone, and feelings are not bounded by the associations common to place names or to persons with whom the reader is unexpectedly familiar.'

Henry Green's observations on prose in his autobiography *Pack My Bag* (1940) have often been quoted by his critics, and rightly.[1] This is a key passage for anyone attempting to come to terms with the work of this distinguished novelist and much of what I shall have to say about what may seem a comparatively minor aspect of his work, his art of naming, will take the form of a gloss, or series of interlinked glosses, on some of its terms. But it should be said at the outset that generalization and the prescriptive manner are not all that common in Green's work. His considered views on the novel appeared, for the most part, when his ability to create substantial works of art was waning. In a number of articles, talks and interviews, he expounded what constituted a programme for, or a rationalization of, the brilliant but comparatively lightweight 'conversation' novels, *Nothing* (1950) and *Doting* (1952).[2] I would not underestimate the power of these comments to illuminate his practice in general, but what is more characteristic of his career is reticence about method and a very individual, largely intuitive approach to the composition of each book. I would prefer to begin by focussing on what one might call, after Eliot, the 'workshop' criticism, what Green had to say when he was in the midst of creating his most challenging and successful fiction, *Caught* (1943), *Loving* (1945) and *Back* (1946).[3] At or near the beginning of the Second World War Green produced two fascinating works of non-fiction, the interim autobiography and 'Apologia', the only critical article that Green devoted to another writer, a celebration of the eccentric author of *Arabia Deserta* (1888).[4] Both works contain reflections, however oblique and glancing, on the craft of fiction and throw considerable light on the sources of his inspiration.

The essay on Charles M. Doughty has a double focus. Green pays tribute to a master of mannered prose whose mastery was achieved 'not so much by conscious art as by the constraint of his adventure' . . . 'this finding of himself'. 'This monumentally lonely man' had a great need 'to get away unnoticed', travelling among the totally alien Arabs, penetrating the hostile company of the Bedouin. Green then speculates on the application of the lesson of Doughty for the contemporary writer. 'Now that we are at war, is not the advantage for writers, and for those who read them, that they will be forced by the need they have to fight, to go out into territories, it may well be at home, which they would never otherwise have visited, and they will be forced, by way of their own selves, towards a style which, by the impact of a life strange to them and by their honest acceptance of this, will be pure as Doughty's was, so that they will reach each one his own style that shall be his monument?'[5] Here Green lays bare the motivation for most of his finest work and especially for the three 'war' novels.

Caught is the most directly inspired by such a conception. Richard Roe, the upper-class widower, is Doughty's 'rich stranger', forced to confront a new area of social experience when he volunteers for the Auxiliary Fire Service and shocked at last out of his habitual aloofness and neurotic self-pity by what he finds there. *Loving*, set in neutral Ireland during the war, evolved from an anecdote told to Green when he was himself serving in the A.F.S. and explores, in a manner marvellously empathetic yet grimly comic, the below-stairs world of an English-staffed castle. In *Back* Green again exposes a grief-stricken hero to a strange world; 'this finding of himself' is for Charley Summers, the ex-prisoner of war who has lost a leg, an arduous quest for stability in a civilian world that his trauma represents to him as a malign conspiracy. Heroes like Roe and Summers are as lonely as Green conjectured that Doughty might have felt in Victorian England, but long before the war, as he tells us in *Pack My Bag*, he felt 'different, desperate now, estranged' (p. 102). His tone is hysterical, for he is at Oxford, at the nadir of his life so far, yet the epithet 'strange' (and variants) is everywhere. He often felt 'a stranger in England' because he had not yet found 'the sort of English life' he liked (p. 230).

His escape from the restrictions of his conventional upper-class education came with the discovery of his own Arabia, the world of skilled manual labour on the factory floor of his family's engineering works in Birmingham, where he was introduced to 'a life bare of almost everything except the essentials and so less confusing, to a new world which was the oldest' (p. 236). His Arabia, it is important to add, was, though tough, full of fun and laughter; and the 'plot' of the autobiography is, in spite of the two wars that frame it rather tendentiously, that of a comic romance, in which the hero eventually finds the community of shared work, his place in society (albeit equivocal) and his love. The impact of these experiences on his second and third novels is unmistakable. *Living* (1929) is remarkable for his portrayal of the life of the ordinary factory-workers with uncondescending sympathy and *Party Going* (1939) for the macabre comedy of his exhibition of the futile lives of a group of frivolous young rich people whose deficiency in 'fellow feeling' is thrown into relief by the capacity for companionship among their servants and 'the vague incoherent, yet somehow friendly unity of the crowd' (as Arnold Kettle puts it in his fine appreciation of the book in the last chapter of his *Introduction to the English Novel*).[6]

But the model that Green was to propose two years later in 'Apologia' throws light on this novelist's typical reservation. Doughty's 'constraint' of sharing precludes a total identification with others. It is not just a matter of his Victorian Christian, violent resistance to Arab 'fanaticism'; for, in spite of being accepted at times like a friend, he has no love for the company he chose to travel among. This may seem to pass too stern a judgement on Green's real and imaginative extensions into a wider world, but for him, as the novels all show, loving recognizes differences. Green, like Doughty, knew the necessity of self-protection and preserves his sense of being different in a style of estrangement, that is, a style which emphasizes the writer's detachment from his subject (compare the linguistic term 'words of estrangement'), which is also a style of pure individuality like Doughty's 'idiom'. In 'Apologia', and a single sentence of 'The English Novel of the Future', Green acknowledges the artificiality of this idiom and it has been remarked that some of the mannerism of Green's own style may derive from this model.[7] (For an interesting but incomplete comparison of the styles, see chapter Two of John Russell's *Henry Green: Nine Novels and an Unpacked Bag* [New Brunswick, New Jersey, 1960], pp. 41–9).

But Green, taking Doughty to heart, has striven for a style of his own, less monumental and of a more complex tone. His responsiveness to strangers and his own wilful strangeness are in an invigorating relationship to each other. His autobiography, his most personal, most mannered book, offers a clear image of his self-division, of that tension between withdrawal and a shy reaching for communion which animates his best work. It was V. S. Pritchett, Green's most sensitive critic, who recognized most surely these contradictory impulses in the novelist and, more unusually, realized their common ground: 'I suspect he felt *himself* to be mysterious. He was a rare being and he was sensitive to that core of rarity which is buried in people who outwardly might be commonplace.' He was 'a master of the comedy of what I can only call the *human underground*.'[8] The perfect validation of Pritchett's imagery appears in the too little known short story 'Mr Jonas', published between *Pack My Bag* and the article on Doughty.[9] It is a true story, born of the 'constraint' of Green's 'adventure' in the fire-fighting service during the war, telling of the rescue of a man trapped underground during a night of spectacular fires. According to Green, in a letter to John Lehmann, the 'spectacular' style matched the blaze, but the convolutions of style are more importantly made to render a mixture of physical confusion and subtler apprehension. The narrator is appropriately just one of the group of rescuers and also the sensitive register of some mystery. On their mission each man becomes aware of having to visit 'a place foreign to himself', 'such a frontier of hopes or mostly fears as it may be in the destiny of each, or almost all, to find, betwixt coma and the giving up of living' (pp. 11–12). Intermittently blinded or choked by the deadly smoke and steam, the firemen still succeed in releasing the man whose emergence, now laconically described, seems grotesquely casual. Hours more of vain fire-fighting are condensed into a few sentences; then the magnificent, multiply suspended last sentence restores the rescued man to 'normality':

'When the other crew took over we had fought our way back to exactly the same spot above that hole out of which, unassisted once he had been released, out of unreality into something temporarily worse, apparently unhurt, but now in all probability suffering from shock, had risen, to live again whoever he might be, this Mr. Jonas.' (p. 17)

Superficially the successful rescue against the odds, by dint of co-operative labour, is a celebration of solidarity, but the mystery is subterranean, the stress falls on the isolated individual, for in finding Mr Jonas the men have found something adequate to their secret imaginings.

Mr Jonas, very much alive, triumphs over their fears of death. He is a resplendently comic figure; far from being drowned (by the rescuers' hoses), he is bone dry, not even coughing (like the rescuers), he is self-sufficient, absolutely silent. It is most particularly in the *naming* of the stranger that Green's oblique comedy resides. At first, he is just a man, 'this man', 'that man', just a case. Then the leader of the crew calls down to him, using the unexpected proper name, 'incongruously' (p. 16) since the firemen remain anonymous. The finding of Mr Jonas is like the finding of oneself, a recovery of the obscured dignity of the real life of proper names, biographies, complex fates. This is a resurgence of the commonplace in a nightmare world. But the name, I take it, invented or not, reaches further, suggesting the fate of the Old Testament prophet who was entombed for three days in the belly of a whale and whose release is the type of Christ's resurrection (Matthew 12. 39–41). And beyond this lurks Doughty's story of a visit to the sepulchre of Jonas in Palestine, where its blind guardian warns against passing beyond the ruinous chamber into the tomb because men have been struck blind by the trespass. Green might well have recollected Doughty's invective against the credulity of the Arabs who attributed miracles even to him, citing an uplifting by night of great stones 'out of the great ruined well-pit, and with no more than a touch of the fingers.'[10] Green's own story, with its victories over blindness and entombment, assigns the miracle to the efforts of the human group, but it is he who, with the lightest of touches, makes the miraculous visible.

But to return to our point of departure: the quotation from *Pack My Bag*. 'Prose is . . . a gathering web of insinuations which go further than names however shared can ever go. Prose should be a long intimacy between strangers with no direct appeal to what both may have known . . .' (p. 88). Behind this concept of communication there lies what I have called the model of Doughty. Communication is with strangers, an adventure in a strange land, a slow and devious intercourse. The long intimacy of writer and reader corresponds to Doughty's sojourn among the Arabs, which resulted in a temporary and qualified rapport. But it would be foolish to attribute the reluctance to rely on shared names to Doughty and to ignore the immediate context of Green's words. He is here refusing to give the proper names of his schools or his schoolfriends. He is plausibly motivated by tact and by the urge to protect his very personal vision of things. The defence of the gambit grows more eccentric, however, when he maintains that this namelessness corresponds to his usual way of remembering people. 'Names distract, nicknames are too easy and if leaving them both out does make a book look blind then that to my mind is no disadvantage.' (p. 88) This is a curious and quintessential conceit of Green's. By typical hypallage it is the book which is deprived of sight, not the reader. (Green's other ways of blinding a book are the lightening of punctuation, the removal of numbered or named chapter divisions or parts, the dropping of epigraphs, and the reduction of titles to a single multivalent word.) Taking away the proper names is intended to blind the reader to irrelevant material or associations, making him concentrate on that idiosyncratic vision.

The effect is unsuccessful. In autobiography the blurring mystifies, the vagueness is a tease. An anecdote from Crabb Robinson is apposite:

> 'I have heard of a lady, by birth, being reduced to cry "muffins to sell" for a subsistence. She used to go out a-nights with her face hid up in her cloak, and then she would in the faintest voice utter her cry – "Muffins to sell, muffins to sell! Oh, I do hope nobody hears me." '[11]

The precedent in autobiographical writings for Green's kind of temperamental obfuscation might be De Quincey's works in the mode; but it is more likely that it was Virginia Woolf's commentary on them, in her article 'Impassioned Prose' in *TLS* (16 September, 1926), that lodged in his mind. As confessional writing De Quincey's work is odd, she considers, not through absence of names, but in deficiency of fact, chronology and observation. Although this reticence cannot prevent the growth of a 'curious sense of intimacy' (of the mind), 'it is odd to reflect how little, after all, we have been admitted to intimacy' . . . 'he is always self-possessed, secretive and composed.' As poetic prose, however, his impressionistic flights become potential models for the modern novelist. He exhibits, what he cannot solve, the problem of making the transition from the extraordinary to the ordinary moments: 'For prose has neither the intensity nor the self-sufficiency of poetry. It rises slowly off the ground; it must be connected on this side and on that.' But his veiled representation of things may indicate a new way for prose fiction, for 'it is not the actual sight or sound itself that matters, but the reverberations that it makes as it travels through our minds. These are often to be found far away, strangely transformed; but it is only by gathering up and putting together these echoes and fragments that we arrive at the true nature of our experience.'[12] Here we may detect an influential anticipation of Green's famous passage in *Pack My Bag* (slow prose, the gathering up of echoes) and a hint that what might be a limited and limiting effect in autobiography could be a useful technique for 'making it strange' in fiction. The novels are, what V. S. Pritchett called the characters in Green, 'echoing chambers', discovering the truth of events in their, often grotesque, repercussions.[13] The young Green had first learned of war by the echoes of gunfire and of the secrets of adult life only through 'the echoes of it all' (*Pack My Bag*, pp. 40, 77). The novelist was able to preserve and cultivate the innocent ear that from 'echoes and fragments' could construct an image of the times. He was especially successful in the 1940s in conveying the war climate (even the absurd out-of-it atmosphere of the Irish castle in *Loving* makes its contribution), but earlier works too show him capturing the war at odd, revealing angles. *Party Going* has long been understood, on one level, as a 'pre-war' book (' "What targets," one by him remarked, "what targets for a bomb!" ', p. 483) and even *Blindness*, Green's first novel, may be regarded as a post-war novel, using the metaphor of blindness to express the guilt of those who had missed the chance to prove themselves in the First World War and needed a substitute ordeal. (Compare Christopher Isherwood's account of his first projected novel *Lions and Shadows* in the autobiographical novel of the same name.)

This metaphoric use of blindness may recall us then to Green's willingness to make his book 'look blind' by eliminating the names (in part of it). In the novels such a refusal to name should be seen as another example of that induced 'sensory failure' which is, as Frank Kermode puts it in his stimulating account of *Party Going*, 'an interruption in the conventional processing of information, in our knowing dully, for the sake of convenience, where and what we are.'[14] Sensory failure should incite the characters or the readers to find out, even to create for themselves. John Haye, the blinded hero of the first book, is the pattern, probing beneath 'the superficial appearance of things' and discovering 'a whole new set of values' (*Blindness*, pp. 502, 437). In fact, it is the loss of place names which is more impressive than the loss of personal names in the fiction. The anonymity of the railway station in *Party Going* or the estate in *Concluding* (1948) is patently conducive to an interpretation of the novels (an interpretation by no means exclusive) as fables about society in general.[15] The failure to grant a proper name to the many-voiced stranger who flits through *Party Going* or to the much-mourned wife of Roe in *Caught* fosters a sense of rather sinister unreality, suggesting that the supposed hotel detective is a perambulating *memento mori* and that Roe's wife is a disabling wraith, a dangerous obsession.

Nevertheless it is rare for Green to omit the names of important personages in his fiction. The passage about prose in *Pack My Bag* may, at first glance, seem deeply suspicious about names in what may be thought the radically Symbolist manner. Mallarmé had claimed that 'to *name* an object is to destroy most of the enjoyment derived from the poem, an enjoyment which consists in a gradual working-out: to *suggest*, that is the dream.'[16] But, although the novels insinuate their meanings, their metaphoric designs, to use Jakobson's terms, are extended from a metonymic base. This novelist habitually exploits the indispensable proper names, and spins from mere denotative function a complex of connotations. The foundation of his onomastic art is thoroughly traditional, the shared world of the verisimilar. Miss Fellowes, the maiden aunt who comes to see her niece depart for a holiday abroad, is the first named character in *Party Going*. The name is neutral at first, mingling with the others unresonantly. But one of the reasons for our sense that she is not as slight and peripheral to the design of the book as she seems at first is an appellation that links her boldly, near-allegorically, to the repeated phrase 'fellow feeling' (pp. 473, 493). Her mysterious almost fatal illness exposes the lack of this virtue in the self-concerned party-goers, of whom her niece is one. She is 'the party' (p. 407) who is almost 'a goner' (p. 498) and, as such, enforces the most general 'moral' of the book: that all the cast are travellers, all must participate in the fellowship of death. To name, *pace* Mallarmé, is to suggest. Names become insinuations in Green's gathering webs and *nomen et omen* might be the motto of his elusive, reverberant fictions.

II

Evelyn Waugh, an admiring friend, objected that the Hon. Henry Vincent Yorke, old Etonian businessman, should publish fiction 'under a pseudonym of peculiar drabness.'[17] It was not the first choice; that was Henry Michaelis 'of all names', as we hear in *Pack My Bag* (p. 163). 'Green', inscrutable to Waugh, seems to have been modest camouflage, muting those 'loud shouts' about literary ambition, those 'yells about self' in the early literary efforts (pp. 163, 165). The central figure of a series of satirical sketches about life at Eton called 'The Type' was, prophetically, Brown.[18] The connoisseur of colour and ordinariness chose well.

Yet in his first novel, begun while he was still at Eton and published when he was an Oxford undergraduate, the tension between his desire to 'get away unnoticed' and the assertion of quirky individuality betrays itself in a paranomasiac glee that foreshadows later, less evidently self-reflexive games. (It is remarkable how Green will strive for a style to realize the unique subject of each book then 'sign' his work again and again with a common motif like the notorious bird imagery.) The schoolboy diary in the first section of *Blindness* is manifestly in-joky. Eton appears as Noat (near anagram) and Haye, the selfconscious hero, responds to 'the one forced note' of some harassing horn-players with, 'Really, it might be Eton.' (p. 345) Green as common word and proper name (always attached to very insignificant characters) winds it way through the book. The casual reference to a boy called Greene then draws attention humorously to the slight strangeness about Haye's own name (presumably signifying a hedge, his defensive posture) with its excrescent 'e' pointing back at the supposedly suppressed Mr Yorke. *Blindness* is, indeed, Green's *Portait of the Artist as a Young Man*.

If we look for the portrait of the man in early middle age, we might find him in the intricacy of *Caught*. The extravagant name-game is, in part, kept up. The naming of the officers in the A.F.S. verges on the Dickensian, retaining likelihood and insinuating a mania: Dodge, Trant, Pye (a cunning trick or a wily person). The world of the fire service is the world of *Caught* in little, replete with plots, traps and betrayals, both petty and portentous. Given Green's artful naming, it seems probable that the man who knew his naval nicknames – Wright is Shiner, in the book, and White is Knocker – might also have known that a Green was often a Dodger![19] The novel is certainly singularly devious in structure for Green, who nowhere else plays so elaborately with time-shifts, and the deviousness derives from the conception of the central relationship between the wealthy Roe and the proletarian fireman Pye. They have been seen as doubles, in the manner of Virginia Woolf's Mrs Dalloway and Septimus Smith, their names proposing the surprising meshing of their fates. To A. Kingsley Weatherhead in his book *A Reading of Henry Green* the names conjoined spell out the dangerous element that brings the men together, *pyro*, the fire.[20]

What has not been noticed is that Richard Roe, whom most agree is the real hero of the book and whose adventures in the A.F.S., as well as temperament, reflect more than usually the experiences of the author, is given the name of the fictitious defendant in the now obsolete 'mixed action' of ejectment. This Roe was set up to be the 'casual ejector' of a fictitious plaintiff, one John Doe, in a legal action designed to recover the real plaintiff possession of his land, with a payment of costs and damages for wrongful with-holding, and to try the title to the land.[21] As an aristocratic landowner, not unlike the hero of his novel, Green might well be familiar with such law. His knowledge of legal language and procedure is amusingly in evidence in his review of Gower's *The Complete Plain Words*[22] and, in an interview with Harvey Breit (where he makes mention of John Doe), he describes in these terms the way in which he constructed his books: 'In English law a practitioner can't depart from his opening statement. I have to make my opening statement and for the remaining seven-eighths of the novel revolve around it.'[23]

Caught is principally about the quest for a real self-possession, Roe's finding of himself, but the scope of the novel is wider than that; as so often in Green the larger issues are felt in the reverberations. The novel begins and ends on Roe's country estate, where he spends his leave from his fire-fighting duties in London. The estate is not literally menaced, like Chekhov's cherry orchard, but, described in evocative language on the first leave, it is barely seen on the last; it is associated with Roe's debilitating preoccupation with the past, embodied most forcefully in the grieving for his wife. Roe's privileged insulation from society is steadily eroded by the new world that life in the substation leads him into. The decisive figure is Albert Pye, the newly promoted commanding officer, whose increasingly erratic leadership is significantly conditioned by his embarrassment and resentment when he finds that it was his mentally disturbed sister Amy who had abducted Roe's son Christopher. The anxiety surrounding the abduction contributes to the mounting dread; Pye loses control at work and commits suicide. Roe finds the body and suffers his own breakdown, ostensibly because he was too near a falling bomb. By the end of the novel, as Roe reviews his experiences in the Blitz of shared danger and shared achievement, he can feel remorse for his failure to communicate with the tragic Pye.

Through Roe's name Green makes an ironic allusion to a legal fiction in which Roe's, possibly Green's, feelings of guilt are symbolized. Roe establishes his 'title' by the accident of birth and education; it is by the wild mischance of Amy's attempted abduction of Christopher that Roe has become the 'casual ejector' of Pye. It is grossly unfair that Pye should be the dispossessed, losing sister, girlfriend, office, all peace of mind (he suspects he has committed incest with his sister) and, finally, his life. In contrast with Roe, Pye is generous and sympathetic, especially to those who are to injure him. Pye is the John Doe in the case, the common man who here must lose the action. That he and Roe are 'brothers-in-law' is something Richard may obscurely feel, but the reader may recall that in Amy's attempt to become Christopher's mother, as it were, Pye is being brought into some such relation to the hero. Although Green, very characteristically qualifies Roe's angry outburst against his sister-in-law's conventional upper-class recoil from Pye, casting doubt on how long Roe will sustain his new valuation, there are constant rumours in Green's work that in the inevitable changes proceeding in society the dispossession of his own class must come and the coming is somehow just.

That Roe's name is a patent fiction seems to suggest that Green is trying his title to the land and, if we compare *Caught* with the directly autobiographical book which preceded it, we may see an analogue, if not a source, for the literary expression of insecurity and guilt. In *Pack My Bag* he recounts wryly how his parents turned their ancestral home into a temporary convalescent home for the soldiers of the First World War 'with a view to self-preservation, to keep the privileges we set such store by, and which are illusory, after those to whom we were kind had won the war for us,' (p. 68) and how the very young Green spotted the awkwardness and instability of men promoted from the ranks to officer and was especially affected by the Pye-like case of a gassed, nerve-racked Australian who was later to commit suicide. Only after going on a bike ride with the man did the ten year old boy realize 'how hopelessly far gone he was'. 'We grow up by sharing situations, what we share of another person's increases us, and my memorial to all of them in my heart now is my anguish remembered as I saw him stagger in disclosed, wondering whether perhaps it were not my fault.' (p. 67)

'Real life is an inextricable tangle,' Green went on to declare (p. 213) and the appropriate design for such a vision is the 'gathering web of insinuations'. Green's deployment of names helps to compose his funny-dreadful images of entrapment in the novels. It seems entirely proper that probably the most considerable character in his fiction should be the scheming butler of *Loving*, Raunce, whose name is suggestive of 'bramble'. Simply by repeating certain forms of naming within a book he can achieve some of this entangling effect. In *Back*, for instance, the encroachment of a faceless, bewildering bureaucracy on post-war life is indicated in the designation of all Government departments by initials only: B.R.N.Q., V.B.S., P.M.V.O., etc. In *Concluding* all the girls being trained in the Civil Service school of Green's levelling dystopia have names beginning with the letter M: Mary, Merode, Moira, etc. Less heavy-handed than this is the tradition in *Loving* whereby the Tennants (an ironic naming that echoes the legal image in *Caught*) comically assert themselves by calling all their footmen Arthur.

Occasionally Green will introduce into a book two characters with the same name in a manner slightly reminiscent of the intricate sagas of Faulkner (in *Blindness* there is John the postman and John Haye the would-be man of letters, in *Loving* there are the contrasted Alberts of Raunce and Mrs Welch, in *Back* there is the waitress Rose and Rose the hero's dead mistress), but Green's use of namesakes is much less deliberately, and much less richly, disorienting than Faulkner's. It should be related to Green's repeated use within his nine novels of a handful of Christian names. Richard/Dick is a favourite (in *Blindness*, *Living*, *Party Going*, and *Caught*), but John, Albert/Bert, Arthur/Art, Philip/Phil, Liz, Diana/Dy, all recur. That Charley should be used as a name for major characters in consecutive novels (in *Loving* and *Back*) is testimony to Green's differentiating skill. Yet, if we contemplate the total effect of all the casual overlapping of names in the fiction, we may feel how extraordinarily small the world seems, how domesticated, and in what a thoroughly pedestrian and cluttered medium his people move. When these names are abbreviated, frequently to curt monosyllables, this air of intimacy is intensified (for it is the rare character who is not curtailed in Green's fiction).

Nicknames and diminutives function ambiguously, representing in part an authentic sharing, a pleasing familiarity or companionship, in part a mere simulacrum of this. Both are present in the world of the substation in *Caught*, for example, where at first it seems a matter of convention, but as experiences involve the characters in genuine collaboration it binds the group together. The nickname in particular, can be a kind of deception or disguise, a way of telling stories, whether to others or oneself. In *Caught* it is typical of the gossip-haunted and secretly competitive atmosphere of the substation before the Blitz that sobriquets abound. Upper-class Roe, felt to be stuck-up and effete, is quickly suspected of treachery by Pye; he launches a Homeric epithet, 'savoury Roe', to be taken up by Chopper (and others), though Chopper ironically misses the fishy associations and connects it with a smart tailor's in Savory Row (p. 88). Some nicknames are not straightforwardly derogatory like this. When Pye is called 'Peewee' by Hilly in *Caught* (p. 71) or Summers is called 'Charley Barley' by the three women who know him best in *Back* (pp. 121, 153, 202), the tone is affectionate, if patronizing, as they are characterized as sweet and child-like respectively through the nursery-style duplicative forms. In *Loving* the nickname is part of the bouncy self-dramatization of Raunce; secure in his status in the servants' world he tags himself 'Uncle Charley', 'Lucky', 'Busy', 'Broadminded' and 'Clever'. But this tactic of self-promotion and reassurance fails as things get out of hand in Kinalty Castle and he finds himself dutiful son, patriot, and in love. The last use of the device occurs near the end of the novel and exposes sharply the change that has overtaken the hero. ' "You leave all the brain work to your old man. Lucky Charley they call him," he said in a threadbare return to his usual manner.' (p. 200)

The names in Green's world can all too easily deceive. They are very much part of his world of shifting appearances. Green puts it lightly, whimsically, in the interview with Breit: 'I believe that when things are named they're named by people, some individual, some genius at naming things. And you'll find they always name the biggest things with the smallest names. Like the horrible cat-o-nine tails in England.'[24] Green's fascination with the business of naming goes hand in hand with a suspicion of names. His attitude to these matters cannot be divorced from his feeling for the wonder and treachery of language in general. His position is very like that of his first hero, John Haye, to whom language is all-important. (Pritchett rightly insisted that Green was a *listener*.)[25] 'Voices had become his great interest, voices that surrounded him, that slipped from tone to tone, that hid to give away in hiding.' (*Blindness*, p. 436) That last devastating phrase is the mark of the novelist who has taken very seriously James's description of the novel as the 'admirably *treacherous* picture of actual manners'[26]; for whom 'faces aslant' reveal most and lies 'give the underlying truth away' (*Pack My Bag*, pp. 125, 186); and who, in his article on 'The English Novel of the Future', maintained that 'you learn more from the lies of someone who is speaking to you, if you can find these out, than you will from direct statements which generally only represent a portion of what the person you are speaking to believes. A direct lie can be infinitely revealing.'[27] Names in the novel will often behave like the voices 'that hid to give away in hiding'. When, at the beginning of the third part of *Blindness*, John Haye rejoices in the thought of the company of the slatternly country girl Joan Entwhistle, he thinks of her as 'June' and, when they actually meet, establishes that she will answer to that name, in full consciousness that 'June was an illusion – a lovely one.' (p. 442) The blind and inexperienced boy, desperate to make contact with the world, lays down the terms, refashioning plain Joan into the girl of his dreams, a June patently improvised from the associations of the season, the rosy fantasies of the poets. For a time, the fiction of sharing, of an interchange between the incompatible, seems to work: her 'Poor John' chimes with his 'Poor June'. But the masquerade of June can be sustained by neither the quick intellectual nor the slow sensuous girl, and when Joan chooses to abandon it, alleging that he will only tire of her and leave her, she aptly counters his high romantic fiction with a name of her own: ' "There was a story I read called The Love of White Hope. The young man in that left the girl whom he had promised to marry . . ." ' And her fiction lays bare how much her mind is on her attachment to her drunken scapegrace father rather than on John, for after the girl committed suicide in the story the young man gave up drink: ' "Yes, that was it, he used to drink in his young days, and then after that he gave it up. He was lovely when he was young." ' (p. 468) When the break finally comes, John appears to be shocked into reality for a moment and calls ' "Goodbye, Joan." ' Then, abandoned to his darkness, he falls back on his pathetic dream. ' "But June," he shouted, to the wood, "June, what do you – June, I – June . . ." ' (p. 473) Here the coalescence of 'June' and 'I' insists on his private imagining, exposes his terrible need.

The reverberation of June's name has a haunting effect. The repetition of a person's name makes that absentee, whether dead, lost, or just temporarily remote, formidably present and emphasizes a secret relation whether of pleasure or of pain. Dissociation of the painful and pleasurable is often extraordinarily difficult as Green represents such situations, and it is possible that great things like the last scenes in *Loving* or *Back* have been conditioned by the experiences recounted in *Pack My Bag*. Green, very much aware of being the youngest of three sons and of being compared unfavourably throughout his school career with the gifted brothers whom he hero-worshipped, had to confront death for the first time in his life when the eldest brother Philip died while he was still at Eton. Unable to react spontaneously to the event, he felt his grief complicated by guilt. 'After the funeral I had a great sense of shock whenever Philip's name was mentioned, and for some months had difficulty in not crying when someone said it out with no warning. So, much later, when in love and I heard the person's name unexpectedly, – is there anyone who has not felt their heart lurch then and, if it happens to be secret, combined with that same sense of guilt I had over Philip's death.' (p. 82) I would stress in this the strange inter-relation of grieving for the dead and longing for the beloved. The link is the name; a name repeated is the 'Open Sesame' that unlocks the sealed chamber of the feelings. And the feelings that are released from the underground source are peculiarly mixed. Green's dwelling on the constant admixture of guilt is his most individual touch. Philip's name, always on the lips of his brother's insensitive prep-school headmaster and always to Henry's disadvantage, buried grief under feelings of shameful inadequacy. Later in life Green would grimly assert that 'the emotion of grief is no longer available; that in our day it is replaced by guilt.'[28]

In *Caught* Roe's grief for his wife is steadily removed from the centre of his attention and it is Pye, the objectification of Roe's sense of guilt, who, now dead, usurps it. To render Pye as an inescapable presence in the story Green has developed the echoic technique of *Blindness* in the direction of the macabre. Pye's name is kept before us, not only by direct reference, but through the constant parrot-like repetitions of the treacherous ex-soldier Piper. Piper's very name includes his skipper's. Piper is Pye's grotesque aural shadow. Exasperated by Piper's repeating him all the time, Pye volleys back: 'For God's sake pipe down.' (*Caught*, p. 21) Piper with his 'pied' skin (p. 21), is known in the substation as the 'old Pied Piper' (p. 102). There is more than comedy in this, for Piper has got to know that Pye's sister has led away Roe's child, like the Piper, and, worse, he is to betray Pye to his superiors and so precipitate the suicide when the Sub Officer has, from a different motive, repeated his sister's act, picking up a stray boy and lodging him illegally in the firestation.

But the most extensive, elaborate, and moving example of the use of the repeated name occurs in *Back*. The partially disabled Charley Summers, suffering from some unspeakable prisoner-of-war experience, finds his already slow adjustment to civilian life that much more difficult because he is grief-stricken by the death of Rose, his mistress and wife to a friend. Rose died 'about that identical week' (p. 9) when he was wounded and he only heard of her death when he was in the prison-camp. As if the horror of his war-experience, which he must keep nameless to remain sane, has found its protective camouflage in the dead girl, Charley projects Rose's likeness on to her half-sister Nancy, convincing himself that Rose is still alive and that she is being unfaithful to him. Very gradually he is weaned from his obsession and he comes to accept the love which Nance offers in her own person, able to tell her one small part of the past that was so dangerous to evoke. The highly contrived plot which Green rears on this simple outline conveys to perfection, in its chime and rhyme of character and incident, word and phrase, the haunted inner world of the protagonist. In the echo chamber of his mind the world vibrates to the memory of the dead Rose. Rose's name is repeatedly recalled to our attention, whether by direct reference or through persistent punning (the flowers in the churchyard, the namesake waitress, 'to rise' in the past tense, etc.). The familiar name, through wild word-play, is made strange, detached from context and given new meaning.

In all his novels Green has manipulated theme words in some such manner. Every title triggers off a set of variations that gives back to the ordinary little word a mysterious resonance. In *Back* the play on the proper name represents an intensification of the normal method (it is not confined to Rose; there are puns on the names of her father, Grant, and son, Ridley). Verbal repetition such as this may result in what I. M. L. Hunter, quoted in Allen McLaurin's study of Virginia Woolf's patterns of repetition, has called 'semantic satiation', an emptying out of meaning.[29] This may be seen as a stage on the way toward the reconstitution of meaning. 'A rose is a rose is a rose': Gertrude Stein's notorious sentence is quoted by Sigurd Burckhardt as an instance of the near nonsense that the writer might deliberately produce through repetition (or punning) to break down conventional sense and transform the word into 'something rich and strange'.[30] Charley's 'rose after rose after rose', is deeply infected with a falsifying nostalgia, the 'picture postcardism' of *Blindness* and the rose-garden associations of Roe's dead wife, that is, the traditional romantic significance of the name. Charley, nevertheless, grows forgetful, has to force himself to remember, in a manner that recalls Green's commentary on his dead brother ('And that is so obviously the saddest thing about good friends who die, that one forgets.' (*Pack My Bag*, p. 83). At the point where Nance and Charley are falling in love, the famous name has become the vehicle of self-pity and a pathetic evasiveness: ' "Oh Rose, Rose," he cried out in himself, not noticing that he did this without having real regret.' (p. 179) Rose, as a person (what the proper name shadows), has lost substance, been devalued. The monstrous punning and the verbal saturation that has composed Charley's hallucinatory image of the world, and of Rose, has effected, without his conscious contriving, a shift of attention from the girl, gradually exposed as trivially promiscuous and self-centred, to Charley, morally not superior but touching now in his desperate, living need. Rose as a delusion, is not, however, so easily exorcised. The guilt, the sense of betrayal, that Green had analysed in his own case, maintains a flickering existence to the end. (Charley thinks that Rose's son, Ridley, might be his and that the boy has shared his own vision of Nance as Rose *rediviva*.) But the culmination of Charley's instinctive effort to re-relate himself to the ordinary universe is reserved for the very last page of the book. Here he prepares to make love to Nance 'for the first time in what was to be a happy married life'.

> 'Then he knelt by the bed, having under his eyes the great, the overwhelming sight of the woman he loved, for the first time without her clothes. And because the lamp was lit, the pink shade seemed to spill a light of roses over her in all their summer colours, her hands that lay along her legs were red, her stomach gold, her breasts the colour of cream roses, and her neck white roses for the bride. She had shut her eyes to let him have his fill, but that was too much, for he burst into tears again, he buried his face in her side just below the ribs, and bawled like a child. "Rose," he called out, not knowing he did so, "Rose."
>
> "There," Nancy said, "there," pressed his head with her hands. His tears wetted her. The salt water ran down between her legs. And she knew what she had taken on. It was no more or less, really, than she had expected.' (p. 208)

Robert S. Ryf has written very plausibly in his short study of Green, 'The only unambiguous thing about this scene is its ambiguity'.[31] The dead Rose haunts the hero still, it seems, in the floral glamour cast over Nance's body and in the naked double cry: suggestions of mania, betrayal, infertility, crowd in. The counter-movement within the passage is the assertion of Charley's love and Nance's acquiescence, the suggestion that his child-like crying is a necessary regression, an up-welling of spontaneous feeling which might signal that he is born again into the real world of human relationships, and that Nance, transformed into Rose, may redeem the weakness of the original, give substance to delusive shadow. I would affirm that the tendency of the last page is optimistic. Not merely does the narrator assure us of the eventual happiness of the couple, but the scene which qualifies such an assurance in some respects, a realistic expression of the hidden tensions and costs in the achievement of any union, uses the repetition of the name to evoke previous contexts that will undermine the negative force of the moment. The last time Charley had twice called out the name, as has been noted, he cried it without 'real regret' and had wept self-pitying tears. The occasion immediately precedes the scene of Mr Grant's death and Charley's virtually simultaneous recognition that he loves Nance. Mrs Grant's role in this scene may be seen as a foreshadowing of Charley's own fate. Early in the novel she had been so shocked by Rose's death that she had withdrawn into amnesia; mistaking the returned Charley for her brother who was killed in the First World War, she 'sung out, "John, John" twice.' (p. 15) As her bullying husband Gerald begins to ail, she recovers her memory and when he dies, while Charley is staying in the house, shouts twice: 'It was Mrs Grant calling so loudly that he could only just recognize her voice. "Gerald". "Gerald".' (p. 185). Confronting real loss in the present, Mrs Grant is able to utter 'crude animal cries'. (p. 186) Charley has to shut out the noise that he senses might let in intolerable memories, but Gerald's death is the turning-point of the book. The death of Rose, unreal for both Mrs Grant and Charley and eliciting from both the self-protective response of hallucination, has at last been realized in the death of Rose's father. Mrs Grant now mourns with the real name, with authentic vigour. Charley's end is prefigured. When Nance shuts her eyes ('that was too much'), she is like Rose *dead*, his old self dead, and burying his face in Nance's side, he buries that self, freed to mourn at last with a loud crying. We have an intensification of the 'Oh, Rose, Rose,' which turns the scene towards the promise in the name of 'rose again': the bawling is the essential grieving that alone can usher in re-birth. It must be admitted that Charley's return to reality is, compared with Mrs Grant's, less direct, very dependent on the goodwill of another. Painfully tentative still, it is very much in character; yet the narrator repeats the governing phrase 'for the first time' reassuringly.

The conclusion of *Back* turns on the reiterated crying of Rose's name, itself a recollection of an earlier doubling up in agony of proper names. Green makes much of the ingemination of names in his fiction, exploiting in the manner of Faulkner or Virginia Woolf (the contemporary novelists whom he seems to have admired most), the poetic resonance of the primitive ejaculation, of minimal syntax and maximum intensity. The tragic outcries of 'Caddy! Caddy!' in *The Sound and the Fury* or the title *Absalom, Absalom!*, the poignant calling of 'Jacob! Jacob!' in *Jacob's Room* or 'Mrs Ramsay! Mrs Ramsay!' in *To the Lighthouse* are memorable instances. Something of Hermione Lee's perceptive characterization of Mrs Woolf's occasions – 'the aimless, hopeful crying out of names' – is consonant with Green's practice.[32] The names haunt the helpless characters – who are positively inviting a haunting, as they grope for some value, some meaning. 'Mr Jonas' has furnished us with a simple paradigm of Green's way with the 'names to conjure with'. The leader of the rescue crew had called the name into the hole 'incongruously' and had apparently received some response. Mr Jonas, emerging, preserves his silence, bearing with him some of the 'unreality' from which he has been released. The name is familiar (to the leader, the caller, but not to the men) and strange, like a familiar spirit invoked from some unreal, some underground realm.

That someone should appear in response to the call is not the typical event. More usual in the novels is the unanswered call, and the call, as in *Blindness* and *Back*, is strikingly for a lost girl. A casual-seeming but pointed example comes from *Party Going*, when Thompson, one of the servants left to guard the luggage in the crowded concourse of the fogbound station, makes a pass at a strange girl, who appears to have 'come up out of the bloody ground', and unexpectedly receives a warm kiss. But the girl is at once called away: ' "Emily, where are you Emily?" ' (p. 472) Very moved, he too calls: ' "Emily," he cried in a falsetto voice echoing the old lady who had called her back. "Where are you Emily, my lovey-dovey?" ' (p. 473) The apparently trivial echoed cry is a serious representation of Thomson's yearning for what he calls 'fellow feeling', a precious commodity in those parts, as mysterious in origin and as elusive as the girl who has vanished forever from his sight. The familiar duplicative form of address, 'lovey-dovey', becomes in the context of his aspersions on the coldness of the upper-class woman a parody of the romantic dove-symbol of his employer, Miss Wraye.

By *Concluding* the elaboration of the outcries forms part of an elegant and extremely mystifying pattern. Rock, the old retired scientist, in calling anxiously, but unmysteriously for his escaped pet goose Ted, throws into relief the tripled call of the name of Mary, which is heard near the beginning and end of the book (pp. 7–11, 245–50). The girl has gone missing from the Civil Service training school in whose grounds Rock lives and the calling, coming from an unidentifiable voice, echoing enigmatically from the school's façade, toneless, seems the embodiment of mystery itself. Not only does the cry come out of fog and darkness, but it is heard by the deaf old man, whose relation to the missing girl is ambiguous in the extreme. Is Rock the only one to care about the girl's disappearance (whether she is rebelliously escaped or dead), or is he guilty, fearing retribution for a sexual offence, or worse? The clamour of the name is on this occasion the medium of a fine-spun comedy of menace.

Much more substantial comedy, however, is made from the disturbing crying out of names in Green's richest entertainment, *Loving*. The novel opens with a mystery, but a more familiar one. The old butler of the castle lies dying. 'One name he uttered, over and over, "Ellen",' (p. 18); '"Ellen", came the voice again, "Ellen".' (p. 19) '"Ellen", the old man called faintly.' (p. 20); 'Upon this came yet another double pitiful appeal to Ellen' (p. 21). Here is the perennial fascination of 'last words', a fascination in evidence in the title of Green's autobiography (alleged to be the last words of F. H. Bradley, the famous philosopher who died in 1924 in Oxford when Green was up)[33] and in the pathetic comedy of Joan's recollection in *Blindness*: 'Mother, when she lay dying, with Father and her at the bedside, instead of whispering something she ought have, had cried out quite loud 'John' as if she was calling. Right in front of the doctor and the village nurse and that. Then she was dead. Those were her last words. John was still the postman.' (p. 409) But Eldon's Ellen is unknown, his 'dead secret'. Formerly all-powerful in the servants' hall, he ends powerless to affect the onrush of the busy, self-interested world of his fellows. The pathos of his lonely death, his utter dependence on some named but absent woman, colours the presentation of the fate of Charley Raunce, successor to his position as butler and master-operator. By the end of the novel Charley himself lies stricken, not dying, but sick from dyspepsia, sick, perhaps, from loving. ' "Edie," he appealed soft, probably not daring to move or speak too sharp for fear he might disturb it all. Yet he used exactly that tone Mr Eldon had employed at the last when calling his Ellen. "Edie," he moaned.' (*Loving*, pp. 203–4) The 'it' which he fears to disturb is a rapt vision of Edie, the servant girl whom he plans to marry and take home to England, even though England is still at war.

The narrator's observation on the similarity of tone, taken with the pattern of the deathbed exclamation, seems to shadow the picture of promised happiness in a way that recalls the complication of the close of *Back*. 'Lucky Charley' having fallen for Edith, finds his enjoyable authority in the castle endangered. The 'absurd look of sweet pain' he has when he has proposed to her is echoed in the narrator's guess 'that he was in pain with his great delight' when he catches sight of Edie at the end. (pp. 132, 203) Love induces pain, loss of ease. Charley grows increasingly anxious about the welfare of his mother in the air-raids and unnaturally scrupulous about his mistress's missing ring (which Edith for a time has had in her keeping). Love entails responsibility, the submission to another's will. The last scene seems to show Raunce as the prisoner of love, as Green had shown old Craigan in *Living* tied down by his love for his Lily: 'We are imprisoned by that person whom we love.' (*Living*, p. 369) The repetition of Edie's name in the last scene, the opening of his eyes upon her, the moaning, all are reverberations of another scene, the one in which Charley loses the initiative in the relationship to Edie. He tries to embrace her. ' "Edie," he muttered breaking away only to drive his face down into hers once more. But he was pressing her back into a bow shape. "Edie," he called again.' (p. 180) But Edie pushes him off, accusing him of neglect; ' "I was kidding myself you would fancy me above any other to open your eyes on first thing," she repeated softly grumbling. "It's the rest," he moaned.' (p. 181) Raunce is forced into a confession of love again and is committed more firmly to marriage and the practical arrangements this will involve. But there is no missing the ecstatic note, too, in Raunce's 'picture'. Edie may be idealized, but she is not an absent, longed-for Ellen. She is present and has been, will be again, responsive to Charley's needs. Even more emphatically than in *Back* the novelist evokes a fairy-tale framework, circumscribing his action in the ring of comic romance: from 'Once upon a day an old butler called Eldon lay dying . . .' to 'The next day Raunce and Edith left without a word of warning. Over in England they were married and lived happily ever after.' In fairy-tales the name is magically potent, a key to the mysteries. Although the last recorded words of both butlers in the novel have the same intonation, the names which they utter point us in very different directions. 'Ellen', the lost girl, effectively seals off the world of Eldon, it is the echo of a dying world (the echo of Eldon in Ellen suggests a narcissistic enclosure); whereas 'Edie' is the girl *found*, opening up the surprisingly complex interior of the hero.

In *Pack My Bag* Green writes of his first experience of class divisions, of 'those narrow, deep and echoing gulfs which must be bridged' (p. 68). All efforts of communication in Green seem to be figured here. The names, the cries, typically betray an abyss of estrangement, of misconception, of secret fears. But they are a new effort to cross over. His finest work makes plain the ambiguous and costly nature of the enterprise; but the imperative, too, is clear. The gulfs must be bridged, the names ultimately shared. So the last word – the last name – should be, perhaps, a shared name, the name of the family firm where work, and life, was first a sharing: H. Pontifex and Sons, Ltd.

Notes

1 *Pack My Bag* (London: Hogarth Press, 1979), p. 88.
2 *Nothing/Doting/Blindness* (London: Picador, 1979).
3 *Caught* (London: Hogarth Press, 1978); *Loving/Living/Party Going*, with an introduction by John Updike (London: Picador, 1978); *Back* (London: Hogarth Press, 1979).
4 *Folios of New Writing*, IV, edited by John Lehmann (Autumn 1941), pp. 44–51.
5 *Ibid.*, pp. 47, 46, 50–51.
6 *An Introduction to the English Novel*, Vol. II: *Henry James to the Present Day* (London: Hutchinson, 1953), p. 195.
7 'The English Novel of the Future', *Contact*, I (Aug. 1950), p. 22.
8 'Henry Yorke, Henry Green', *London Magazine*, XIV (June/July 1974), p. 29.
9 *Folios of New Writing*, III (Spring 1941), pp. 11–17.
10 C. E. Doughty, *Travels in Arabia Deserta* (London, 1926), I, vi, pp. 173–4.
11 Quoted by Ivor Brown, *Chosen Words* (London, 1955), p. 83.
12 Reprinted in *Granite and Rainbow* (London, 1958), pp. 32–40 (pp. 39, 35, 40).
13 Review of *Blindness*, *New Statesman* (23 Sept. 1977), pp. 403–4.
14 *The Genesis of Secrecy: On the Interpretation of Narrative* (Cambridge, Mass., and London, 1979), p. 14.
15 *Concluding* (London: Hogarth Press, 1978).
16 *Oeuvres Complètes* (Paris, 1945), p. 869.
17 Review of *Living*, *Graphic* (14 June 1930), p. 588.
18 Reported by John Russell, 'There it is,' *Kenyon Review*, XXVI (Summer 1964), p. 441.
19 See, for example, Julian Franklyn, *A Dictionary of Nicknames* (London, 1962), p. 30.
20 *A Reading of Henry Green* (Seattle, 1961), p. 66.
21 See 'John' (4) and 'ejectment' in *OED*; and 'ejectment in *Wharton's Law Lexicon*, edited by A. S. Oppée (London, 1938).
22 *London Magazine*, II (February 1955), pp. 88–91.
23 *The Writer Observed*, edited by Havey Breit (Cleveland and New York,

1956), p. 105. Reprinted from the *New York Times Book Review* (19 February 1950), p. 29.

24 *Ibid.*, pp. 104–5.

25 'Henry Yorke, Henry Green', *London Magazine*, XIV (June/July 1974), p. 29.

26 Henry James, 'The Future of the Novel', *The Future of the Novel: Essays on the Art of Fiction*, edited with an introduction by Leon Edel (New York, 1956), p. 38.

27 *Contact*, I (August 1950), p. 23.

28 'There it is', *Kenyon Review*, XXVI (Summer 1964), p. 440.

29 *Virginia Woolf: The Echoes Enslaved* (Cambridge, 1973), pp. 108–10.

30 'The Poet as Fool and Priest', *ELH*, XXIII (1956), pp. 284–5.

31 *Henry Green*, Columbia Essays on Modern Writers no. 29 (New York and London, 1967), p. 31.

32 *The Novels of Virginia Woolf* (London, 1977), p. 66.

33 'There it is', *Kenyon Review*, XXVI (Summer 1964), p. 435.

The Uses of Fiction
Edited by
Douglas Jefferson
and Graham Martin

16

Surviving The Course, Or a Novelist for All Seasons: Graham Greene's *The Honorary Consul*

Miriam Allott

In a recent celebratory radio symposium, 'Graham Greene at 75', John le Carré brought out the ambiguous nature of the 'modern' in Graham Greene by referring at one moment to his being a man of the thirties with strong resemblances to Auden (a view shared by Bernard Bergonzi in *Reading the Thirties*) and at another to his remarkable universality:

> 'He is one of the very few novelists of his generation to have survived the course. It's astonishing how international Greene is . . . he's done something amazing in making his form of Englishness a universality for artistic purposes. I can't think, offhand, of any other writer who's done that. So that our drawing-rooms and our manners, even if they're translated to distant South America or whatever, still serve him as the material of human intercourse, and still serve an enormous readership as a metaphor for their own lives.'[1]

Greene's comment, in one of his rare interviews, is that as a period the thirties marked 'anybody who was writing at that time – the inevitable approach of war, and so on'. As for himself:

> 'I think I was lucky enough to be able to bridge over into the Fifties and Sixties. I found it difficult at first, when the war was over, to find what I

wanted to do in a novel; I wasn't very happy about *The Heart of the Matter*, which seemed to me to be a rather exaggerated book. I was trying to find my way into the later period. But I wouldn't say that I was really a Thirties man more than a Fifties man.'[2]

Or than a sixties or seventies man? The answer must be no, if we accept as evidence nothing more than the twin facts of his productivity throughout these decades and the topicality of his 'international' subject matter, which, as I have said elsewhere, is sometimes so remarkably up-to-the-minute that it looks like an act of *clairvoyance*.[3] But what is remarkable is the resourcefulness and resilience with which he has been able to develop his art, drawing upon older while profiting from newer technical methods. His novels span the long period from the tag-end of modernism in the thirties, through the revival of documentary realism in the fifties, to the indulgence in narrative games about the fictionality of the real and the reality of fiction which have become familiar to us since the sixties. The 'topicality' of his first major work in the seventies, *The Honorary Consul* (1973), derives as much from its manner of reflecting upon the nature of fictions as it does from its use for the plot of a political kidnapping, a form of activism which began to establish itself in those early years of the decade. The exchanges between Doctor Eduardo Plarr and his friend and patient, the once-popular South American novelist Jorge Julio Saavedra, take the form for the most part of a serio-comic debate about realism and abstraction in fiction. The debate, introduced fairly early on in the book, turns with characteristically quizzical irony on the problem of making a novel both politically topical and timeless. 'If one is to write a political novel of lasting value,' Saavedra says, 'it must be free from all the petty details that date it. Assassinations, kidnapping, the torture of prisoners – these things belong to our decade. But I do not want to write merely for the seventies.' A 'poet', that is a creative writer, 'deals in absolutes. A novelist today who wants to represent tyranny should not describe the activities of General Stroesser in Paraguay – that is journalism not literature – Tiberius is a better example for a poet.' (p. 57) As it turns out, Saavedra's creator works his cunning to eat this particular cake and have it too by seeing to it, as often before, that those 'things of our decade' (assassination, kidnapping, the torture of political prisoners, revolutionary activism, all feature in some way in his story) shall exist in a symbiotic relationship with a particular kind of inquiry into the nature of certain absolutes. The terms of the inquiry are penetrated by that sense of the ambiguous surrounding concepts which human beings use often and understand little – their terms for them are love, honour, God – which gives to Greene's novels their unmistakable personal flavour. And as the 'things of the decade' have altered, the tone and mood of the inquiry have altered with them, together with the author's manner of telling.

References to literature in his fictions are of course nothing new. We have long been accustomed to his characters talking about being affected by it in some way or another. Instances occurred even before the heightening of Raven's lonely misery in *A Gun For Sale* (1936) as he listens to Tennyson's *Maud* broadcast in the National Programme –

> 'Ah Christ, that it were possible
> For one short hour to see
> The souls we loved, that they might tell us
> What and where they be . . .'

– and have continued all the way to the reading of Trollope's *The Way We Live Now* by almost everyone who is anyone in the cast of *The Human Factor* (1978). In all the novels, playing in and out of them like leit-motifs, are echoes of Greene's 'presiders', especially Conrad, James, Stevenson, Mauriac, Péguy. Probably the most noticeable effect on Greene of his literary enthusiasms has been, paradoxically, a heightening of his idiosyncratic personal style, a phenomenon with its own fascination for the student of 'influences'. The single sign of anxiety appears in the early period, between the first novels and *A Gun For Sale*, when Greene abandoned Conrad 'because his influence on me was too great'.[4] There is little to suggest such anxious self-scrutiny in *The Honorary Consul*, where the literary exchanges seem at first sight to be doing no more than point to the tricksy narrative games which the modern novelist sometimes feels drawn to play. It is true that Greene is believed by some to have played his own game of now-you-see-me-now-you-don't in the parable about the jeweller in *A Burnt Out Case* (1960), which focusses themes such as the callousing of the creative sensibility by pride and success and the capsizing of critical intelligence when in collision with the fashionable established reputation.[5] The parable certainly enshrines observable truths about the risks besetting a particular kind of creative sensibility, especially one that is skilful, admired and prolific, and in which the first fresh driving impulse is the realization in art of a strong personal vision which, in the closing stages of a career, may be held to more complexly, and perhaps with more difficulty, than at its beginning. That Graham Greene is particularly well equipped to explore such a situation is suggested by the changed tone and emphasis separating his dryly ironic novels of the 1970s from, let us say, the strongly coloured metaphysical drama of *The Power and the Glory* or *The Heart of the Matter*, which he now describes as 'exaggerated'. And also by his recently adding high on his list of 'presiders' Dostoevsky's The Legend of the Grand Inquisitor.

In *The Honorary Consul* Saavedra's fictions, together with his discussions with Plarr, form an integral part of the narrative. Saavedra's darkly romantic themes, written 'in a heavy pulsating style, full of the spirit of *machismo*', are set before us in the first pages of the book and their presence is felt like an undersong during the events and emotions unfolding themselves in the rest of the story with a totally unSaavedra-like stylistic sparseness. And yet Greene's own brand of romanticism suffuses all, establishing itself from the beginning in an opening sequence constructed with his customary narrative skills: there are the haunting visual memories of a foreign setting; the evocation of a strange and sorrowing atmosphere of isolation, loss and exile 'on the edge of things'; and an accomplished orientation of the reader in the 'present' of the story while paradoxically awakening in him the sense of long sad passages of time already lived through. The Saavedra undersong, then, does not act simply as a kind of satirical counterpoint to the 'biter bit and bitter bite' of a Greene mainsong. The relationship is more complex and, indeed, more affectionate. Plarr's stance is not the novel's. His melancholy, irritation and distaste are reflections of his own complication of distresses, for he is one of that lengthy line of would-be 'uninvolved' Greene characters (he bears a close family resemblance to Fowler in *The Quiet American*).

When we first encounter him in the opening pages Plarr, a doctor in his early thirties, is walking alone in the evening by the riverside in the small quiet South American town north of Buenos Aires. In the same way, Mr. Tench, a dentist and like Plarr daily engaged with human pain, walked alone by his Mexican waterside at the opening of *The Power and the Glory*, which *The Honorary Consul* complements and replies to, its terms and procedures suggesting a transposition of that earlier dialectic into a totally different key (a 1970s key). It is as intensely concerned with pain and loneliness, with spiritual deprivation and social injustice, and with the conflicting attempts, often tragically at odds with each other, made by human beings in their struggle for comprehension and betterment; but it is now spare, wry, often ironical, and always meticulously directed to the non-melodramatic. Plarr's thoughts turn (as many times before) to his English father, the exiled espouser of humanitarian causes who vanished years ago on some courageous libertarian venture across the border, departing from this same quayside, where the fourteen-year-old Eduardo and his once beautiful South American mother waved goodbye for the last time. 'We all of us seem to live with dead fathers,' Plarr says on the last day of his life, which takes place not long afterwards, (p. 217) and this key theme, also emerging in the opening sequence, is related to the other theme which centres on the idea of love, honour and courage as the staple materials of certain fictions ('myths' would be the fashionable word). In the Argentinian tradition honoured by Saavedra the qualities are united in the simple romantic conception of '*machismo*':

> '*Machismo* – the source of masculine pride – was the Spanish equivalent of *virtus*. It had little to do with English courage or a stiff upper lip. Perhaps his father in his foreign way was trying to imitate *machismo* when he chose to face alone the daily increasing dangers on the other side of the Paraguayan border, but it was only the stiff upper lip which showed on the quay.' (p. 10)

The solitarily perambulating Doctor Plarr carries with him a copy of *The Taciturn Heart*, the earliest of Saavedra's long series of long novels. Brought up on Dickens and Conan Doyle (one of his creator's early enthusiasms), Plarr finds it enough to read a few pages at a time and not only, it turns out, because 'Doctor Saavedra was far from taciturn'. Greene's lively talent for parody often indicates affection as well as amusement (as with many of the best parodists) and does so in this 'extract' from Saavedra's novel while keeping in play Plarr's resentment:

> ' "Julio Moreno would sit for hours in silence, on those days when the wind blew continuously from the sea and salted their few hectares of dry earth, shrivelling the rare plants which had survived the last wind, his chin in his hands, his eyes closed as though he wished to live only in some hidden corridor of his nature from which his wife was excluded. He never complained. She would stand beside him for long minutes, holding the maté gourd in her left hand, and when he opened his eyes Julio Moreno would take it from her without a word spoken. Only a relaxation of the muscles around the stern and unbeaten mouth appeared to her like an expression of thanks." ' (p. 13)

We are allowed to enjoy the flavour of the rest of this novel-within-a-novel for Plarr summarizes it sourly to himself. He guesses rightly that a hundred pages further on Moreno will encounter his wife's lover in the city (she had run away briefly with a more talkative companion), they will fight with knives, Moreno will be killed, his eyes as always showing 'the expression of an exhausted swimmer who surrenders to the dark tide of his ineluctable destiny'. Plarr will not put up with this.

> 'Life isn't like that. Life isn't noble or dignified. Even Latin-American life. Nothing is ineluctable. Life has surprises. Life is absurd. Because it's absurd there is always hope. Why, one day we may even discover a cure for cancer and the common cold.' (p. 16)

He looks at the last page where 'Julio Moreno's blood was draining away' and then closes the book 'with a bang of irritation'. (p. 10)

But the pattern of ironies in *The Honorary Consul* suggests that everything is true in a different sense, life being indeed 'full of surprises'. By the end of the story Plarr will have been caught up in political action and will have lost his life trying to save his mistress's husband, accidentally the victim of a revolutionary kidnapping. He will also have forgiven with his last breath the idealistic leader of the band, the failed priest, Léon Rivas, an old school friend who himself loses his life trying in turn to save Plarr. How's that for *machismo*, one might well ask. Love certainly is at the heart of Greene's matter as well as Saavedra's, and 'the taciturn heart' is a good name for both, since in Plarr, in Charley Fortnum (the Honorary Consul for whom he dies), in Clara (Charley's pathetic little wife from Senora Sanchez's well run brothel), and in the failed priest himself, love is either feared, dissembled or unexpressed. But it finds a measure of release, at last, through 'a relaxation of the muscles' so to speak, for example when Rivas permits himself to talk of his feeling for the slow painful conquest of the 'dayside' over the 'nightside' in both God and man: he makes sense of things only by seeing both as united in a long process of learning and suffering. It does so again when Charles Fortnum comforts Clara's grief for her dead lover in a generous and moving conclusion.

The difference between these figures and Saavedra's lies as much as anywhere in the self-scrutiny and self-distrust which Greene articulates in them but which is countered by his own agile feeling for the interplay of the comic with the profoundly serious. We learn early on, for instance, that Moreno, the first in Saavedra's long line of noble, simple, *machismo* heroes, was modelled on someone met in the bar of a small holiday hotel who was not South American at all but Welsh. ' "Who ever heard of a Welshman with *machismo*," says the old friend and jealous enemy who reveals all to Plarr, "There are lots of Welshmen in these parts. He was drunk, that was all. His weekly drunk when he came in from the country." ' (p. 15) This part-bracing, part-poignant, commentary of the actual on the ideal has its focal centre in the tragi-comic kidnapping of the ageing, whisky-drinking and, politically speaking, totally unimportant Honorary Consul, who is seized in mistake for the American Ambassador. This amateurish bungling brings the principals, including the pathetic revolutionary band, face to face with pain and fear, the taking and saving of life, and brings a new need to understand the nature of whatever it is in whose name their actions are carried on. So the issue long ago dramatized in *The Power and the Glory* through the relationship between the whisky priest and his captor, the communist police lieutenant, are reassembled in a different pattern, the religio-political conflict centred this time in the priest-turned-revolutionary and the alcoholism transferred to Charles Fortnum, who as it happens is, like Plarr, a 'bad' Catholic. And with the different assembly, the temper and outcome are also different. Browning's 'dangerous edge of things', which Greene refers to with special emphasis in his autobiography, *A Sort of Life*,[6] reappears here as the more ambiguous region indicated in the epigraph from Hardy, 'All things merge into one another – good into evil, generosity into justice, religion into politics . . .' This image, drawn from frontiers and border regions as so often in Greene's novels, expresses characteristic compassion towards human efforts to find a path through the complexities of the 'real'. Saavedra's novels irritate Plarr, the 'English' side of whose temperament cannot tolerate their elevated notions. Yet his antagonism speaks for itself, since he is also partly South American and inhabits a borderland region whose things 'merge into one another'; moreover the creator of the *machismo* stories, living in a dingy room in straitened circumstances and keeping up appearances in his single carefully pressed grey suit, is in his own way a heroic figure, single-mindedly dedicated to discovering accurate artistic expression for the truth of things as he sees them.

The point is that this 'truth' is glimpsed – if seen at all – only here and there, and in different ways according to different lights. Greene's use of his own and Saavedra's fiction to comment obliquely on each other in this manner is an allusion to current narrative devices (such as those of John Fowles). With the cunning of an old hand, Graham Greene exploits fashionable literary expectations in the interests of his own permanent concern with what Kafka called 'the rumour about the true things'. In this novel his characters strain their ears to catch a sound of the 'true things', at times seeming to hear something distantly and half-consciously, like voices coming over the radio to the kidnappers and their victims in the hut at the heart of the *barrio popular* among the dwellings of the wretchedly poor.

Since there can only be 'rumour' about absolutes, seeing and hearing as uncertainly as we do, the narrative makes itself responsible for demonstrating that whatever is captured in our myths about 'the true things' may at least be 'true in a different sense'. From the outset, for instance, it is apparent that there is more than one explanation for Doctor Plarr's irritation with *The Taciturn Heart*. He lingers reading by the riverside because of his anxiety to avoid chance phone calls at home. He is anxious because he is involved, in spite of himself, with Rivas and his friends who will call him later that night; and he has become involved because he believes their assurance that his father is still alive, a political prisoner across the border, and that if he agrees to help them an attempt at rescue will be made in reward. Since their plan is to kidnap the American Ambassador during his official visit, holding him to ransom for the lives of political prisoners across the border, he undertakes to secure details about the Ambassador's itinerary from the Honorary Consul who will be of the party. This promises to resemble still more closely the raw material for a Saavedra story when we learn that one call especially dreaded would be from his mistress Clara, the wife of the Honorary Consul but pregnant by her lover. Here, then, is a situation heavy with the potentialities of love, courage, honour, *machismo*. But facts are one thing, the human motives and feelings behind them another.

To begin with, the revolutionaries know that Plarr's father is already dead, so it is through deceit that he comes to their hideout to attend Charley Fortnum, like a son attending a surrogate father, and so finally meets his death. Then there is the matter of love. Clara is nothing like the wealthy and voracious well-upholstered Latin-American married ladies of Plarr's casual affairs. Nor has she much in common with the silent subservient females in Saavedra's novels. Like Plarr she is a character with a familiar Graham Greene lineage. Her kindred include Rose in *Brighton Rock* and Helen Rolt in *The Heart of the Matter*, immature, vulnerable figures who must be reckoned among life's losers unless we count as dark victories their uncomplaining acceptance of pain and loss. But Clara, structurally speaking if nothing else, has a more positive rôle than theirs and becomes an important agent for the humane counterpointing ironies of the novel containing her. She is the childlike prostitute with the grey birthmark on her forehead with whom Charley Fortnum fell in love when frequenting Senora Sanchez's establishment and whom he has taken as his second wife. The girl who arouses both Charley and Eduardo Plarr makes her first appearance as one of Senora Sanchez's girls, glimpsed through an open door tidily straightening the bed after her last customer. This is Plarr's first visit, instigated by Saavedra, who uses the establishment weekly for physical relief and also for procuring information 'about human nature', particularly the life of the poor since otherwise in this city, he explains, 'there was no contact between the classes'. (p. 54) He and Plarr discuss literature throughout the evening, starting at the run-down Hotel Hacional and continuing at the brothel. So the beginning of Plarr's 'obsession' with Clara as he calls it, to avoid the word 'love', is bound up with the drunken conversation about life and art which becomes one of the narrative's comic set-pieces. Saavedra speaks of the disciplines to which his 'daemon' submits him.

> 'A talent is friendly. A daemon is destructive. You cannot conceive how much I suffer when I write. I have to force myself day after day to sit down pen in hand, and I struggle for expression.'

Castillo, the fisherman in his last novel,

> 'wages an endless war with the sea for a small reward. You might say that Castillo is a portrait of the artist. Such daily agony and the result five hundred words. 'A very small catch . . . (pp. 53–4)

The 'daemon' is indeed peculiarly destructive: artistic dedication 'merges' in the Hardyan sense into something else when Saavedra later refuses to sign a letter which might save Fortnum because he disapproves of the style. At this moment, however, Plarr comments dryly:

> ' "I seem to remember Castillo died from a revolver shot in a bar defending his one-eyed daughter from rape."
>
> "Ah yes, I am glad you noticed the Cyclops symbol," Dr. Saavedra said. "A symbol of the novelist's art. A one-eyed art because one eye concentrates the vision. The diffuse writer is always two-eyed. He includes too much – like a cinema screen . . ." ' (p. 54)

If Saavedra fails to practise which he preaches, his creator certainly does not. It comes as no surprise to learn that Greene made seven drafts of this most undiffuse novel, paring it hard down in the interests of density and concentration.[7] Once at the brothel Saavedra is joined by Teresa, a girl from Salta where he plans to set his next novel. Plarr fears that his daemon will insist on giving the fictional Teresa only one eye, and leads him on to further explanations when Saavedra says that he has the idea of giving her only one leg.

It is hard not to see amused authorial self-comment in this juxtaposition of Saavedra's disabled heroines and the thin girl with the birthmark. But it makes us think of something else as well. Saavedra's 'one leg' is to be 'a symbol of the poor crippled country where we still hope . . .', part of his attempt to free his political novel 'from all the petty details which date it'. Greene, taking another route, concentrates on making his 'metaphors' as close to 'metonymy' as the resources of narrative will allow. Plarr's irritation – 'Your fisherman is timeless because he never existed,' he says tartly – is accounted for by 'realistic' psychological motives. He is angered by recollections of the harsh actualities of his father's life and distracted by his unlooked-for emotional response to the girl with the blemish on her forehead. Long afterwards, when Clara has become Mrs Fortnum and he is called to examine her slight malady, he passes a sporting print on the wall outside her bedroom. It shows a hunting scene in a landscape with 'a narrow stream shaded by willows situated in that small northern island where his father had been born'. Thereafter this becomes a 'symbol' of his own, representing 'a kind of peace, a kind of truth' associated with the girl whom he soon makes his mistress and whom he treats casually, even cruelly, to protect himself against the demands of 'love'. Her body haunts him,

> 'like the site of an old country battlefield where pale grass grew which had abolished the scars of war, and a small stream flowed peacefully between the willows . . .' (p. 73)

To the end he flinches from understanding the nature of her feelings for him, hoping always that she plays 'the comedy of love' like one of Senora Sanchez's well-trained girls, but the real 'comedy' is her sad pretence that she is indifferent to him, biting back the expressions of pleasure which it would anger him to hear. Charley Fortnum too falls to distrusting her when he learns of the affair with Plarr and finds that the child, whose advent had filled him with pride and happiness, is not his. Yet all these unSaavedra-like characters, and with them Léon

Rivas, the failed priest torn by his pity for God and man, experience something for which 'love' is probably the only possible word – 'the rumour of the true things' in this book. The Honorary Consul at the heart of it, old Charley Fortnum, ungainly, alcoholic, with 'increasing spots of melancholy like mould in his well-bottled bonhomie', and nothing at all like Julio Moreno, not only forgives Clara but comes to cherish her with new unselfishness when he understands the strength of her feeling for the man who deceived him but cancelled his debt when he walked out to plead with the police for a stay of time and was shot by the parachutists. 'There's nothing wrong in love, Clara,' he tries to say, 'It happens. It doesn't much matter who with. We get caught up,' adding as 'a feeble joke' to reassure her, 'we get kidnapped . . . by mistake.' His last speech meets her anguish ('He wanted to kill the baby . . . He really wanted it. I knew then he could never love me') and speaks to the book's principal theme.

> ' "Perhaps he'd begun, Clara. Some of us . . . we are a bit slow . . . it's not so easy to love . . . we make a lot of mistakes." He went on for the sake of saying something, "I hated my father . . . I did not much like my wife . . . but they were not really bad people . . . that was only one of my mistakes." '

Her denial ('I never loved him, Charley') is belied by her tears but in place of grief or jealousy he experiences

> 'immense relief. It was as though, after what seemed an interminable time of anxious waiting in the anteroom of death, someone came to him with the good news that he had never expected to hear. Someone he loved would survive . . . ' (pp. 267–8)

In Saavedra's *The Taciturn Heart* the lover survives, the husband dies displaying *machismo*, and the events leading to the dénouement are intended to show the working of 'ineluctable destiny'. In *The Honorary Consul* the events seen in retrospect look predestined; at the same time these events as they fall impress us as supporting Plarr's notion of life as 'absurd . . . full of surprises'. But the 'surprises' are surprising, we come to see, because of the characters' 'clouds of unknowing'. The sense of a considered tricksiness at the heart of things is most explicit in those mischievous conversations devised for Plarr and Saavedra but the ideas set moving there are felt throughout this subtle and complex book. It is these ideas and the feelings they generate which help to make *The Honorary Consul* Graham Greene's most accomplished novel to date. And that, after all, is saying something.

Notes

1 *The Listener*, 4 October 1979, p. 443.
2 *Loc cit.*, p. 442.
3 'Graham Greene and the Way we live now', *Critical Quarterly*, Vol. 20, No. 3, p. 12.
4 On this see David Lodge, 'Graham Greene', *Columbia Essays on Modern Writers*, No. 17 (1966), reprinted in his *The Novelist at the Crossroads* (1971), pp. 96, 98.
5 *A Burnt Out Case*, p. 155. All page numbers in references to Greene's novels are those in the Penguin edition.
6 '. . . if I were to choose an epigraph for all the novels I have written, it would be from "Bishop Blougram's Apology" ' [ll.396–401, beginning, 'Our interest's on the dangerous side of things/The honest thief, the tender murderer . . . '], *A Sort of Life* (1971), p. 115.
7 From a letter addressed to the present writer.

The Uses of Fiction
Edited by
Douglas Jefferson
and Graham Martin

17

William Golding's View of the Human Condition in *Free Fall*

Sylvère Monod

Free Fall is the fourth of William Golding's novels in the order of publication. Very little is known about the order in which they were written and even less about the period when each book was first conceived or came to maturity. But it is fairly obvious that the first three which saw light of print in quick succession (*Lord of the Flies*, 1954; *The Inheritors*, 1955; *Pincher Martin*, 1956) form one phase of the Golding *oeuvre* and result from one initial spurt of creative energy. The interval of three years between *Pincher Martin* and *Free Fall* (1959) is the first of its kind; it was not entirely barren since *The Brass Butterfly* appeared in 1958; but that comedy, though it reads pleasantly enough and is not unlike a minor late play by G. B. Shaw, can neither be regarded as a major achievement nor comfortably placed at any point of the line leading from *Pincher Martin* to *Free Fall*. The next Golding novel was to come only five years later (*The Spire*, 1964).

Free Fall thus occupies a curious position in the Golding canon, as, for that matter, Golding's work as a novelist occupies an intriguing position in the life and career of that writer. William Golding is still in full possession of his remarkable powers; but the fact is that he published no new novel between *The Pyramid* (which came out in 1967) and *Darkness Visible* (1979). This makes it possible for the critic to cast a retrospective glance at the bulk of William Golding's early achievement in that field. Admittedly, *The Scorpion God* had come in 1973, six years after *The Pyramid* and six years before *Darkness Visible*, which might seem to imply a desire to keep in regular if remote touch with the writing of fiction, but *The Scorpion God* is a collection of three short stories, one of which was by no means recent at the time of publication, and parts of the book were clearly in the vein of *The Inheritors*, others in that of *The Brass Butterfly*. It is tempting to see Golding's earlier fiction in two main blocks, with *Free Fall* as a kind of belated appendage to the original three novels, followed by the looser pair of *The Spire* and *The Pyramid* (linked by the striking similarity of their titles, if by nothing else).

If *Free Fall* is in the nature of an appendage to William Golding's first three published novels, it is nevertheless markedly different from them. It has something in common, undoubtedly, with *Pincher Martin*, in that both novels concern themselves with the retrospective glance cast by a man over his past life and particularly over his misdeeds. But even with *Pincher Martin* the differences are much more striking than the similarities; *Free Fall* has none of the sensational purgatorial gimmickry used in the earlier novel to explore Christopher Martin's psychology and morality. The least insular of Golding's novels so far, *Free Fall* is in many ways a new departure in the author's career.[1]

Curiously enough, the position of *Free Fall* in William Golding's own liking and estimation seems to be consistently low. I find that I am by no means the only person, or the only Frenchman, to whom the novelist has said as much (in the course of a private conversation held in May 1976), quite unambiguously. It is of course readily understandable that Golding should have a special fondness for *Lord of the Flies* which made him famous. As for the rest, perhaps *Free Fall* is in fact too different from those other children of his brain to have endeared itself to him. If it was, as suggested above, a new departure, the author may feel that it took him into a dead end. However that may be, William Golding has not expressed himself about *Free Fall* as he has done about *Lord of the Flies*, a state of things which, as will appear later, is not without its advantages.[2] In default of the author's own comments, however, let us consider a few representative opinions. The originality of the novel is generally recognized. Oldsey and Weintraub see it as 'unique in Golding's work'.[3] Kinkead-Weekes and Gregor call it 'the most elusive and difficult of Golding's novels'.[4] And Henri A. Talon, who clearly resents or deplores *Free Fall* on the whole, defines that novel as 'of his works the one most fraught with experience'[5]. Talon goes on to add, with lavish use of inverted commas, that *Free Fall*, rather than 'a "true" novel', is 'a "montage" of situations'. (p. 66) Oldsey and Weintraub are less reserved in their admiration: 'Golding's ability to hold, balance, and juggle scenes so that eventually they come down in place is extraordinary . . . it has gone . . . probably high enough to be fairly compared with Camus's classic structure'.[6] And Mark Kinkead-Weekes and Ian Gregor write, yet more reassuringly, that 'it is surely not perverse to claim the book as a considerable achievement'.[7] Reassuringly to me, for that is precisely the claim I wish to make for *Free Fall*.

A vivid liking and admiration for *Free Fall* (or even, as in my case, a preference for *Free Fall* over the author's other works of fiction) may seem to imply a lack of appreciation for the other Golding, or Goldings. One cannot speak of the *ordinary* Golding, for he is never ordinary and never made it a habit to write one specific kind of fiction, but one may speak of the *real* Golding and there is reason to believe that he would accept such a definition of himself as the author of *Lord of the Flies*, *The Inheritors* and *Pincher Martin*; a preference for *Free Fall* thus boils down to a preference for the *realist* Golding over the real Golding, or creator of fables, allegories and myths.[8] Not that there is no myth in *Free Fall*.[9] Not that the early trio had contained no realistic elements or had not been concerned, like *Free Fall*, with the human predicament. But they had expressed that preoccupation less straightforwardly.

The major question about *Free Fall*, considering Golding's constant ambition and also taking into account his specific aim, the question by the answer to which the novel stands or falls, may well be: what does Golding tell his reader through that novel about mankind and mankind's fate that is true, important, and, if not entirely new, at least worth hearing?

Oldsey and Weintraub in their detailed comparison between *Free Fall* and Albert Camus's *La Chute*,[10] have convincingly shown that the two works have more in common than their names. The central theme of Golding's novel – if not all his fiction – brings to mind another great French work of our time, André Malraux's *La Condition humaine* (the human predicament).

The two words of Golding's title are significant in themselves as well as through their association, they possess 'both theological and scientific connotations'.[11] The theological, or at any rate moral, aspect probably predominates over the scientific, which serves only as a metaphor. But the very real and acute problems faced by the narrator,

Sammy Mountjoy, are those of freedom (and/or free choice, free will) and of the Fall, the fall of man, the fall of Everyman, regarded as ineluctable and inborn. Sammy repeatedly asks himself the same question or questions: when did he lose or alienate his freedom, when did he fall from his childhood state of grace? The loss of freedom and the fall of man are one and the same event, which Sammy Mountjoy (predestined by his ironical name, it would seem, to descend into sorrow rather than mount in joy) finds it very hard to pinpoint, however hard he tries. As the loss of freedom and the fall result from a man's use of his free will, the whole problem is one of guilt and responsibility. Mark Kinkead-Weekes and Ian Gregor's masterly chapter on *Free Fall* is based on Golding's essential concern 'with *Being*, not *Becoming*'.[12] But, even through their careful analysis and discussion, it appears that Being and Becoming cannot be wholly separated. 'What I was,' Sammy claims, 'I had become.' (p. 100)[13]

A complementary aspect of the human predicament also examined in *Free Fall*, and on which Golding lays great stress, is the lack of stability and even permanence in the human personality. That view is not new of course. Oscar Wilde had been much struck by the impossibility of identifying oneself (i.e., one's present self) with the remembered image of oneself (i.e., one's past self) acting, feeling, or writing, some time ago – not even necessarily very long ago. In his essay 'Pen, Pencil and Poison', Wilde wrote: 'The permanence of personality is a very subtle metaphysical problem, and certainly the English law solves the question in an extremely rough-and-ready manner.'[14] Closer to us, two remarkable though unaccountably neglected novels by Rayner Heppenstall, *The Connecting Door* and *The Woodshed*, both published in 1962 and thus of later date than *Free Fall*, explored the same psychological and moral difficulty. *The Connecting Door*, in particular, goes one better by staging in a spectacular and graphic manner the confrontation between three of a man's successive selves. I do not wish to go into details here, having already done so elsewhere.[15] But I would like to point out that this perception of an important phenomenon belonging to the condition of man, of modern man at any rate, forms part of the value, interest, and modernity of Golding's *Free Fall*. The author has not invented a device comparable to Heppenstall's in *The Connecting Door* (where Harold Atha, in the course of his third visit to a city in the East of France, meets, and holds converse with, both Harold and Atha, i.e., with the persons he had been on the occasion of his two earlier stays in the same city). But his procedure for placing

Sammy Mountjoy face to face with several of his earlier selves is nonetheless original and effective.

How is it done? In great part through narrative technique and, more precisely, through the manipulation of time. Without going into details of plot, we note that an obvious characteristic of *Free Fall* is the absence of chronological sequence in the narrative. But there is a deliberate purpose behind the shuffling of the sections. In the first three, Sammy Mountjoy looks back, fairly consecutively (but not quite) at his childhood; in sections 4, 5, and 6, his story has taken a great leap forward to the period when he has become an art student, lives in London, seeks out his former schoolfellow Beatrice Ifor, courts her, forces her to become his very unsatisfactory mistress, and finally deserts her as soon as he has fallen in love with another woman whom he marries. Section 7 takes another jump ahead to a time when Sammy is a prisoner-of-war in a German camp, being questioned by one Dr Halde, who attempts in vain to make him denounce the prisoners planning to escape; because of his refusal to answer Dr Halde's questions, Sammy is locked up in a dark room. The scheme becomes slightly more complicated at this stage, for in section 8, before the two following sections relate his harrowing experiences in the dark cell, Sammy reminisces; it is not quite clear whether he does so in the cell itself (in which case we should have him in the book, as so often, reminiscing about reminiscing) or by recalling the experiences in the cell at some later period, beyond the point reached by the narrative by the end of the book, at the time when he is conducting his searching self-examination. Section 8 begins with the query 'How did I come to be so frightened of the dark?' (p. 117) The answer to that question enables him to bridge a great part of the gap left between sections 3 and 4, explaining in passing, that although originally the pauper orphaned son of a decayed prostitute, he had been adopted by Watts-Watt, a kindly but tormented and ridiculous clergyman, and thus enabled to go to art school. Sections 9–10, then, deal with the experiences in the dark cell. Sections 11 and 12 make up another extended flashback and complete the stop-gap narrative begun in 8 (of the period of Sammy's adolescence and schooldays, originally left unfilled-in between 3 and 4). Section 13 has to do with a much later, i.e., more recent, post-war, time, when Sammy visits Beatrice Ifor in a mental hospital where she carries on her incurably wrecked existence. There remains only a very brief fourteenth section reverting to the end of the dark cell episode and disclosing one essential fact about it, i.e., that the terrors of the cell (in fact an ordinary cupboard) had been made up solely by Sammy's own imagination and sick fears.

So that the real, historical chronology of Sammy's *Bildungsroman* rests on the following sequence of the sections in the book: 1, 2, 3, 8, 11, 12, 4, 5, 6 (here, a still unbridged time-gap), 7, 9, 10, 14, 13. The number of these sections calls only for brief comment. Unlike *Lord of the Flies*, which has just twelve (like *The Inheritors* and *The Spire*, while *Pincher Martin* runs to fourteen, twelve being reputedly the most harmonious or classical figure), *Free Fall* is thus composed of thirteen units and a coda (or *cauda*), the units being of uneven length and irregularly organized.[16] Whether or not Golding chose the figure thirteen deliberately, it so happens that thirteen as a number is small, odd, prime, supposedly unlucky (or, through inverted superstition, lucky), and in every way adapted to this story and study of Sammy Mountjoy, the bastard, the eccentric, the artist, the odd man out in so many ways.

The technique of shuffling the time-units may well be regarded as owing something to such predecessors of William Golding as Joseph Conrad and the founding father of flexibility in the novel, Laurence Sterne. The technique has some traditional weight and significance. In fact, the resulting time-pattern is both psychologically and morally convincing: psychologically, because as far as we know, the human mind is much less methodical than any form of printed narrative; memory never yields a continuously chronological sequence of events (that is a significant distinction between memories and memoirs, or – in French – between *une mémoire* and *un mémoire*); it jumps back and forth, juxtaposes and conflates episodes, etc. Morally, the quest for guilt and responsibility is much assisted by the potentialities of such a time-pattern: Sammy can thus short-circuit many impeccable chains of explanations, and embrace at one glance the consequence and the cause, however remote from each other in time, and conversely he can send his mental searchlight at will further and further back into his past. To say that the time-pattern in *Free Fall* is convincing is not to say that it is life-like; it is of course arbitrary and contrived (like all organized narrative); but it makes the book readable as well as meaningful, and it enables the narrator to be constantly confronting and comparing segments of his past, as though his life were given back to him on index-cards instead of in a bound volume or on an unbroken recorded tape. 'Time,' Sammy writes, 'is two moods. The one is an effortless perception native to us as water to the mackerel. The other is a memory, a sense of shuffle fold and coil, of that day nearer because it is more important, of that event mirroring this, or those three set apart, exceptional and out of the straight line altogether.' (pp. 5–6) Mountjoy thereby gains the possibility of conducting his search more profoundly, of investigating really meaningful relationships between persons or incidents, of producing what Talon finely called 'the superficially sinuous yet profoundly coherent evocation of the past'.[17] A straightforward chronological narrative can perhaps achieve similar results, though at a greater cost, and with less of the fruitful freedom that a book called *Free Fall* demands and deserves.

The method is not everything. The method is only, after all, the medium, and the medium is not *all* the message, though there would be no message without a medium to convey it. In spite of the current unpopularity of the notion that art must, or even that art may, have a message, that a work of art may be, or may include, a statement, I find it extremely difficult to discuss Golding in other terms, or, for that matter, to believe that he would have greatly cared to write *Free Fall* if he had not wished to say something, to convey ideas to his readers. No doubt that is what he means when he says: 'I have been trying to write the sort of thing I would define as "significant literature" ' or when he refers to 'the novel which tries to look at life anew'.[18] Let us therefore review such general statements as *Free Fall* contains, and attempt to define their overall significance.

I suppose many readers will have been mildly irritated by the opening pages of *Free Fall* which are almost entirely made up of general statements, many of them sufficiently portentous: 'Free-will cannot be debated but only experienced' (p. 5, in fact the very first page of the novel). 'We are dumb and blind yet we must see and speak . . . To communicate is our passion and our despair'. (p. 7) They are interspersed with Sammy Mountjoy's self-questionings (as a man) and posturings (as narrator) in a way reminiscent of the tricks and manners of the garrulous Victorians, even including an address to the reader, though not, of course, to the dear, or the gentle, reader. 'Then why am I writing this down?' (p. 6) 'To communicate . . . With whom then? You? . . . No. Not with you . . . And who are you any way? Are you on the inside, have you a proof-copy? Am I a job to do? Do I exasperate you by translating incoherence into incoherence?' (p. 7) Golding's or Sammy's reader is thus treated as someone clearly neither dear nor gentle, someone to be met with a mixture of arrogance and cunning. It would be a pity to let oneself be irritated, to the point of being deterred, by the slightly pretentious note in this beginning. Every reading after the first one will provide evidence that the opening section has its uses, that the archness and slackness belong to Sammy and indeed characterize him thus early.[19] Besides, every word counts, it will be discovered on returning to that section, or on remembering it, and contributes in striking the keynote and heralding the treatment of the major themes.

Among the general statements in the later portions of *Free Fall* we find: 'Man is not an instantaneous creature . . . He is an incredible bundle of miscellaneous memories and feelings, of fossils and coral growths' (p. 36); 'No man can tell the whole truth' (p. 140); 'Perhaps consciousness and the guilt which is unhappiness go together' (p. 60); 'Only the things you cannot avoid, the sear of sex or pain, avoidance of the one suffering repetition and prolongation of the other, this constitutes what your daily consciousness would not admit, but experiences as life' (p. 110); 'What men believe is a function of what they are; and what they are is in part what has happened to them' (p. 161); 'Useless to say that a man is a whole continent, pointless to say that each consciousness is a whole world because each consciousness is a dozen worlds' (p. 189). Such phrases and questionings add up to a valid, coherent view of life, profoundly pessimistic in tone. Sammy Mountjoy is not a pleasure to contemplate, least of all to himself. He may be a great artist, but he is a sorry specimen of humanity, although at the same time a representative specimen, being very much (apart from his artistic gift) the *homme moyen sensuel*, trapped in the shackles and limitations of the human predicament.[20] Golding seems to have intended his reader to become conscious, to *gain* awareness, of his (or her) kinship with Sammy. There are Mountjoy-like trends and impulses in all human beings because such trends and impulses, unpalatable as they are, are part of human nature. But for this awareness to be a gain, and not a dead loss of hope, we must step beyond the desolating perception.

Sammy is bound to accept responsibility for some misdeeds, or for acts of his which involved enduring unhappiness for others. But he repeatedly finds that he could not have acted otherwise than he did, being what he was ('I had lost my power to choose. I had given away my freedom . . . What I was, I had become.' (p. 100) Probably part of Sammy Mountjoy's theorizing amounts to special pleading. It is comfortable or at least comforting for him to think that what men are is in part what has happened to them. He deceives himself, is a 'self-swindler', as Dickens put it in *Great Expectations* (Ch. 28). But again Sammy is not unlike other human beings in this respect. All his elaborate effort to see, to understand, to communicate with himself, is adulterated by unconscious insincerity and by moral blindness.

The general conclusion, to put it simply, appears to be that evil and unhappiness are unavoidable, that it is man's fate both to inflict and to endure suffering. Evil and pain are everywhere. As all readers of *Lord of the Flies* know, 'the Beast is in us'. And presumably readers of *Lord of the Flies* realize that the *deus ex machina* in the guise of a naval officer will not always come to rescue us from ourselves; or if he comes it may be only to take us back into the uncertainties and potential horrors of nuclear warfare.

From William Golding's *Free Fall* there are two ways of deriving encouragement. One seems to me mistaken. I admire and envy the readers who find moral support in their view of Sammy as redeemed by his ordeal in the dark cell and as emerging from it victorious in the end. B. S. Oldsey and S. Weintraub, for instance, claim that Sammy 'emerges from the cell with some portion of victory'; they believe that in the cell he 'has finally made use of man's last resource, prayer'. But it takes great ingenuity to perceive this, and more to demonstrate it. M. Kinkead-Weekes and I. Gregor, who comment in detail on the final section, do not reach the same conclusion. H. A. Talon, however, also believed that Sammy's cry in the dark cell – 'Help me!' (p. 140) – is the sign of his conversion.[21] In a way one wishes such readers were right, but I fear the ultimate significance of *Free Fall* is as bleak, as devoid of any explicit expression of hope as the view of mankind and mankind's fate at the core of *Lord of the Flies*, *The Inheritors*, and *Pincher Martin*.

Is Golding then an out-and-out pessimist? He has contrived to make contradictory pronouncements on this very issue: 'I am by nature an optimist; but a defective logic – or a logic which I sometimes hope desperately is defective – makes a pessimist of me.'[22] Fortunately he has said nothing specifically about *Free Fall*, unless, as Kinkead-Weekes and Gregor contend,[23] the last line of the book ('The Herr Doktor does not know about peoples', p. 192) is a statement about hero and author as well, a view which I find attractive rather than convincing. William Golding has all too often been impish in his statements about his own writings.[24] But he has always been intransigently honest in his fiction. Let us trust the tale, rather than the teller.

The saving grace of Sammy Mountjoy and of the world depicted in *Free Fall* lies in the potential for compassion and communication. Lucid perception is saddening, because mankind offers at best a sorry sight; you may respond with Lady Macbeth: 'A foolish thought, to say a sorry sight', but William Golding apparently believes that it would be a more foolish thought, *not* to say a sorry sight, and most foolish of all to content oneself with the saddening perception. Clear-sightedness is better than illusion; but it is not enough.

The writer's duty may be to denounce weaknesses and frailties and perils. But he must at the same time lead his readers to realize that beyond his denunciation there may lie something else. Denunciation in itself would be meaningless and useless (or worse than useless, for it might act as an inducement to commit suicide), if it did not carry with it some positive possibilities, which need not necessarily be formulated by the writer. But his very act of denunciation cannot be accomplished in a moral or spiritual vacuum; preaching for nihilism is self-defeating. At any rate Golding does not espouse the Schopenhauerian form of pessimism echoed by George Gissing[25] or by Thomas Hardy; his most pessimistic hope does not reside in an expectation that mankind will cease to desire life and its continuation and thus become peacefully extinct. William Golding's view comes closer to George Eliot's 'meliorism'; what he has created is a darker version of meliorism, tailored to suit the disillusioned, predominantly gloomy mood of our own century. In the face of evil in man and doom in the world, little can be done, but that little must be done. Mankind is of little value and cannot reasonably entertain or inspire very exalted hopes, but through sympathy, compassion, communication, solidarity, sharing, men and women can alleviate one another's sufferings. We may remember at this point that Sammy Mountjoy wrote: 'To communicate is our passion and our despair' (p. 7) and also that, after he has seen Beatrice Ifor in her decrepit state, he is genuinely moved: 'Suddenly the image of thick Beatrice started up behind my eyes, green, tense, and nittering. I covered them with my hand.' (p. 188) To me, there (rather than in the self-centred and cowardly fears experienced in Dr Halde's cupboard) lies the one redeeming moment. Realizing the unhappiness of one other human being, realizing that it has come to that other being through one's own act, is the most agonizing experience imaginable. Shedding tears over that experience is, however fleetingly, cathartic. It enables Sammy to make contact with Kenneth, whom he hates and whose own motives are impure and selfish. I do not believe that Sammy ever prays, but at that point he feels.

Golding seems to be telling us that an honest mind which is not foolish or simplistic, unless it pins its faith and hope on another life in another world, has very little to build on in its struggle against utter pessimism. Dim is the solitary light that shines over the bleak landscape of the modern world. Yet it is enough to save man from utter hopelessness and to impart meaning and purpose to artistic creation.

And after all what do we find in Golding's greatest predecessor in English literature, in Shakespeare himself, if not a view of man as endlessly, ineradicably disappointing, but at the same time perennially and infinitely pathetic?[26]

Notes

1 See Mark Kinkead-Weekes and Ian Gregor, *William Golding. A Critical Study* (London: Faber and Faber, 1967). While noting the link with *Pincher Martin* (pp. 161, 165), they consider that in *Free Fall* Golding for the first time abandoned the 'isolated and isolating settings' (p. 165) hitherto familiar to him.

2 He did, however, introduce one gimmicky reference (with a quotation) to *Free Fall* in 'Tolstoy's Mountain' (see *The Hot Gates and Other Occasional Pieces*, London: Faber and Faber, 1965, p. 123), as the work of 'a contemporary'.

3 Bernard S. Oldsey and Stanley Weintraub, *The Art of William Golding* (New York: Harcourt, Brace, and World, 1965), p. 11.

4 Kinkead-Weekes and Gregor, p. 165.

5 Henri A. Talon, *Le Mal dans l'oeuvre de William Golding* (Paris: Lettres Modernes, 1966), p. 65. Talon's resentment is connected mainly with the hero's persistence in making love to his impotent mistress (see pp. 76–7).

6 Oldsey and Weintraub, p. 122.

7 Kinkead-Weekes and Gregor, p. 198.

8 Although the best 'realistic' episodes in *Free Fall*, i.e., the early sections about Sammy's childhood comprise a powerful element of creative imagination; at any rate they could hardly be more different from Golding's own childhood, as described in 'Billy the Kid' (see *The Hot Gates*, pp. 159–65).

9 As is recognized by Kinkead-Weekes and Gregor and also, with reservations, by Talon, who finds their analysis 'too subtle' (Talon, p. 66).

10 See Oldsey and Weintraub, Chapter 5: 'Double Vision: *Free Fall* and *The Fall*.'

11 Oldsey and Weintraub, p. 105. Talon calls *Free Fall* by a French title of his own coinage: *Liberté de la chute*.

12 Kinkead-Weekes and Gregor, p. 157.

13 All quotations from *Free Fall* are taken from the Penguin edition (Harmondsworth, 1963, reprinted 1964). Section and page numbers are given parenthetically in the text.

14 See *Essays by Oscar Wilde*, edited by Hesketh Pearson (London: Methuen, 1950), p. 94.

15 See my 'Rayner Heppenstall and the *Nouveau Roman*' in *Imagined Worlds*, edited by Maynard Mack and Ian Gregor (London: Methuen, 1968), pp. 461–75.

16 In at least *Lord of the Flies* the ideal figure is not achieved without artifice or deliberation, for the twelfth section would have lent itself to subdivision between its two disparate parts.
17 Talon, p. 78.
18 'On the Crest of the Wave', *The Hot Gates*, pp. 126, 132.
19 Albert J. Guerard, in the 'Note on Method' prefixed to his book *The Triumph of the Novel* (New York: Oxford University Press, 1976), rightly insists on the essential difference between our first reading of any novel, and all later readings of the same.
20 As is fully recognized, e.g., by Samuel Hynes, who writes that Sammy is 'an ordinary, unheroic man, who insists on his representativeness' (*William Golding*, New York: Columbia Essays on Modern Writers, 1964, p. 33). And Golding himself has explained that in the 1950s he 'believed then, that man was sick – not exceptional man, but average man. I believed that the condition of man was to be a morally diseased creation' ('Fable', *The Hot Gates*, p. 87).
21 See Oldsey and Weintraub, pp. 118–19; Kinkead-Weekes and Gregor, pp. 194–9; Talon, p. 70.
22 In 'On the Crest of the Wave', *The Hot Gates*, p. 126.
23 Kinkead-Weekes and Gregor, p. 198.
24 As when he says that *Lord of the Flies* is a 'highly and diversely explicable book' (*The Hot Gates*, 'Fable', p. 98) or, 'I regard myself as a religious, but possible incompetently religious man' (quoted by John Bowen in a 1959 essay reprinted in *William Golding's Lord of the Flies. A Source Book*, edited by William Nelson, New York, 1963, p. 57).
25 See, specifically, 'The Hope of Pessimism', a long essay written by Gissing in 1882 and published for the first time by Pierre Coustillas in *George Gissing. Essays and Fiction*, Baltimore, 1970. But the deaths of Biffen and Reardon in *New Grub Street* illustrate the same attitude.
26 This article was written before I even heard of the appearance of *Darkness Visible* (London and Boston: Faber and Faber, 1979). After reading that truly impressive novel, I see no reason to modify my conclusion that the author was and is starkly pessimistic about both the modern world and the nature of man.

The Uses of Fiction
Edited by
Douglas Jefferson
and Graham Martin

18

Iris Murdoch: The Novelist and the Moralist

Douglas Jefferson

Perhaps the most obvious feature of Iris Murdoch's work is the extraordinary variety and abundance of her fictional art. In her early phase especially she seems deliberately to have composed each novel in a different idiom. *Under the Net*, for example, has some affinity with the picaresque: Jake has no stable way of life nor fixed abode, he kidnaps a famous dog, he dodges the police in comic circumstances, he helps a patient to escape from a hospital; but what goads him on through his adventures is his quest for two people, a man and a woman, who appear but only to disappear again, as they were allowed to disappear from his life in the past. His renewed contact with them has the promise of meaning and human value, but all is episodic and much of the atmospheric charm of the book lies in the elusiveness of these people, who are never allowed to settle down for our inspection. Jake reveals facts about his own character: 'I hate solitude, but I am afraid of intimacy. The substance of my life is a private conversation with myself which to turn into a dialogue would be equivalent to self-destruction'[1] (p. 31), which relate him to more modern types of anti-hero. Out of the wry and largely accidental convergence of events a new way of life suggests itself and is accepted at the end, so it is a moral novel, and a little masterpiece too, but in the lightest possible manner and with the focus often, it would seem, on the brilliant and extravagant sequence of events for their own sake.

A Severed Head is another kind of comedy. The situation at the beginning, that of a man who is happy with wife and mistress, has a classic comedy of manners pattern. Martin Lynch-Gibbon describes his condition in language that establishes the urbanity of the mode: '. . . it was important to me, even very important, that Antonia should think me virtuous; and, with that degree of self-deception which is essential to a prolonged and successful masquerade, I even felt virtuous.' (p. 21) But he has the uneasy feeling that he has not suffered enough, and in his dreams has 'glimpses of a punishment that would perhaps yet find its hour' (p. 13): portentous words which herald the strange events that follow. The pattern of the novel is that of a *reductio ad absurdam*. What if everybody is doing it? Secretly or unabashed the six characters, three men and three women, achieve eight out of the nine relationships that are mathematically possible. (Martin's brother, Alexander, who has been his wife's lover from the outset and becomes briefly engaged to his mistress, omits to have any sexual connection with Honor Klein.) There is a familiar note of poetic justice here. Why should one person enjoy a monopoly of infidelity? But if there is comedy in Martin's discomfiture on learning of his wife's liaison with her American analyst, Palmer Anderson, there is a special flavour in the portrayal of this egregious figure with 'his smooth clever American face all gentleness and concern,' and his easy talk about the way Martin will save the situation:

> ' "How do you know I'll keep on liking you, Palmer?" I said. I felt my faculties slipping.
> "You will," said Palmer.
> "Loving one's successful rival?"
> "The psyche is a strange thing," he said, "and it has its own mysterious methods of restoring a balance. It automatically seeks its advantage, its consolation. It is almost entirely a matter of mechanics, and mechanical models are the best to understand it with." ' (p. 32)

Palmer and Antonia are distressed and gently reproachful when they learn about Martin's secretiveness in his relationship with Georgie, and this enhances the monstrous moment when Martin catches Palmer in bed with his half-sister Honor: a state of affairs which moves Palmer to the most earnest and morally assured plea for silence. As for Antonia's relationship with Alexander, well, that is clearly quite different: 'You must have known for ages,' she says to the astonished Martin (p. 189). If we are looking for a moral outcome we can regard Martin's tentative understanding with Honor as a new beginning, with the hope of a life without illusions. But it would be a mistake to discuss outcomes too simplistically, as if this were a straight study of social and moral realities. Probability has been distorted to produce a schematic, sardonically-conceived reversal of Martin's whole existence, and Honor is part of the design. But though the last words of the book are an endearment they are in response to her challenge: 'You must take your chance.' Instability has been of the essence throughout, and the unexpected union at the end between Georgie, the only character who has attracted our sympathy, and Palmer, has the effect of leaving us suspended in the realm of the anomalous.

In *The Bell*, perhaps her best novel, there are elements of comedy, sometimes flamboyant, but the most important relationship is handled with an imaginative insight and a sense of moral truth that place her in the central tradition of the English novel. *The Flight from the Enchanter* begins on a note of levity. Annette Cockayne, who has just decided to walk out of her finishing school, chooses a suitable gesture of repudiation. She would have liked to carve her name on a bust by Grinling Gibbons: 'There was something solemn and florid about this work which made Annette itch for a blade.' But she had mislaid her pocket knife, so she indulges another craving: that is, to swing on the chandelier in the dining-room. This performance is interrupted by the appearance of the headmistress, whose spinsterly grandeur is all that could be wished. Later in the novel (Ch. 12) there is an extravagantly absurd meeting of the shareholders of the periodical *Artemis*: all eccentric viragoes, one contingent drinking tea, their rivals champagne. It is clear that Iris Murdoch could have done extremely well as a producer of fiction aiming at no more than elegant light entertainment; and equally apparent from *The Nice and the Good* that she could have written stories of criminal investigation; while the very effective opening of *The Unicorn*, with the combination of setting and mystery, shows an affinity with the Brontë tradition. In the same novel and in others there are elements of fantasy and 'myth' the role of which is less easy to state briefly.

In some of her artifices she goes out of her way to cultivate old-fashioned conventions. When Adelaide marries the decidedly shaky Will Boase at the end of *Bruno's Dream* the chapter concludes with a Dickensian glimpse into their future in which Will becomes a famous actor and a knight. *The Nice and the Good* ends with a neatly-ordered group of happy solutions for various couples, in the style of traditional comedy; and in Chapter 39, where Ducane and Mary reach their understanding, the first thoughts of the one (John's dismayed realization that he has 'so infelicitously, inopportunely, improperly and undeniably fallen quite madly in love with [his] old friend Mary Clothier') follow comically the same verbal pattern as those of the other. Iris Murdoch likes physical adventure with exciting rescues, such as Pierce's exploit in *The Nice and the Good* and Donald's in *The Sandcastle*. She is a connoisseur of the elaborately designed comic or macabre episode, in the manner of E. M. Forster. The events culminating in the prodigious misadventure of the bell; the piquant circumstances of Marcus's entry into his brother Carel's rectory through the coalhouse during a power-cut in *The Time of the Angels*; the smashing of the goldfish tank at Mischa's party in *The Flight from the Enchanter*: these and many other passages testify to an inveterate appetite for fictional invention, a great strength in a novelist but also a temptation. The bizarre encounter in the museum engineered by a faking of letters in *A Fairly Honourable Defeat* is a rather infelicitous revival of an Elizabethan comic convention. The scheme of coincidences in *The Red and the Green* whereby no fewer than four men on their bicycles find their way during the same night to the house of the over-committed Millie, might seem at first to be an artistic error, an unfortunate intrusion into a serious novel of devices more appropriate to lighter books; but actually it has thematic point. These events synchronize with the series of disasters whereby the Irish nationalists ('God, what a nation of dunces!') throw away all their chances of success. 'All that [German] stuff sitting in Tralee bay and no one there to land it.' (pp. 202–3) Want of convergence ruins the Irish movement; excess of convergence spoils everything for the expansive, somewhat feckless Irish Millie and her male friends; so all is waste and anti-climax, absurdity and confusion, though for some who have the will for it there is also heroism and tragedy.

This extraordinary profusion of fictional play and variety of style must be in the forefront of our consideration in discussions of the intellectual and moral implications of her work. She is often approached in very abstract terms, far removed from the spirit in which the books are plotted; and here, in her own theoretical writings and in interviews, she has given the lead. A. S. Byatt, at the end of her valuable chapter on *Under the Net*, in *Degrees of Freedom* (p. 39) writes: 'One feels uneasily that any analytic explanation of the book weighs it down, adds a portentousness to what is in fact, light, amusing and rapid.'[2] Some of her interpretations are perhaps a little schematic. In her comments on Lefty Todd, for example, she is concerned primarily with what he stands for. In demanding socialist plays from

Jake he becomes, as it were, one of the tempters in his life, comparable with but more wholesome than Madge, whose offers of easy money Jake is to reject later. But do we take his suggestions so seriously, and are Jake's options quite so pointedly placed? Jake, with his friends, encounters Lefty in a pub on their hunt for Hugo, and the episode has the true picaresque flavour: travellers in the old novels are always running into talkers. Lefty, with his red bow-tie and his enormous eyes, 'sad and round, luminous as the eyes of a wombat or a Rouault Christ', is referred to at the outset as the 'eccentric' leader of a new socialist group (p. 97). With his confident, didactic, slightly hectoring manner he is a lively figure, but how much of his socialist analysis deserves to be pondered? The scene is a digression and, with Hugo by this time forgotten, the night's events conclude felicitously with the zany enterprise of swimming the Thames, in which Lefty participates. It then turns out that Hugo is immensely impressed with Lefty, and in the glorious episode of the film set (Ch. 12) when Jake sees what must surely be 'Catiline inflaming the Roman plebs', it is really an oration to the workers by Lefty, and Hugo is anxious not to miss a word of it. His reason for giving money to Lefty is not that he shares his political views: he has none, and is 'bad at understanding these things'. Lefty, he says, is 'decent' (p. 224), and we can agree, but without having much evidence of his political wisdom, only a few scraps of his great speech. It is in keeping with Hugo's sublime integrity that he should in some respects be simple-minded – he is also inept in matters of love – and his munificence to Lefty has some of the character of a generous and touching joke.

The place of abstract ideas in Iris Murdoch's novel can be more effectively brought out by reference to the work of Sartre,[3] on whom she published a critical study before she appeared as a novelist, and who certainly influenced her as a philosopher seeking to develop ideas in fiction, though in her method of doing this she has resisted his influence. In her account of *La Nausée* Iris Murdoch describes a kind of novel that is strikingly and significantly different from those she was to write. Sartre's hero, Roquentin, 'amid the raw material of metaphysical discovery' (p. 19) has virtually no other life, nor has the novel. He is 'a pure case' (p. 14), and *La Nausée* is a pure case of the novel of ideas. Had she followed Sartre the central figure in *Under the Net* would have been Hugo, and with his 'nostalgia for the particular' we could have had an equally pure case, co-extensive with the life of the novel. But her method is to place Hugo as an elusive figure in the experience of the narrator Jake, who only has glimpses of him and always finds him surprising. At the end, he says, Hugo 'towered in my mind like a monolith: an unshaped and undivided stone which men before history had set up for some human purpose, which would remain for ever obscure' (p. 238).

A similar method is used in *The Time of the Angels* where the theme 'the death of God', which occupies Marcus academically, has become a terrible but also mysterious fact in the life of his brother Carel. Again, a novelist like Sartre might have made over the whole novel to Carel's obsessed consciousness; but Iris Murdoch causes Carel to be seen or discussed by Marcus, the crudely positivist Norah and the inscrutable bishop, while he is also known more intimately by the West Indian servant Pattie, who has enjoyed his love and is now still close to him, though painfully aware of the incomprehensible developments that have made him a changed man. The early part of the novel where Carel is established for us is beautifully written. In the first pages there is little more than the two voices, with strange endearments from a person whose identity eventually becomes more apparent with the reference to a black cassock. We hear his voice, we sense an atmosphere, subtly evoked, before we learn who he is, or of the 'facts' that cause talk. Chapter 3, which traces Pattie's early memories and her changing experience of Carel, is a fine example of how a simple but responsive sensibility can be used to reflect the behaviour of a complex and unfathomable one. With both Hugo and Carel Iris Murdoch uses the novelist's art to considerable advantage, but at the expense of course of any thoroughgoing treatment of a 'pure case' in the manner of Sartre.

What makes Roquentin a 'pure case' is that he has no '*être-pour-autrui*, no close connexion with other people and no concern with how they view him . . . ' (*Sartre*, p. 14) This does not mean that he has no sexual life. He receives nothing, he gives nothing, but there is the woman Françoise of whom he can ask, 'Have you got time this evening?' and whom it is unnecessary to consider as a human being with feelings: she enjoys sex too, and she has many men. This is as convenient for Sartre as for Roquentin. As Iris Murdoch points out, Sartre, in *L'Age de Raison*, 'is not really very interested in the predicament of Marcelle' (who is pregnant) 'except from the technical point of view of its effect on Mathieu' (p. 40), who is interesting, like Roquentin, because of the philosophical implications of his predicament. Sartre's characters 'are never deeply involved with each other . . . Sartre bypasses the complexity of the world of ordinary human relations which is also the world of ordinary moral virtues.' (p. 24)

Here we can simply say that Iris Murdoch as a novelist moved as far away from this position as it was possible to go. Her novels become more and more concerned with human relationships: some would add 'to a fault', because the programme of sexual partnerships is occasionally more crowded than one book can conveniently accommodate, though this criticism would not apply to *A Severed Head*, where the extreme congestion is required by the comedy.

She is very much engaged by moral issues. In *The Sovereignty of Good*, a book deeply admired by some who are not attracted by her fiction, she urges most seriously and eloquently the supreme importance of being good, of seeking goodness in the face of all the obstacles inherent in our nature. Her novels on the whole do not give as much prominence to characters involved in this strenuous endeavour as one might expect, and this is a difference between the novelist and the moralist which may disappoint some students of both. But Gunnar Jopling's desperate attempt to overcome hatred and achieve reconciliation with the man who has destroyed his life is an outstanding example, and its failure brings the most powerful of her later novels, *A Word Child*, to a terrible climax. The exchange of letters between Ludwig and his father on the painful subject of draft evasion in *An Accidental Man*, may be cited as an exemplary exercise of fine consciences within a relationship of deep affection. In a different vein is her handling of John Ducane, whose conduct of the enquiry into Radeechy's suicide ends in his sacrificing his own career in order to save that of a man he has never liked and whose reunion with his wife he also helps to bring about. Ducane is a man of conscience haunted by a 'Calvinistic devil'. He wants to be good, and also to feel good: he 'liked his life to be simple, did not care for concealments and feelings of guilt' (p. 26), so the sexual deception in which he has become entangled is intolerable to him. He is aware of 'one of the great paradoxes of morality, namely that in order to become good it may be necessary to imagine oneself good, and yet such imagining may also be the very thing which renders improvement impossible, either because of surreptitious complacency or because of some deeper blasphemous infection which is set up when goodness is thought about in the wrong way.' (p. 76) Iris Murdoch's preoccupation with the problems of goodness is reflected here, and Ducane's predicament is of the kind to which she brings her best analytical skills.

But what gives Ducane's adventures a flavour one recognizes as typical of Iris Murdoch is her introduction of elements that make them a sequence of comic temptations of St Antony. This decent and very personable puritan is repeatedly exposed to the good-humoured blandishments of Judy McGrath, who on two occasions is naked. But there are other ways in which her ethical ideas would seem to have influenced her practice as a novelist. One of her key words, to which Simone Weil, an important influence on her thought, gave a special profundity, is 'attention'. 'Love' means something very similar and is based on 'the imaginative recognition . . . of otherness', the 'non-violent apprehension of difference' to quote phrases used in one of her essays.[4] One of the most individual features of her characterization is her ability to devote her understanding and imagination to people of the kind that in real life would provoke disapproval, and to treat them in such a way as to discourage this response. This does not necessarily involve either positive sympathy or advocacy, but rather an intelligent, controlled acceptance. Randall in *An Unofficial Rose* is of the type that takes from others. He wants to leave his wife, and in order to afford a handsome way of life with his mistress he asks his father, Hugh, to sell a Tintoretto. His wife is of the kind that cannot take. Though it is virtually certain that she has lost Randall, she is unable to respond effectively to another man whom she loves: 'She had let go of the exceedingly dear and precious Felix whom she needed with all her heart, almost, it seemed to her, because of a naked meaningless incapacity to take what she wanted' (p. 321). Ann's problem is handled with considerable imaginative subtlety. She realizes the dreadful fact that 'keeping pace demonically with her love for Felix there had developed in her a new dark passion for Randall. It was as if one were the infernal mirror image of the other' (p. 261). When she feels that it is her duty to let Randall go, to set him free, she is then plagued with the realization that this would set her free too. This quality in Ann is precisely what has thwarted Randall. Ann is 'bad for him'. 'I ought to have people around me who have *wills*, people who take what they want. Ann has no will. She saps my energy. She's got a kind of openness that makes whatever I do meaningless.' (p. 36) His father has already seen the ironical fact that such people as Randall 'compel love . . . and merit the love they compel. While the worthy and deserving ones, such as Ann, are, by a terrible justice, unloved.' (pp. 14–15) When Randall has achieved his ends, his sheer pleasure in affluence and freedom, and his knowledge later that he can, in fact, have Ann and 'as many other women as he pleased' (p. 306) is presented with no suggestion of disapproval; and Hugh's final reflection on the transaction to which he has contributed is of a certain satisfaction at 'the beautiful, extravagant, feckless setting of Randall free'. He had not claimed his own freedom in comparable circumstances, so 'this crime squared his account with the tipsy gods' (p. 332). Austin in *An Accidental Man* and Julius in *A Fairly Honourable Defeat* may also be briefly cited as disconcerting characters whom we are nevertheless not allowed to reduce to simple terms or relegate to a ready-made category. But in some cases the author's obvious zest for novelty, a pleasure in experiment, seems at least as strong a motive as the moral imperative to exercise 'attention'.

Iris Murdoch's attitude sometimes reveals a kinship with that of George Eliot as expressed in the latter's affirmation that 'the greatest benefit we owe to the artist . . . is the extension of our sympathies',[5] and occasionally she commits herself to a belief in unselfish love. The central subject of *Bruno's Dream*, beautifully handled in some scenes, is the care of the old, and their need for affection. The two women, Lisa and Diana, have learnt to love Bruno in all his repulsive physical decay and Diana's thoughts about this all-important reality ('Yet love still existed, and it was the only thing that existed'), as the old man dies, bring the novel to an end. This is the voice of the novelist, but it must be said of this page that we honour the sentiments more than the writing. *Bruno's Dream* is rich in what are called 'positives', but it contains several passages where their expression has this slightly rhapsodizing note. An increasing readiness to concern herself with characters who are in need has been one of the marks of her later development, and it has not always been accompanied by artistic rigour. There have been too many stretches of distended dialogue in which demoralized figures such as Morgan in the early chapters of *A Fairly Honourable Defeat*, and the hopelessly miserable and rejected Patricia in *The Black Prince*, just go on and on, compulsively. Here she exercises a Samaritan's patience with this fatal fluency; but the effect on the reader is obtunding, his sympathy is not quickened. This element of weakness in the later Iris Murdoch, and its connection with one of her best human qualities, presents a critical problem. Her reaction against 'dryness' has indeed taken her a long way.

Throughout the novels there are references, touching and sometimes half-humorous, to the forbidden and unexpressed sexual longings of middle-aged or elderly people for the much too young. Homosexual love is treated with profound insight and compassion in *The Bell*. The crucial problem for Michael is expressed in the reflection that 'his religion and his passions sprang from the same source and . . . this seemed to infect his religion with corruption', but, turning the argument about, 'why should his passions not rather be purified by this proximity?' (p. 105). There is no resolution. He loses the possibility of ordination as a result of the episode with Nick at school, and his commitment now to his community has meant the renunciation of this kind of love. He avoids close contact with Nick when he comes to live at Imber. But the issue comes to life again, not with Nick but with Toby, whom he kisses in an unguarded moment, and all his old uncertainties return. They *are* uncertainties, and it is unjust to Michael, who is a genuinely good man, to stress too much the self-deception in his desire to see Toby again. The sensible recognition that he must terminate the connection as soon as possible is in genuine conflict with his conviction that his affection for the boy is due to the way God has made him; and his conclusion that at least, 'in any world in which he would live' homosexual love must be judged as wrong, is not easy to accept. He has warning thoughts of another, more dangerous aspect of the situation: its effect on Nick; but he fails to recognize the full weight of it. With Nick's suicide, which brings this wonderfully well plotted novel to its culmination, he has a total revulsion of feeling and suffers agonies of remorse for what he has failed to give him. This and this only was what mattered:

> 'Michael had concerned himself with keeping his own hands clean, his own future secure, when instead he should have opened his heart: should impetuously and devotedly and beyond all reason have broken the alabaster cruse of very costly ointment.
>
> He had the image of Nick continually now before his eyes, seeing him often as he was when a boy, seeing him in flight across a tennis court, agile and strong and swift, conscious of Michael's glance; and sometimes it seemed to him as if Nick had died in childhood.' (pp. 308, 307)

But it is in the nature of remorse that it selects, and indeed shapes its object. The fineness of Michael's grief lies in his passionate regret for ideal possibilities not attempted, not in a realistic sense of what could have been achieved in any such relationship. In view of the circumstances, and especially of the destructive side of Nick, his is a generous sorrow. But there were mistakes and he cannot forgive himself. These passages, where her moral imagination is especially kindled, may remind us of some of the notable places in *Lolita*, and are even in the tradition of very much greater pages towards the end of *The Wings of the Dove*, where in both cases the theme is a more palpable guilt.

Notes

1 Page numbers of Iris Murdoch's novels are those of Panther editions.
2 A. S. Byatt, *Degrees of Freedom. The Novels of Iris Murdoch* (1963).
3 Iris Murdoch, *Sartre. Romantic Rationalist* (Cambridge, 1953).
4 Iris Murdoch, 'The Sublime and the Good', *Chicago Review*, XIII (Autumn 1959), pp. 52, 54.
5 George Eliot, 'The Natural History of German Life', in *Essays*, included in the same volume with *The Impressions of Theophrastus Such* (n.d.).

The Uses of Fiction
Edited by
Douglas Jefferson
and Graham Martin

19

Susan Hill's Fiction

Kenneth Muir

When Susan Hill, to the dismay of her admirers, announced that she had decided to write no more novels, her reasons were complex. It was partly her feeling that the novel on which she was working, and which she destroyed, was inferior to her best, partly her newly found happiness in marriage and motherhood, and partly, one suspects, her realization that she ought to let her talent lie fallow. She had been writing since her schooldays and her mature work, written between the ages of twenty-six and thirty-two, included two volumes of short stories, a collection of radio plays, and six novels. She had won several prizes and was increasing her reputation with each successive volume, varied as they were. This seems, therefore, to be a convenient moment to consider her present achievement. It will be necessary in this brief essay to confine our attention to the six novels and the volumes of short stories. These are: *Gentleman and Ladies* (1968); *A Change for the Better* (1969); *I'm the King of the Castle* (1970); *Strange Meeting* (1971); *The Albatross* (1971); *The Bird of Night* (1972); *A Bit of Singing and Dancing* (1973); *In the Springtime of the Year* (1974).[1]

Elspeth Thackeray, a character in 'The Peacock' (in *A Bit of Singing and Dancing*) who is taking a correspondence course on Creative Writing, is gently satirized for following the instructions on how to create character:

> 'After observing people carefully you could then take a step farther on, you might invent a background for them, imagine them in their home environment, or at their place of work.' (p. 125)

So she observes Daisy Buckingham, another guest at the hotel, and the central character of the story; but her observation tells her nothing of the inner thoughts and feelings – that she hated living in Africa, although she looked back on her stay with nostalgia, that she hated the hotel when she had stayed at it with her father years before, although it had been transformed by memory into a charming place, that she hoped her husband, although she recognized that he was a good man and a good husband, would die of a heart attack.

Obviously Susan Hill's method differs from Elspeth Thackeray's. She possesses to an extraordinary degree the quality which has been called the essential *dramatic* gift,[2] the power of identifying herself with a wide variety of characters, all very different from the young graduate who wrote the novels and stories. Only one of them is told in the first person, but we look at events through the eyes of an eleven-year-old schoolboy, a mentally defective boy, a soldier in the trenches, a middle-aged railway clerk, a mad poet and his Egyptologist friend, the old man in 'The Custodian', the dying old woman in 'Missy'. It was presumably this quality that led one critic to compare Susan Hill to Tolstoy, though she is more akin to Turgenev or Chekhov.

When we are reading (as to Susan Hill when she was writing) *I'm the King of the Castle*, we see nearly everything through the eyes of Charles Kingshaw – his genteel, husband-seeking mother, his enemy, Edmund Hooper, his friend, Fielding, and his terrors, his hopes and his ultimate despair. He is given no idea of feeling that such a boy might not have, and the style never calls attention to itself, but only to the object, the feeling, the idea, or the landscape. Although an extraordinary tension is built up in the course of the book by the ordeals that Charles undergoes and by the temporary turning of the tables on his persecutor in Hang Wood, the story unfolds so naturally that we become conscious of the art only when we close the book and come to analyse it.

Susan Hill often uses old and middle-aged women as her personae; but the only one of her tales where a young woman is so used is *In the Springtime of the Year*, where the bereaved Ruth Boyce, widowed at twenty-one, is the character through whose eyes and memories we watch the action and her gradual recovery. This is accomplished through the affection and care of her fourteen-year-old brother-in-law, through the healing power of the countryside and of the village rituals (such as the decorating of graves for Easter Day), and through her ministering to the griefs and troubles of others. But although the dedication of the book may suggest that Susan Hill had herself suffered a bereavement, the heroine is differentiated from the novelist in almost every other way.

The second quality displayed by Susan Hill is what may be called the innocent eye. This is apparent not merely in the vividness of her landscapes, so that we seem to be seeing them for the first time, but also in the apparent avoidance of sophistication in the way in which she presents people's behaviour, however eccentric or cruel. This is what they did; this is how it happened. Another kind of novelist, for example, would have made explicit the sexual element in the friendships described in *Strange Meeting* and *The Bird of Night*. Here, and elsewhere, Susan Hill gains considerably from her reticence about sex and from her avoidance of psychological analysis. Her husbands and wives are mostly divorced or widowed or aged, and although the middle-aged booking-clerk in *Gentleman and Ladies* does marry for love at the end of the book, Mr Hooper has sexual fantasies about his life with Mrs Kingshaw, and the motor salesman in *A Change for the Better* picks up any available woman, Susan Hill is as reticent as the hero of *Gentleman and Ladies* when he proposes to Florence Ames at the seaside:

> 'They began to climb one of the long, steep wooded paths up from the shore.
>
> "You will marry me?" Gaily said suddenly, "won't you? When things are – are clear? That will be all right?"
>
> They paused for a moment to recover breath.
>
> "I would like that," she said. "Yes. I would like that very much." '
>
> (p. 221)

They pause because they are middle-aged people going up a steep hill, not for a kiss.

To speak of the innocent eye does not imply that Susan Hill is unaware of the 'dark' side of life; many of her readers, indeed, feel that the atmosphere of her world is sombre and depressing. Her favourite English novelist is not George Eliot, but Dickens; and though she lacks his melodramatic intensity, his grotesque humour, and his flamboyance, she shares his appreciation of the odd and eccentric, a compassion for the aged, the lonely and the persecuted, and his obsession with violence. A summary of her plots would read like headlines from one of the more lurid Sunday newspapers. A half-witted boy murders his mother (and burns the house down), a teenager commits infanticide; two old men engage in a suicide pact; an eleven-year-old boy drives another to suicide; an old man is saved from death by cancer by dying of a heart-attack; a young agricultural labourer is killed by a falling tree; a nurse murders a geriatric patient because she fouls her bed; an old woman dies of food poisoning; a boy watches his father drown; a mad poet kills himself; and, sadder than all this violence, are the aimless and meaningless lives of many of her characters.

In *Gentleman and Ladies* the self-deceived Alida Thorne intrigues to have her invalid mother placed in a home, feeling guilty about it, although the mother is happier for the change. In the same book neurotic Isabel bullies her meek sister Kathleen, is furious that her other sister has left money to a hospital and jewelry to a friend, instead of to her, and buries the jewelry in the garden when the legatee refuses to accept it. The significance of the title *A Change for the Better* is that it is ironical. Mrs Fount, who runs a draper's shop with her mother, dreams vaguely, like the three sisters of Chekhov's play, of starting a new life; but when her mother dies she is unable to make a new start. Another character comments:

> 'She is very young . . . not yet forty, and already she has given in, she is afraid of life, she will have nothing to look forward to in the future.' (p. 222)

Susan Hill extracts some bitter comedy from the continual bickering between Mrs Fount and her dreadful mother. She is always defeated and by the end of the book she has become very like her mother. Such characters are defeated by life, defeated ultimately by their own personal inadequacies. The author treats them compassionately, but ruthlessly and realistically. The painful effect of the stories would be alleviated only by our recognition of their truth, if it were not for characters in all the novels, and in some of the stories, who stand out against the prevailing hopelessness.

Susan Hill, for all her objectivity, uses the novel, in Auden's famous phrase about the greatest art, to teach men to unlearn hatred and to learn love. The characters are divided into sheep and goats: those who are loving, life-enhancing, and filled with a purpose beyond themselves, and those who are possessive, unloving, and dying inwardly. In

Gentleman and Ladies, the genteel rentiers of Haverstock are either snobs, who regard Hubert Gaily as common, or sympathetic, like Dorothea Shottery, who appreciates his goodness. The snobs are also the selfish ones, Alida Thorne and Isabel Lavender. It is characteristic of the good people that they admit to mixed motives and evil thoughts. Dorothea, for example,

> 'had expected to get satisfaction from refusing Faith's jewellery, because it seemed an action on principle, and because there was always a surreptitious pleasure to be gained from snubbing Isabel.' (p. 64)

Later in the book, when she is praised for her generosity, Dorothea thinks:

> 'I am not generous. If the truth were known, it is only because I have for so long been lonely that I welcome demands for help. It is only that I feel that I may make a new friend and be rewarded with company.' (p. 129)

Kathleen, on hearing of Isabel's death, thinks

> 'I am not a vindictive woman . . . but I am glad that my sister is dead, for all my life I have suffered under her.' (p. 248)

Even Hubert, whose affectionate and grumbling relationship with his mother is beautifully presented and who had dutifully stayed with her all his life, had wished at one moment that she were dead, since he could not apply for promotion elsewhere so long as she was alive.

Hubert's 'goodness' is illustrated through the book by his thoughtfulness for others – his joining in the funeral service in the first chapter, his helping an old woman to her seat in the bus, his mending of Mrs Shottery's gate, his organizing the village fair (not without satisfaction to himself). The goodness of Gaily is made explicit when Florence arranges for him to meet Mrs Shottery:

> ' "I'd like to meet anyone – if you say so."
> "Then you shall. She is a good person."
> "Good?"
> Nobody ever said a person was good, like that. They were nice, or all right, kind or likeable or easy to get on with. Not good, right out like that.
> "I can't say I know any of what you'd call *good* people."
> She turned to him in surprise.
> "Not," Gaily said, worried, "not that I meet bad people. No, it's just

– well, it's not a word you tend to apply, is it? You know . . ." He began to confuse himself. "I'm not sure what it means," he finished up, "a good person."

"Why," she said, "*you* are a good person! It is quite easy. That is what it means." ' (p. 95)

There is the same contrast in *A Change for the Better* between the life-enhancers and their opposites. The Founts, as we have seen, are spiritually dead or dying; but James, although born into a strange household from which adult males have been extruded, is saved, partly by his talents as a musician, partly by his determination to stand up against his mother and grandmother, and partly by the encouragement of his music teacher, Ralph Porlock. There is one very funny episode when James's grandmother goes off to interview Porlock because she suspects him of homosexual tendencies. He confronts her on the doorstep holding a meat-cleaver and causes her considerable alarm. She does not know that he was about to cut up a hare. He reluctantly invites her inside but does not ask her to sit down; so she perches on the back of a chair. She funks a direct accusation and her hints are too vague and confused to be understood. Porlock finally says:

' "Madam, I do not yet know why you have come to see me. I am, as you have said, a busy man. I would be grateful if you would now speak out plainly."

Mrs Oddicut flushed. She could not now say anything about the time he and the boy spent here together, she could not ask what they talked about, and say that she did not think it altogether suitable.' (p. 51)

So she pretends that she had come because James was in danger when he came down the cliff path at night:

' "Things have happened there, girls have been – have been set upon. Accosted."

"Once, yes. In the middle of a summer afternoon."

"Nobody knows what may be the danger, then, on a dark winter's evening."

"Tush, madam. No more than the danger outside your own house." '

Mrs Oddicut goes away 'red about the neck with anger'. Porlock smiled to himself 'because as he got older, he found the quest for the risible more and more fully rewarded.'

The foul-tempered Major Carpenter behaves intolerably to his sweet-tempered wife; but there is some comedy in his irrational behaviour, in his snobbery, and in his Blimpish prejudices:

> 'The people of whom Major Carpenter disapproved were – almost all summer visitors, all conference members, the Jewish businessmen from Hampstead and engineering executives from the Midlands, solicitors and retired Diocesan Bishops.' (p. 31)

Mrs Carpenter spends her time in making up for her husband's rudeness, and when he dies she is able to make a new, and happier, life for herself. Yet the reader can feel some pity even for the Major, who is upset by the death of an old friend, and himself afraid of dying.

We are given a glimpse of one happy household in the town, to which James Fount is invited by a school friend, Schwartz. He persuades his mother to let him go on holiday with the Schwartzes, although she had arranged for him to stay in an hotel with her. But at the end of the book she finds herself behaving just like her mother:

> 'James Fount got off the cane chair and picked up his satchel.
> "I'm going to tea with Schwartz," he said.
> "I *beg* your pardon? How dare you tell me what you are or are not going to do, without so much as asking my permission."
> "I'm sorry. *May* I go to tea with Schwartz?"
> "Oh go on, go on, do what you like, I do not care for you. You have more feeling for your friend Schwartz and his family than you have for me."
> James Fount left the shop.
> I am saying all the things to him that I vowed I would never say, thought Mrs Fount. I am becoming more and more like my own mother was with me and I cannot help myself, for now I understand. I see it all and I am miserable and afraid.' (p. 213)

We know that James will get his way and go to a boarding school on a music scholarship.

In *I'm the King of the Castle*, the victim, Charles Kingshaw lives in an unsympathetic or hostile environment. His mother, because she is so anxious to marry Mr Hooper, cannot be his confidante; Mr Hooper, though generous according to his lights, is unable to understand either his own son or Charles; and Edmund resents the invasion of his territory by Charles, and therefore persecutes him. The persecution takes understandable forms: locking his victim in a room containing a frightening collection of moths, putting a stuffed crow on his bed in the middle of the night, locking him in a shed, and so on. Near the end of the book, when Edmund is away, Charles meets Fielding, the son of a neighbour, normal, good-natured and friendly; but this friendship is ruined by the return of Edmund. This and his mother's imminent marriage to Mr Hooper increase Charles's unhappiness; and when Mr Hooper arranges to pay his fees so that he can join Edmund at his school, he despairs and commits suicide. When Edmund finds the body, he

> 'thought suddenly, it was because of me, I did that, *it was because of me*, and a spurt of triumph went through him.' (p. 222)

There had been many unpleasant and selfish and foolish characters in the previous books, but Edmund is evil. When all excuses have been made – family pride, snobbery, his motherless state, his father, the barbarous ideology of his school – Edmund is cruel and evil. This is made apparent not merely by his bullying, but by his refusal to respond to Charles's acts of kindness. In Hang Wood, when he is terrified of a thunderstorm, when he is afraid that they will starve to death, and when he is nearly drowned, he is cared for by Charles; yet when they are found Edmund accuses Charles of trying to drown him. Later in the book, when he breaks his leg in a climbing accident, he accuses Charles of having pushed him, although Charles had tried to help him to safety. The Fieldings merely provide a climpse of a world outside the nightmare of schoolboy cruelty: to have given them a larger share in the book would have lessened the tension.

Characters in the earlier books had been cruel and selfish – Isabel Lavender, for example, or Mrs Oddicut – but here Susan Hill faces directly the mystery of iniquity: Edmund, although his cruelty is adolescent and merely verbal, is as evil as the demi-devil, Iago.

Strange Meeting was suggested by the first performance of Britten's *War Requiem* in Coventry Cathedral (1962), although some nine years elapsed before the novel was written. During the interval Susan Hill read a large number of books about the First World War, including those by Graves, Blunden, and Chapman. The Owen poem which provided the title is about the meeting after death of a German and an English soldier: in the novel the strange meeting is the close friendship between two English officers on the Western Front, and the death of one of them. The authenticity of the setting is the result of an amalgam of multitudinous sources, so that no direct borrowing can be detected. This is a remarkable imaginative feat. But the real subject is friendship rather than war: war provides a threat, a background, a quickener to the friendship. John Hilliard, the older of the two men, comes from a cold, respectable and conventional family, and he is himself reserved and emotionally inexperienced. David Barton comes from a warm, out-going, affectionate family, and he himself is loving and beloved. The contrast between the two families continues what we have seen in the previous novels; but Hilliard undergoes a conversion by love, so that when David is killed he is absorbed into the Barton family.

When he is home on leave at the beginning of the book, John is revolted by the uncomprehending attitude of his family to the realities of the war and by the sentimental attitude of a retired cavalry major. He hopes to be able to talk openly with his sister Beth, to whom he used to be close, and hears that she is to marry a middle-aged solicitor for security. When he gets to know David, he is astonished at his openness and the difference between their two families.

> ' "No. I didn't want to come out here at all, I was in a blue funk. I'd have done more or less anything . . . but I'm fit and of age, I couldn't slip through the net. So I suppose I'd better make the most of it."
>
> "Do you always tell people everything you're feeling?"
>
> Barton looked round at him in surprise. "Generally. If I want to. If they want to hear." He paused and then laughed. "Good Lord, we're not at school now, are we?"
>
> Hilliard did not reply.
>
> "Besides, it's the way we were brought up. To say things, tell people what you feel. I don't mean to force it on anyone. But not to bottle things up." ' (p. 55)

The letters from the Barton family begin to include messages to John, and then letters to him:

> 'He said again and again. "They don't know me. They don't know me," holding the envelopes, looking at the writing upon them, feeling the smoothness of the letter paper between his fingers.
>
> As always, Barton laughed. "Of course they do!"
>
> "They haven't seen me, we have never met."
>
> "Oh, that's practically superflous by now." ' (p. 100)

These friendly letters contrast painfully with those he receives from his own family; and, when he is badly wounded and in hospital, the affectionate letters he gets from Mrs Barton contrast with the visit of his mother:

> ' "You look very beautiful, mother. You always look very beautiful."
> She inclined her head, smiled at him, as Royalty would smile. She wore a dark fuchsia dress, full-skirted, and with a coat of deeper, more purplish red, a hat with purple feathers. When she walked away, the other men in the room looked up from their books and letters, and watched her go.' (p. 176)

The theme of friendship is continued in the next novel, *The Bird of Night*, in more difficult circumstances. For Francis Croft is a great poet, who suffers from recurrent periods of madness, and the narrator, Harvey, looks after him with selfless devotion for many years. The title is taken from a Hölderlin poem, and the novel was written at Aldeburgh, where Britten composed his Hölderlin settings. Of the mad poets to whom Susan Hill refers, – Clare, Smart, and Blake – none was given to violence, whereas Hölderlin and Croft were. But we are meant to understand, perhaps, that when poets are mad, it is because the society in which they live is at fault. Harvey says:

> 'And if he is mad, it is because one man's brain cannot contain all the emotions and ideas and visions that are filling his without sometimes weakening and breaking down.' (p. 141)

Harvey tells the story thirty years after Croft's death and his narrative is interspersed with prose quotations from the poet's notebooks. Susan Hill does not, however, risk quoting any of Croft's poems (as Pasternak quoted Zhivago's), for Croft is supposed to be the greatest poet of his age, one who had written during the First World War, and afterwards developed, as Owen might have done if he had survived. Harvey is himself a writer so that by using him as the narrator Susan Hill can allow herself a more 'literary' style than in her previous books, with a good deal of imagery and some splendid Suffolk and Dorset landscapes.

It will be remembered that the start of Hölderin's madness coincided with the death of the lady he called Diotima: Croft seems to have no interest in women – his madness begins when his brother shoots a bird. Harvey is jealous; and his resentment of the academics who pester him for information about the dead poet, although suggested by the theses and articles about Sylvia Plath after her suicide, may have been due to his possessive love.

Towards the end of the book Croft's father comes to visit him in the Battersea asylum, and there is a meeting between him and Harvey, which brings out the difference between the two men, and between

Croft and his father. The father disapproves of Harvey for not having the poet sent to an asylum years before, 'in the privacy of some clinic – Austria – Switzerland . . . There is no history of insanity in my family.' (p. 139) His reputation as a poet adds to his father's fear that his madness will become public knowledge; and when Harvey remarks that 'very many men of seventy had lost their sons in the war', he rplies:

> 'I had rather he were dead than this, there would have at least been no shame in it. I should not have had to wake every morning of my life and fear for his future. At least I should have known.' (pp. 146–7)

Harvey realizes that 'there was no hope at all of sympathy left between us'.

The last of the novels, *In the Springtime of the Year*, has a less ambitious theme but a tauter construction. In the place of the first person narrative, the action is viewed through the eyes of Ruth. We learn nothing except what she sees and hears;[3] our knowledge of the other characters in the book is her knowledge or her opinion, which we are willing to accept as true because she emerges as a kind and loving person. She is proud and independent and determines to come to terms with her bereavement on her own. She stays on in the cottage, refusing to see the clergyman who comes to bring spiritual comfort, and visited only by Jo, the one member of the family who is like her dead husband in temperament. He is one of the Hill characters who is sensitive, caring, and open-hearted, whereas his mother, Mrs Boyce had resented Ruth's marriage with Ben, is conventional in her ideas, and regards Ruth's behaviour after the death of her husband as unfeeling because she does not weep in public and refuses to take a last look at the corpse.

> 'She saw the expression on Alice's face, remembered what she had said that night. "You've not even feeling enough to cry." But she could not go upstairs, the sight of his body, lying in a coffin, which would soon be sealed up forever, would be more than she could bear. And it would mean nothing, now. She looked around the room. So they had all been up? Yes. She imagined the file of dark mourners mounting the stairs and peering down into the coffin. At Ben. Ben. How could they? How could so many people have touched him and looked at him, unasked, since the moment of his death, when she herself had not?' (p. 47)

Mrs Boyce is a self-deceiver, hoping to live a vicarious life through her daughter, Alice, who would marry a gentleman and become the lady she might have been herself:

> ' "I could have been Someone, Miss, had a real life, I could . . ."
>
> "We all know what you fancy you could have been. A lady! we've heard it all our lives and do you suppose we believe it? Why should we? And does it matter? Because whatever you might have been is a day-dream, isn't it, an escape from the truth? You live in a day-dream. But *this* is real, this is what you are, here, a woman of fifty, married to a farm hand. Well why can't you be satisfied, why not make do?" ' (p. 87)

Alice, tired of her mother's fantasies, has an affair with a man she doesn't love. Ruth, although she cannot understand[4] how any woman could behave in this way, nevertheless shelters her when she is repudiated by her mother, and goes vainly to intercede on her behalf. Just before this she has tried to comfort the clergyman whose beloved child has died, and who has lost his faith as a result and proposes to resign from Holy Orders:

> 'Because she has died and now I know that everything I believed in and lived for has died with her. Because my life is a lie. I am a lie. How can I visit them, people sick, people dying and in distress, needing truth, what have I to say to them? How can I take services in the church and preach and pray and know that it is all a lie? I used to know what words to say, but there are no words, and there is no help for anyone. I think of how I went to people and talked to them, about death and goodness and consolation, and I feel ashamed, I knew nothing, I had never felt what they felt.' (p. 163)

The naked grief of a professed and professional Christian prevents the reader from feeling that Ruth's grief for her husband had been alleviated too easily in the course of the book; and the clergyman's bereavement has been placed near the end both to show Ruth's concern for others and to remind us of what she herself had suffered. There is also a contrast between the possessive love of the clergyman and Ruth's selfless but reciprocal love for her husband which enables her to endure.

It is too early to assess Susan Hill's achievement, as her future work may well surpass what she has already done. She is younger now than George Eliot was when she published *Scenes from Clerical Life*; and the qualities we have outlined – the purity of her style, her ability to identify with a wide range of characters quite unlike herself, and her sensitive moral discrimination – are the best guarantee of her future development. She is one of the finest writers of the seventies: we may hope that she will emerge as the outstanding novelist of the last quarter of the century.

Notes

1 Page references are to the Penguin editions, except for *Gentlemen and Ladies, A Change for the Better* and *In the Springtime of the Year*.
2 Una Ellis-Fermor, *Shakespeare the Dramatist, passim.*
3 There are two exceptions to this statement, pp. 169–72, and a paragraph on p. 185.
4 There is a story entitled 'In the Conservatory' (in *A Bit of Singing and Dancing*), in which an unpleasant woman commits adultery, not from love or lust, but to be in the swim. When she causes a half-witted lad to commit suicide, she is merely annoyed that the place where the act takes place disrupts her plans.

Appendix: Arnold Kettle—A Select Bibliography 1939–1981

W. R. Owens

This is not intended to be a definitive list. It includes books, articles, teaching material written for Open University courses, and reviews. Articles written for the *Morning Star* are omitted, as are radio and television scripts.

1939

'Marxism and Literature', *University Forward*, 5: 32, 9.

1941

'Report from America', *University Forward*, 7: 2, 18–20.

1943

'One of Our Ancestors', *University Forward*, 8: 5, 24–28.

1948

'The Greatness of Joseph Conrad', *The Modern Quarterly*, 3: 3, 63–81.

1950

'The Mental Traveller', *Arena*, 1: 3, 46–52.

Review of George Lukács, *Studies in European Realism*: *The Modern Quarterly* new ser., 6: 1, 72–81.
Review of Joan Bennett, *George Eliot: Her Mind and Her Art*: *RES* new ser., I, 177–79.

1951

An Introduction to the English Novel. Vol. 1: *To George Eliot* (London: Hutchinson). [Vol. 2: *Henry James to the Present Day*, 1953. Reprinted New York: Harper Torchbooks, 1961; London: Arrow Books, 1962. Second edition, Hutchinson, 1967. Translated into Serbo-Croat, 1959, Russian, 1966 and Japanese, 1974.]
Review of F. S. Boas, *Queen Elizabeth in Drama and Related Studies*: *MLR*, 46, 137.

1952

'The Progressive Tradition in Bourgeois Culture' in *Essays on Socialist Realism and the British Cultural Tradition* (London: Arena Publication). [Reprinted in *Masses and Mainstream*, 7, 1954, 9–20, and in *Radical Perspectives in the Arts*, ed. Lee Baxandall (Harmondsworth: Penguin, 1972).]
'Talks with Soviet Writers', *Anglo-Soviet Journal*, XIII No. 3, 31–33.

1954

'A Blow for Humanism', review of Kathleen Nott, *The Emperor's Clothes*: *The Marxist Quarterly*, 1: 3, 185–87.
'Fairground Mirror', review of Herbert Read, *Anarchy and Order*: *Labour Monthly*, XXXVI, 525–26.

1956

'Impressions of a provincial University', *Twentieth Century*, 159, 151–58.
'Two Working Class Novels', *The Marxist Quarterly*, 3: 4, 248–50.
'Homage to George Meredith', review of Jack Lindsay, *George Meredith*: *Labour Monthly*, XXXVIII, 382–83.
'Life and the Novel: F. R. Leavis on D. H. Lawrence', review of F. R. Leavis, *D. H. Lawrence, Novelist*: *The Gryphon*, January, 29–31.

1957

'E. L. Voynich: A Forgotten English Novelist', *Essays in Criticism*, 7, 163–74.

'The English Romantic Movement', *Philologica* (Prague), IX, 1–7.
'English Blake', *Marxism Today*, 1: 1, 16–22.

1958

'The Early Victorian Social-Problem Novel' in *The Pelican Guide to English Literature*, Vol. 6, *From Dickens to Hardy*, ed. Boris Ford (Harmondsworth: Penguin).
'Rebels and Causes: Some Thoughts on the Angry Young Men', *Marxism Today*, 2: 3, 65–72.
Review of Walter B. Rideout, *The Radical Novel in the United States, 1900–54: MLR*, 53, 253.
'Three Recent Novels', review of Herbert Smith, *A Field of Folk*; David Lambert, *No Time for Sleeping*; Len Doherty, *The Man Beneath*: *Labour Monthly*, XL, 232–35.
Review of Howard Fast, *The Naked God* and Hershel D. Meyer, *History and Conscience: The Case of Howard Fast*: *ibid.*, 477–78.
Review of Franz Stanzel, *Die typischen Erzählistuationen im Roman*: *RES* new ser., IX, 105–106.
Review of Margaret Dalziel, *Popular Fiction 100 Years Ago: Universities Quarterly*, 12: 3, 336–40.

1959

'The Artist and Politics', *Marxism Today*, 3: 5, 139–45.
Reviews of Mary Visick, *The Genesis of Wuthering Heights*; M. R. Proctor, *The English University Novel*: *MLR*, 54, 300, 301.
Review of John Berger, *A Painter of Our Time*: *Labour Monthly*, XLI, 142–43.

1960

'Reply to Discussion on the Artist and Politics', *Marxism Today*, 4: 2, 61–4.
'How New is the "New Left"?', *ibid.*, 4: 10, 302–309.
'Recherche à la Recherche', review of George D. Painter, *Marcel Proust* Vol. 1: *Universities Quarterly*, 14: 4, 419–23.
Review of Brian Simon, *Freedom* and Herbert Aptheker, *On the Nature of Freedom*: *Labour Monthly*, XLII, 429.

1961

'The Consistency of James Joyce' in *The Pelican Guide to English Literature*, Vol. 7, *The Modern Age*, ed. Boris Ford (Harmondsworth: Penguin).

'Dickens and the Popular Tradition', *Zeitschrift für Anglistik und Amerikanistik* (Berlin Ost), IX, 229–52.
[Reprinted in *The Carleton Miscellany*, 3: 1 (1962), 17–51. See 'Mr. Kettle's Reply', *ibid.*, 3: 4, 91–95. Also reprinted in *Marxists on Literature: An Anthology*, ed. David Craig (Harmondsworth: Penguin, 1975).]

'Thoughts on *David Copperfield*', *Review of English Literature*, 2, 65–74.

'Our Morals and Lady C', *Marxism Today*, 5: 4, 123–25.

'Reply to Discussion on the "New Left" ', *ibid.*, 5: 6, 191–92.

'Culture and Revolution: A Consideration of the Ideas of Raymond Williams and Others', *ibid.*, 5: 10, 301–307.

'Communication', *Labour Monthly*, XLIII, 447–48.

'Tolstoy in 1960', *Anglo-Soviet Journal*, XXII No. 1, 13–14.

Review of Albert J. Guerard, *Conrad the Novelist*: *RES* new ser., XII, 100–102.

1962

'Dickens' *Our Mutual Friend*' in *Dickens and the Twentieth Century*, ed. John Gross and Gabriel Pearson (London: Routledge).

'Hamlet', *Zeitschrift für Anglistik und Amerikanistik* (Berlin Ost), X, 117–27.

'Rocco and his Brothers', *Marxism Today*, 6: 3, 75–79.

'Our Theatre in the Sixties', *ibid.*, 6: 9, 276–81.

1963

Karl Marx, Founder of Modern Communism (London: Weidenfeld and Nicolson). [Second edition, 1968; translated into Norwegian, 1966, Italian, 1972 and Swedish, 1976.]

'Communism and the Intellectuals' in *The Challenge of Marxism*, ed. Brian Simon (London: Lawrence and Wishart).
[Reprinted as a separate pamphlet, Lawrence and Wishart, 1965.]

'Charles Dickens: The Novelist and the People', *Marxism Today*, 7: 2, 48–54.

'Higher Education and the Robbins Report', *ibid.*, 7: 12, 358–63.

Review of Maximillian E. Novak, *Economics and the Fiction of Daniel Defoe*: *MLR*, 58, 244–45.

Review of Bernard Bergonzi, *The Early H. G. Wells*: *Notes and Queries*, new ser., 10, 275–76.

Review of Eliseo Vivas, *D. H. Lawrence: The Failure and the Triumph of Art*: *RES* new ser., XIV, 94–95.

1964

Ed., *Shakespeare in a Changing World* (London: Lawrence and Wishart).

'From Hamlet to Lear' in *ibid.*

'In Defence of *Moll Flanders*' in *Of Books and Humankind: Essays and Poems Presented to Bonamy Dobrée*, ed. John Butt (London: Routledge).

'Shakespeare 400 év után', *Helikon*, X, 400–10

'Lear király', *Filológiai Közlöny*, X, 47–57.

'The Value of Marxism Today', *Common Factor*, 1 (October), 30–32.

Review of Ihab Hassan, *Radical Innocence: Studies in the Contemporary American Novel*: *MLR*, 59, 289–90.

1965

'Puritanism and the Rise of the Novel', *Kwartalnik Neofilologiczny* (Warsaw), XII, 235–44.

Review of Maximillian E. Novak, *Defoe and the Nature of Man*: *MLR*, 60, 256–57.

Review of Daniel A. Weiss, *Oedipus in Nottingham: D. H. Lawrence* and Kingsley Widmer, *The Art of Perversity: RES* new ser., XVI, 100–101.

Review of Margaret Schlaugh, *Antecedents of the English Novel 1400–1600*: *ibid.*, 305–307.

1966

Ed., *Tess of the D'Urbervilles*, by Thomas Hardy (New York: Harper and Row).

'Some Tendencies in Shakespeare Criticism', *Shakespeare Jahrbuch* (Weimar), 102, 23–36.

'The Future of the Left', *Marxism Today*, 10: 1, 5–9.

1967

Hardy the Novelist: A Reconsideration. The W. D. Thomas Memorial Lecture (Swansea: University College of Swansea).
[Reprinted in *The Nineteenth Century Novel: Critical Essays and Documents*, ed. Arnold Kettle (London: Heinemann, 1972)]

1968

'Man and the Arts in a Changing World', *Horizons: The Marxist Quarterly* (Toronto), No. 24, 45–61.

[Reprinted in Arnold Kettle and V. G. Hanes, *Man and the Arts: A Marxist Approach* (New York: The American Institute for Marxist Studies, 1968.)]

1969

'What is *Kim?*' in *The Morality of Art. Essays Presented to G. Wilson Knight by his Colleagues and Friends*, ed. D. W. Jefferson (London: Routledge).

1970

'*Felix Holt the Radical*' in *Critical Essays on George Eliot*, ed. Barbara Hardy (London: Routledge).

'The Future of the Book: Books and the Growth of Higher Education', *TLS* (11 December), 1439–1440.

'Charles Dickens (1812–1870)', *Labour Monthly*, 53: 6, 263–66.

'The Artist and Society' in The Open University Course A100 *Humanities: A Foundation Course* (Milton Keynes: The Open University Press), Unit 4.

Review of Grahame Smith, *Dickens, Money and Society*: *RES* new ser., XXI, 233–35.

Review of '*The Quest for Rananim*', *D. H. Lawrence's Letters to S. S. Koteliansky, 1914–1930*, ed. G. J. Zytaruk: *Mosaic*, 4: 1, 123–26.

1971

'The Precursors of Defoe: Puritanism and the Rise of the Novel' in *On the Novel: A Present for Walter Allen on his 60th Birthday from his Friends and Colleagues*, ed. B. S. Benedikz (London: Dent). [Reprinted in *Seventeenth Century England: A Changing Culture*, Vol. 2, *Modern Studies*, ed. W. R. Owens (London: Ward Lock Educational, 1980.)]

'Introduction to Literature (Part II)' in The Open University Course A100 *Humanities: A Foundation Course* (Milton Keynes: The Open University Press), Unit 10.

'A Study Guide to Stendhal's *Scarlet and Black* (1830)' in The Open University Second Level Course A202 *The Age of Revolutions* (Milton Keynes: The Open University Press), Supplement to Unit 28.

Review of Everett Knight, *A Theory of the Classical Novel*; Vida E. Marković, *The Changing Face: Disintegration of Personality in the Twentieth-Century British Novel, 1900–1950*; Bernard Bergonzi, *The Situation of the Novel*: *RES* new ser., XXII, 520–22.

'All for Love', review of E. M. Forster, *Maurice* and *Albergo Empedocle and Other Writings*: *The New Republic*, 165 (9 October), 25–26.

1972

Ed., *The Nineteenth Century Novel: Critical Essays and Documents* (London: Heinemann). [Rev. edn., 1981]

'Balzac and Dickens' in *Literature and Western Civilization, The Modern World II: Realities*, ed. David Daiches and Anthony Thorlby (London: Aldus Books).

'William Blake' in The Open University Second Level Course A202 *The Age of Revolutions* (Milton Keynes: The Open University Press), Units 21–22.

'Stendhal's *Scarlet and Black*' in *ibid.*, Unit 28.

'An Imaginative Memoir', review of V. S. Pritchett, *Midnight Oil*: *The New Republic*, 166 (6 May), 29–31.

'Trying to Reshape the Novel', review of John Berger, *G*: *ibid.*, 167 (7 October), 30–31.

1973

'*Beauchamp's Career*' in *Meredith Now: Some Critical Essays*, ed. Ian Fletcher (London: Routledge).

'Introduction' in The Open University Third Level Course A302 *The Nineteenth-Century Novel and its Legacy* (Milton Keynes: The Open University Press), Unit 1.

'*Cousin Bette*', in *ibid.*, Units 8–9.

'*On The Eve*' in *ibid.*, Units 10–11.

'The Novel in the Mid-Nineteenth Century' in *ibid.*, Unit 12.

'The Late Nineteenth-Century Novel' in *ibid.*, Unit 23.

'*Mrs Dalloway*' in *ibid.*, Unit 30.

'French Critic of the English Social Novel', review of Louis Cazamian, *The Social Novel in England 1830–50*: *Books and Bookmen*, 18: 7, 79.

1974

Review of Paul Meier, *La Pensée Utopique de William Morris*: *Etudes Anglaises*, 27, 105–107.

1975

Foreword to Alick West, *Crisis and Criticism and Selected Literary Essays* (London: Lawrence and Wishart).

'The Eighteenth Century Novel in England' in *Estudios sobre los géneros literarios I: Grecia clásica e Inglaterra*, ed. Javier Coy and Javier de Hoz (Salamanca: University de Salamanca).

'Is Literature a Luxury?', *Umma*, 5, 120–33.

'Modernism and its Origins Part 2: The War Poets' in The Open University Third Level Course A306 *Twentieth Century Poetry* (Milton Keynes: The Open University Press), Units 4–5.

Review of C. Vaughan James, *Soviet Socialist Realism: Origins and Theory: Anglo-Soviet Journal*, XXXV, No. 3, 44–47.

Review of Ioan Williams, *The Realist Novel in England: A Study in Development*: *Literature and History*, No. 2, 114–16.

Review of Joan Rockwell, *Fact in Fiction: The use of literature in the systematic study of Society*: *RES* new ser., XXVI, 512–13.

1976

With Graham Martin, 'Teaching Literature in the Open University' in *Experiments in English Teaching*, ed. David Craig and Margot Heinemann (London: Edward Arnold).

'Literature and Ideology', *Red Letters*, No. 1, 3–5.

'Poetry and Politics' in The Open University Third Level Course A306 *Twentieth Century Poetry* (Milton Keynes: The Open University Press), Units 21–22.

'*Sentimental Education*: A Study Guide' in The Open University Third Level Course A321 *The Revolutions of 1848* (Milton Keynes: The Open University Press), Unit 4.

'Flaubert's *Sentimental Education*' in *ibid.*, Unit 13.

1977

'Shaw and Brecht' in The Open University Third Level Course A307 *Drama* (Milton Keynes: The Open University Press), Units 22–24.

Review article, 'Lawrence, Leavis and Life', *Marxism Today*, 21: 9, 282–84.

Review of Ivanka Kovačević, *Fact into Fiction: English Literature and the Industrial Scene, 1750–1850*: *Literature and History*, No. 5, 123–25.

Review of Raymond Williams, *Marxism and Literature*: *Red Letters* No. 6, 71–73.

'Love and the Writer', review of A. O. J. Cockshut, *Man and Woman: A Study of Love and the Novel 1740–1940*: *Books and Bookmen*, 23: 1, 48–9.

1978

'Bernard Shaw and the New Spirit' in *Rebels and Their Causes: Essays in Honour of A. L. Morton*, ed. Maurice Cornforth (London: Lawrence and Wishart).

'The Gould Report: An Attack on Higher Education', *Comment*, 16: 3, 35–36.

'The Artist and Society' in The Open University Course A101 *An Arts Foundation Course* (Milton Keynes: The Open University Press), Units 1–2A.

'*A Midsummer Night's Dream*' in *ibid.*, Units 6–8.

1979

'W. H. Auden: Poetry and Politics in the Thirties' in *Culture and Crisis in Britain in the Thirties*, ed. Jon Clark, Margot Heinemann, David Margolies and Carole Snee (London: Lawrence and Wishart).

With Dennis Walder and P. N. Furbank, '*Tom Jones* by Henry Fielding: Part One' in The Open University Second Level Course A204 *The Enlightenment* (Milton Keynes: The Open University Press), Units 1–2.

'*Tom Jones* and the Literary Traditions of Eighteenth-Century Fiction' in *ibid.*, Units 4–5.

'Critic of the Thirties', review of Edgell Rickword, *Literature and Society: Essays and Opinions, II, 1931–1978*: *New Universities Quarterly*, 33: 4, 500–504.

Review of Hubert Teyssandier, *Les Formes de la création romanesque a l'époque de Walter Scott et de Jane Austen, 1814–1820*: *Etudes Anglaises*, 32, 86–87.

Review of Raymond Williams, *Politics and Letters: Interviews with New Left Review*: *Marxism Today*, 23: 11, 28–29.

1980

'The Drama of Bernard Shaw' in *English Literature of the Working Class*, ed. F. Garcia Tortosa and R. Lopez Ortega (Sevilla: Universidad de Sevilla).

'Introduction to Mozart's *The Marriage of Figaro*', in The Open University Second Level Course A204 *The Enlightenment* (Milton Keynes: The Open University Press), Units 21b–24b.

'Metaphysical Poetry' in The Open University Second Level Course A203 *Seventeenth-century England: A Changing Culture, 1618–1689* (Milton Keynes: The Open University Press), Block 2.

1981

'Teaching Literature in The Open: Some Thoughts', *Bulletin of the International Association of University Professors of English*, Spring, 1–4.

'English Poetry and the Spanish Civil War' in The Open University Second Level Course U202 *Inquiry* (Milton Keynes: The Open University Press), Unit 17:1.

With W. R. Owens, 'John Bunyan' in The Open University Second Level Course A203 *Seventeenth-century England: A Changing Culture, 1618–1689* (Milton Keynes: The Open University Press), Block 9.

'Restoration Culture and Neo-classicism' in *ibid*.

'Consensus on Conrad?', review of Ian Watt, *Conrad in the Nineteenth Century*: *The Literary Review*, No. 32, 12–14.